"A" is for Adamski:

The Golden Age of the UFO Contactees

"A" is for Adamski:
The Golden Age of the UFO Contactees

By Adam Gorightly and Greg Bishop

ISBN 9781726611671 (black & white edition)

Gorightly Press
info@adamgorightly.com

Cover Design by Red Pill Junkie
absurdbydesign.com

Book Design by Feejee Press
feejeepress.com

Dedicated to the holy trinity of u-fool-ology:

Jim Moseley, Gray Barker, and John Keel

&

To the contactees, past and present

Table of Contents

Helen and Gabriel Green at the Giant Rock Convention. (Photo credit: Joe Fex/APE-X Research)

Foreword

I have often wished that I had come upon the eclectic personalities profiled in this book during the hopeful and richly-textured postwar '50s and '60s, during the truly "Golden Days" of flying saucers and the dedicated Earthlings chosen by the alien visitors to inform and enlighten we humans here on this "Planet of Sorrows," this "Garbage Dump of the Universe," this still revolving and evolving but benighted planet, Earth.

Over the years and tens of thousands of miles I spent photographing the personalities and organizations that eventually culminated in *In Advance of the Landing: Folk Concepts of Outer Space*, I met many of the names found in this compendium, along with other less well known and unexpected humans, but who enthusiastically shared with me their own experiences and vision of the promise of alien contact and enlightenment. Without fail, that vision shared salient points and reflected similar concerns for the future of humankind and our precarious journey into the future.

While the alien message—formed and recognizable within our own core Judeo-Christian philosophies—were related to us by the modern contactees, it was the inclusion of technologies, with capabilities dreamed of, but just beyond our reach, that cemented the attraction for the crowds gathered at early UFO conventions and provided the opportunity for contactees to develop their message and support. It was the promise of free energy, limitless speed, combined with beautiful languid sirens that proved irresistible, that found its way beyond the fringe of hardcore believers into the very fabric of a popular culture daydream, exemplified in films such as Spielberg's *Close Encounters* and *E.T.* As I ventured across North America and encountered the aging remnants of the UFO landscape such as Gray Barker or Wayne Aho, it was the years of Giant Rock conventions that I wished to have seen, to have felt their clean, excited promise of the future.

As a visual anthropologist and photographer, it was the nature of those beliefs, along with the consistent need and regeneration of hope—not the reality of flying saucers themselves—that was, for me, the critical component of the phenomena. At the time of my travels and research there was no internet, no single source by which one could remotely 'armchair' one's way across the fields of history and distance. *"A" is for Adamski* fills a valuable service in compiling the key personalities and backgrounds that created and propelled the UFO phenomena through inception into history and portrays our persistent capacity and need for hope as part of the human experience.

Douglas Curran
August 2017

Jack Parsons

Introduction

Strangers From An Unknown Country

At the dawn of existence—just as WoMan was getting a handle on all the essentials like food, fur and fire—we eventually had the opportunity to raise our eyes to the skies and that first glimpse of infinitude fueled our imaginations.

What was going on up there? What were all those points of light? They must be alive with *something*....

Soon followed stories shared around the campfire, and legends grew of gods who visited Earth on occasion and passed along mystifying words later to be carved on walls and recorded on tablets or papyrus.

Thus was birthed *The Other*—or perhaps it had always been encoded in our DNA—the sense that we're not alone way out here on the edge of nothingness on this spinning ball of mud— and were possibly even seeded by some advanced extraterrestrial civilization that neglected to explain what exactly they had in mind.

The Bible, Dead Sea Scrolls and other religious texts are chock full of such legends, including the fabled Books of Enoch which relate tales of fallen angels who swooped down from on high and seeded Earth's fair maidens with their Nephilim charm. Enoch—according to these apocryphal tales—was the first human to travel into space, visiting a total of seven worlds courtesy of his angelic guides.

Numerous are the accounts in ancient texts of luminous beings in celestial ships from an unknown country—Magonia by any other name; a land inaccessible to mere mortals and inhabited by beings possessed with supernormal powers, described in some instances as angels or Ezekiel's cherubim. Other religions gave other names, but the theme remained the same—whether allegorical or literal—crossing the span of time; the Greek and Norse gods lived in the heavens and traveled back and forth from the stars to Earth with ease. Native Americans considered the Milky Way a stairway between Heaven and Earth.

During the Middle Ages—before science and religion parted ways—astronomy and astrology walked hand-in-hand with men of knowledge like Paracelsus, who explored these diverse disciplines in the same breath. Paracelsus stated that "each person possesses within himself the powers and latent faculties necessary to become aware of a many-dimensioned universe." Many point to Swedish scientist-mystic Immanuel Swedenborg as the first contactee. In 1758, Swedenborg published *Earths in the Solar World*, which chronicled his astral travels to the planets in our solar system and his wondrous encounters with "moon-men."

In the 17th century, Elizabethan magician Dr. John Dee devised a Cabalistic language of "Enochian calls" as a means to contact those same "fallen angels" featured in the Books of Enoch. Ultimately, Dee's use of this Cabalistic system led to encounters with "little men" who moved about "in a little fiery cloud."

In the early part of the 20th century, occultist Aleister Crowley employed a variation of Dee's "Enochian calls" to conjure certain entities that in recent years have been associated with ETs; one in particular named Lam looked similar to your garden variety alien grey that came of age in the late 1980s.

In 1946, Crowley's protégé Jack Parsons joined forces with future Scientology founder L. Ron Hubbard, and the two conducted Enochian rituals in the Mojave Desert that, according to some accounts, brought them into contact with a Venusian. Another legend suggests that Parsons and Hubbard re-opened the same interdimensional doorway that Crowley had used to summon Lam, but afterwards weren't as adept as Crowley in closing this doorway, which in turn allowed a portal of entry for the Modern Era of UFOs.

Kenneth Arnold's June 24, 1947 sighting of several chevron-shaped craft over Mt. Rainier in Washington State was followed shortly after on July 8th by

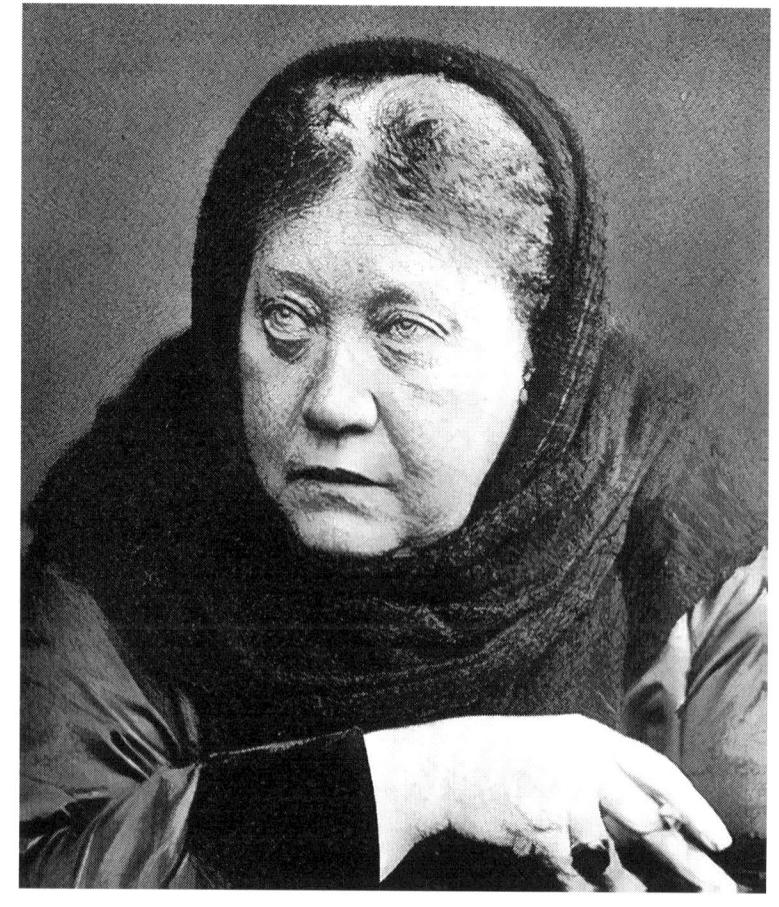

Helena Blavatsky

whatever crashed and burned at a ranch near Roswell, New Mexico. These two events form important data points in ufological history, as suddenly—it seemed—the genie had popped out of the bottle and flying saucers were all the rage. There are those who credit Parsons and Hubbard for opening this crazy bottle.

In the aftermath of World War II, there was an uptick in UFO sightings. In retrospect, this seems only natural, as prior to that time we hadn't completely evolved the concept of "UFO" in our collective consciousness. In fact, the term UFO wasn't coined until 1952 by Captain Edward J. Ruppelt of Project Blue Book who employed it as a catch-all to identify unexplained aerial phenomena.

The Air Force's use of "UFO" illustrated a growing concern—post World War II and into the Cold War era—of an increase of unexplainable things in our skies that posed a potential National Security threat—be it from

George Van Tassel at the 1961 Giant Rock Convention (Photo Credit: Joe Fex/APE-X Research)

Russians or Martians. This post-war upsurge could be attributed to any number of things, including the testing of secret Nazi technologies that had been imported into the U.S. by Wernher von Braun and his Project Paperclip colleagues.

Another theory was that the ETs had observed our atomic tests and traveled to Earth to intervene before we blew ourselves to smithereens. Contactees and Beat poets alike droned on about the dangers of atomic age doomsday devices; technologies that could propel us to the stars and at the same time blast us to Kingdom Come.

In the spirit of Dr. John Dee, psychic mediums continued communications with ascended masters and assorted discorporate entities throughout the first half of the 20th century, including—

Aerial view of the first Giant Rock Convention (Courtesy of Joe Fex/APE-X Research)

on occasion—Martians, Venusians, and other supposed denizens of our solar system. However, Kenneth Arnold's sighting seemed a game changer in terms of triggering the next step in our planet's evolution of otherworldly contact. By the early 1950s—at least according to the likes of George Adamski—these otherworldly contacts had advanced beyond parlor room séances to flesh and bone encounters. This motif of spinning saucers from distant galaxies soon populated the silver screen of the 1950s—as well as Sci-Fi pulp covers—setting in motion, one could contend, the Golden Age of UFO Contactees.

The advent of manned flight—like the splitting of the atom—seemed also to herald the Coming of the Saucers. Leading up to the Wright Brothers' historic flight—and with the onset of the modern mechanical age—witness accounts of mysterious airships appeared in U.S. newspapers. Described as cigar-shaped or dirigible type craft of wood or metallic design—or in some cases constructed of panels of glass—airship reports included wing-like sails, bicycle peddles to power propellers and rudders for steering. Some were even locomotive powered, evoking current images of Steampunk contraptions. The airship pilots—usually human in appearance—often exhibited peculiar behavior.

Integratron under construction in the mid 1950s (Courtesy of Joe Fex/APE-X Research)

When engaged in conversation, they came across as inscrutable strangers from some unknown country conversing in a nonsensical, or cryptic manner.

Airship pilots were a free spirited lot, such as those encountered by Mr. W.H. Hopkins near Springfield, Missouri in April of 1897, consisting of a crew of six beautiful nude women and one nude male. In 1896, Col. H.L. Shaw of Stockton, California encountered a parked airship featuring several seven-foot-tall Martians who gave him a hard time. Another witness—Alexander Hamilton of Leroy, Kansas—observed a craft carrying "six of the strangest people I ever saw" that lowered a red cable around one of Hamilton's prized heifers and hoisted it into the sky. Later, the remains of the hapless heifer—head, hide, and haunches—were discovered a few miles away by one of Alexander's neighbors, and perhaps qualifies as the first recorded cattle mutilation case.

By and large, these accounts have been attributed to urban legends, although The Great Airship Mystery of 1896-1897 seems a continuance of Jacques Vallee's *Passport to Magonia* fairy folk traveling in strange craft from an unknown country for equally unfathomable reasons. These stories—whether real or make believe—serve as a precursor to the Golden Age of UFO Contactees.

Many point to Helena Blavatsky's influence on the early days of contactee-ism. Co-founder of Theosophy—and occasional spirit medium to certain ascended masters (known as The Great White Brotherhood)—Blavatsky's spirit guides were located on planets such as Venus and had visited Earth in times past in an effort to aid in humankind's spiritual development.

A number of contactees were apparently inspired by Theosophy and formed their own religious outfits dedicated to spreading the good space brother word. These included Guy Ballard's I AM, George King's Aetherius Society, and Ruth Norman's Unarius. Channeling ascended masters (who doubled as ETs) was a theme these saucer religions evidently glommed onto via Blavatsky, including a fondness for a Great White Brotherhood of blond haired fair-skinned Venusians (called The Nordics.)

Another deep influence on the Contactee Movement was John Ballou Newbrough's Oahspe, *A New Bible, in the Words of Jehovih and His Angel Ambassadors* (1882). A channeled work received through automatic writing (and typing), *Oahspe* chronicled a sprawling galactic hierarchy inhabited by a host of biblical characters, including cameo appearances by Jesus and angels known as "ashars" who sailed about in ethereal ships. This majestic work would have been lost to the ages had not *Fate* magazine publisher Ray Palmer plucked it from obscurity and made it available again for the growing ranks of flying saucer fandom of the 1950s.

Another channeled work, *The Urantia Book*, dictated to Dr. W.S. Sadler during the 1930s, came courtesy of a group of ET entities known as the "Orvonton Commission." A volunteer organization soon formed around Sadler calling itself, appropriately enough, the Urantia Foundation, which has printed and distributed nearly half a million copies of the book across the globe.

We've adopted the term "Golden Age of UFO Contactees" to define a specific period, (1947–1978). Granted, "contactee" is a relative term and these dates simply provide an arbitrary bench-mark for examining the subject from an historical standpoint and aren't intended to be chiseled in stone. To this end, "UFO contactee" generally describes that brand of 1950s starry-eyed believers chosen by the space brothers to serve as earthly ambassadors. Contactees claimed direct contact—either physically or mentally—and essentially viewed their ET brethren as benevolent ascended masters that travelled to our planet in an attempt to elevate human consciousness and promote interplanetary good will.

1947 is an obvious benchmark. Kenneth Arnold's seminal sighting was followed by an influx of UFO reports worldwide. In 1952, the UFO Contactee Movement reached critical mass, as it was that singular year so many of the All-Star Contactees claimed their first encounters with Orthon, Ashtar, and other space travelers with funny names. From George Adamski and his mythic meeting with a golden haired Venusian named Orthon near Desert Center, California, to George Van Tassel's encounter with a UFO pilot named Solganda who instructed him to build an otherworldly rejuvenation machine called the Integratron. Although never completed, the structure to house this cosmic contraption still sits majestically in Landers, California, resembling some sort of quirky astronomical observatory, a monument to a bygone futuristic age.

The space brothers recruited Van Tassel to host the fabled Giant Rock Interplanetary Spacecraft Conventions, held annually beginning in 1953. Throughout the '50s, '60s and '70s, Van Tassel's conventions served as a Woodstock for the flying saucer set. By the time of the last Giant Rock Convention in 1977, many of the original contactees had ascended to that great Mothership in the Sky. Just the same, there's a good chance Van Tassel's gatherings would have continued on into the next decade had he not died of a sudden heart attack in February 1978. Van (as he was known to friends and followers) was said to be in good health at the time of his death and preparing for a television appearance in Los Angeles to announce to the world that the Integratron was near completion.

In the ensuing years, sinister implications have been attributed to Van Tassel's apparent and premature passing—that he was "taken out" to suppress the soon-to-be-reality of his amazing rejuvenation machine that would basically put the health care industry out of business. Afterwards—according to internet legend—Van Tassel's technical papers and blueprints turned up missing, along with the Integratron's mechanical inner workings. In this regard, Van Tassel's 1978 death denotes another critical benchmark (for the sake of discussion), signaling the end of the Golden Age of the UFO Contactees.

So who put the "Golden" in the Golden age? And what was so golden about it? Granted, this connotation is purely subjective, as most current day ufologists tend to dismiss the old school contactees as either crackpots or conman who tried to cash in on the 1950s saucer craze and are just as happy to have seen that era and its colorful characters washed away in the cosmic debris of time. Just the same, it's hard to deny the sense of innocence and wonder that filled the air in those bygone days, mixed with the heavy doses of naivety and gullibility embraced by the '50s contactee crowd.

In 1979—a year after Van Tassel's passing—Dr. Paul Bennewitz filmed strange and menacing craft over Kirtland Air Force Base in Albuquerque, New Mexico. To a great extent, the Bennewitz Affair—although not well publicized at the time—influenced the 1980s and onwards as much as Kenneth Arnold's sighting informed the late '40s and early '50s UFO subculture. To this end, it could be argued that Bennewitz's ufological investigations ushered in a new era featuring underground bases filled with human-alien hybrids in burbling vats.

Whitley Strieber's *Communion* (1987) further popularized the dark side of the UFO mythos, a sinister spectre that first entered into popular consciousness with Betty and Barney Hill's terrifying encounter of the early '60s recounted in John Fuller's *The Interrupted Journey* (1966). In 1975, a made for TV movie, *The UFO Incident*, further immortalized the Hill's harrowing experience, moving the fringe further into mainstream culture.

By the 1990s, this transformation—from kindly golden-haired Nordics to sinister gray-skinned creeps (armed with probes and implants)—seemed complete, as the '50s contactees had been transformed into abductees—from ambassadors to victims, from the Golden Age to Dark. This change could be viewed as a psychological response to the Computer Age and its promise of technologies that will free us from drudgery and provide us vast knowledge—as all the while these robots sent to serve us silently plot our demise.

Taking this premise further, one could argue that we've gone from a culture of self-reliance to one of dependence and victimization, along the way creating a technological Frankenstein monster that will ultimately destroy its maker. Cast adrift in this modern age maelstrom, we've abdicated personal responsibility, placing blame for the ills of the world on a malevolent power structure that takes many forms. From the artificial intelligence of the Computer Beast 666—to multinational corporations poisoning us with fluoride or GMOs—or government bureaucrats who claim to serve the best interests of *We the People* as they meanwhile monitor and manipulate our every move. This cruel, inhuman hierarchy treats common men as cattle, much like the Dulce Base test tube victims, soulless human-alien hybrids hooked into a hive mind, the products of ufology's Dark Age. But we digress....

There have been more than enough books in recent years about the abductees, but not nearly enough about The Contactees, who—as you've probably figured out by now—are the stars of this show, set in a Golden Age when the future was as bright, vast and limitless as the Universe itself; when Giant Rock was Woodstock and Universal Peace seemed just within reach, brought to Earth by golden haired Venusians and buxom, beret-wearing space babes from Clarion.

We welcome you now, beloved Earthlings, aboard the Mothership. Please step into our time machine for a journey to the past.

"Professor" George Adamski (Courtesy of Joe Fex/APE-X Research)

ADAMSKI, GEORGE (1891–1965)

A Polish immigrant and self-styled philosopher, George Adamski is the UFO Contactee you think of when you can think of only one.

In 1934, Adamski founded The Royal Order of Tibet in Laguna Beach, California, based out of a compound dubbed the "Temple of Scientific Philosophy." It was here that "Professor" Adamski (as his students fondly called him) channeled Ascended Masters not unlike those otherworldly ambassadors he would later allegedly encounter.

During Prohibition, The Royal Order of Tibet secured a special license to produce wine, which some suggest was Adamski's main motivation for starting his mystical order to begin with. In 1940, the good professor and several Royal Order faithful relocated to the slopes of Mount Palomar in Northern San Diego County where Adamski and one of his initiates, Alice Wells, purchased property and opened a small roadside diner, The Palomar Gardens Café. It was there that Adamski served as resident mystic and chief hamburger flipper.

To attract visitors, Adamski set up a couple of telescopes on the property, the intent of which—some have suggested—was to associate himself with the nearby Palomar Observatory and give the impression he was some kind of real life Professor of Astronomy. Not long after, Adamski attached a camera to one of his telescopes and began photographing flying saucers like they were going out of style. In 1949, Adamski started delivering public lectures where he exhibited his many flying saucers photos and the following year authored a *Fate* magazine story titled "I Photograph Spaceships."

Adamski's first face-to-face with the space brothers reportedly occurred near Desert Center, California, on November 20, 1952. On that fateful day the Professor was joined by six other saucer seekers: Mr. and Mrs. George Hunt Williamson; Mr. and Mrs. Alfred Bailey; Lucy McGinnis, Adamski's personal secretary; and Alice Wells. Things started getting interesting when the group witnessed a "gigantic cigar-shaped silvery ship" and after spotting the craft, Adamski decided "to go 1½ miles up the road" to set up his portable telescope. A couple hours later, Adamski witnessed a "scout ship" land and a Venusian with long blond hair step out, an event allegedly observed from a distance by the others in his group.

Adamski's Venusian visitor went by the name of Orthon. "The beauty of his form surpassed anything I had ever seen!" Orthon was outfitted in a ski suit onesie and his hair was not unlike that of actress Veronica Lake. Using a combination of hand signals and telepathy, Orthon explained that he'd traveled to Earth due to his concern about the human race detonating atomic bombs. To emphasize his point, Orthon said, "Boom! Boom!"

During the course of their telepathic chat session, Orthon—who was sporting "unusual shoes"—kept pointing down at his feet as if they were of some cosmic significance. After Orthon departed back to the stars, Adamski was able to get the attention of the rest of his group and waved them over to his location. At Adamski's request, George Hunt Williamson made a plaster cast of the Venusian's footprints, the soles of which were inscribed with some fancy hieroglyphs.

Adamski produced a sixty page account of his Orthon meeting that landed in the hands of Irish author Desmond Leslie who was then working on a book about unexplained aerial phenomena. Leslie added Adamski's story to the mix and whipped up *Flying Saucers Have Landed* (1953) which sold over 100,000 copies and helped launch Adamski's career as "Earth's cosmic ambassador."

Flying Saucers Have Landed wasn't Adamski's first stab at literary immortality. In the 1940s, he submitted a science-fiction yarn called "Pioneers of Space" to *Amazing Stories* that featured an extraterrestrial messianic figure who comes to Earth bearing a message of peace and love. Adamski later self-published a book version of "Pioneers of Space" that fell by the wayside until debunkers rediscovered the work and pointed to it as an early fictional account of his Orthon encounter.

Flying Saucers Have Landed included photos of Venusian "scout ships" (the famous bell shaped flying saucers synonymous with Adamski) as well as cigar-shaped "mother ships" in which—Adamski claimed—he was treated to trips to the moon and Saturn courtesy of his blond-haired, blue-eyed benefactors.

However, Adamski didn't take complete credit for all of his startling flying saucer photos. On one occasion, Orthon did a fly-by and dropped off a canister of undeveloped saucer photos, literally tossing them from the porthole of his passing scout ship, which afterwards Adamski took to the local Fotomat.

Although Adamski took full credit for authoring his books, they were actually ghostwritten by his personal secretary, Lucy McGinnis, and by another follower named Charlotte Blodgett, who came up with the names of Adamski's space people. Like so many alien handles of the time, they sounded like some sort of ultra-modern synthetic fabric: Orthon, Firkon, et al.

In the first three pages of *Inside the Spaceships*, Adamski is willingly removed from a hotel lobby in downtown Los Angeles by Firkon the Martian and Ramu, from Saturn. Later, our hero boards a scout

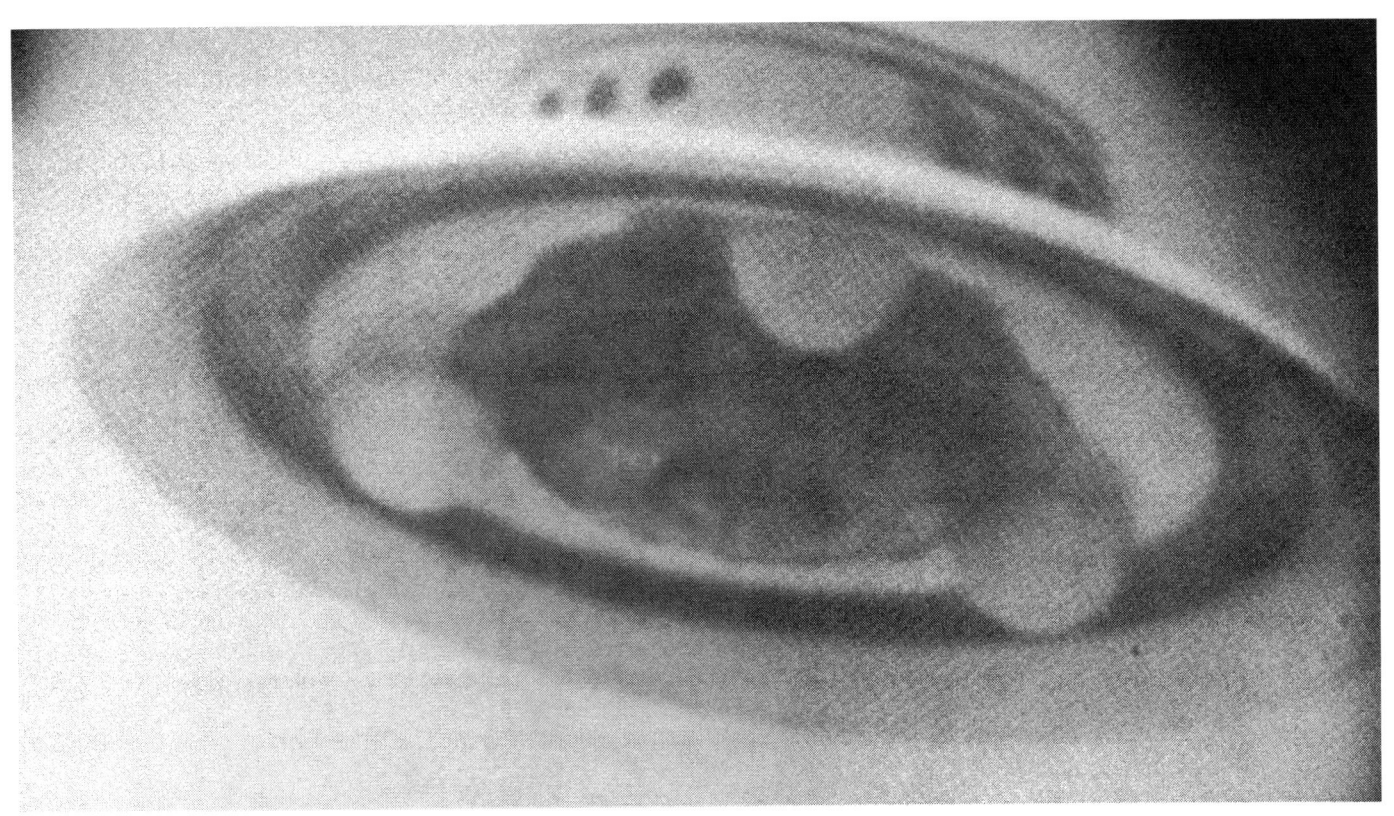

George Adamski's "scout ship" (Adamski Foundation)

ship (complete with one of those thrill-ride safety bars that come down over your lap) and flies off to meet more aliens with monikers like Kalna and Ilmuth, space babes of the highest order. Adamski spares no details in recalling their "draped garments of a veil-like material which fell to their ankles... bound at the waist by a striking girdle of contrasting color, into which jewels seemed actually to be woven." In one of the final scenes, Adamski meets with Firkon in a Los Angeles restaurant over a few cups of coffee and a slice of pie. He teaches Adamski that in the distant past our planet was basically a dumping ground for "unruly ones...what you here on Earth call troublemakers" and reiterates the biblical concept of "fallen angels." Firkon then delivers the usual speech urging humanity to develop spiritually so they may join the universal brotherhood. He refers to the Captain Mantell Incident (where an Army Air Force pilot crashed and died chasing a UFO) as "an accident which we regretted deeply...If his plane had been round, or cigar-shaped, the accident would not have happened." This makes sense.

The religious and philosophical tenets of the Space People—as documented in *Inside the Space Ships*—is, like most other contactee literature, based firmly in the western monotheistic tradition with a few tentative forays into eastern religions like Buddhism and Taoism. Adamski urges that the resemblance between space and Earth religion is due to the fact that we "all worship the same infinite creator."

Desmond Leslie (Courtesey Joe Fex/APE-X Research)

In Curtis Peebles' *Watch The Skies*, a former Adamski follower, Ray Stanford, recounted how the good professor once admitted: "I made enough wine for all of Southern California. I was making a fortune..." and if it hadn't been for the repeal of Prohibition, he wouldn't have got caught up in "this saucer crap."[1] An inebriated Adamski then took Ray and his twin brother Rex on a tour of his workshop and revealed how he'd faked his famous flying saucer photos using a Chrysler hub cap and a set of ping pong balls.

The first in depth Adamski exposé appeared in the 1955 issue of *Nexus*, a result of Jim Moseley's 1953 cross-country trip when he was compiling material for a book on the emerging Contactee Movement. During his travels, Moseley had an opportunity to interview all but one of the witnesses involved in Adamski's Desert Center sighting and discovered several discrepancies in their stories. In response to Moseley's exposé—and a growing number of skeptical critics—Adamski claimed that his debunkers were being manipulated by a "Silence Control Group" that wanted to keep a lid on the truth about flying saucers.[2]

On April 23, 1965, Professor Adamski officially exited the earth plane, ushered through those Venusian pearly gates—one can only hope—by his old chum, Orthon. The following day, a British bloke named Ernest Bryant allegedly witnessed a flying saucer land in his hometown of Devonshire and out popped three space men dressed in what appeared to be diving gear.[3] One of the three, a teenaged male, introduced himself as Yamski from Venus and mentioned that someone named "Des" or "Les" would understand the purpose of his visit. The "Des" or "Les"—in this instance—was assumed to be Desmond Leslie, all of which suggests that Adamski didn't waste any time reincarnating himself as a teenaged youth from Venus with a fondness for underwater equipment. Evidence later surfaced that Bryant's supposed Yamski-flying saucer encounter was a put-on.

The *real* Adamski was probably rolling over in his scout ship.

1. Peebles, Curtis, 1995. *Watch The Skies! A Chronicle of the Flying Saucer Myth*. New York: Berkeley Books.
2. Barker, Gray, 1965. *Gray Barker's Book of Adamski*. Clarksburg, W. Va.: Saucerian Books.
3. Buckle, Eileen, 1967. *The Scoriton Mystery*. London: Neville Spearman.

Further reading

Adamski, George, 1949. *Pioneers of Space*. Los Angeles: Leonard-Freefield Company. (Ghostwritten by Lucy McGinnis.)
Adamski, George, 1955. *Inside the Space Ships*. New York: Abelard-Shuman (Ghostwritten by Charlotte Blodgett.)
Adamski, George, 1961. *Flying Saucers Farewell*. New York: Abelard-Schuman.

Major Wayne Aho at the 1998 UFO Congress in Laughlin, Nevada (Photo credit: Nick Redfern)

AHO, WAYNE (1916–2006)

Wayne Aho claimed otherworldly contacts dating back to his childhood. However, his key encounter with the space brothers occurred in Washington State in 1948:

> I had my first experience telepathically with the beings who inhabit "flying saucers" while I was making use of a rather noisy D-7 bulldozer used in logging. I had read about an airplane crash with no apparent survivors and noted that some observers saw some UFOs near the scene of the crash three days afterward. While engaged in using the bulldozer, I mused, "Who are these strange beings flying in their craft at the scene and why are they here?" A reply that came was startling: "We are caretakers of the souls of the dead!"

In 1957—while attending George Van Tassel's Giant Rock Interplanetary Spacecraft Convention—Aho encountered a "beautiful, majestic egg-shaped light" that telepathically instructed him to launch his own annual flying saucer bash.[1] In 1960, Aho began hosting his "New Dawn" conventions at the base of Mount Rainier (in proximity to Kenneth Arnold's famous sighting) and named the venue *Spacecraft Protective Landing Area for Advancement of Science and Humanities* (SPLAASH.) In a letter sent to state and federal authorities—including the President of these United States—Aho identified SPLAASH as a "Free Landing Zone" (along the same lines of nuclear free zones established by peaceniks across the planet) that would be maintained free of arms and open to all sentient beings, human and otherwise.

Aho claimed he served with Army intelligence during World War II and on the flying saucer lecture circuit referred to himself as Major Aho, an obvious attempt to conflate his name with famed ufologist Major Donald Keyhoe. According to *Saucer Smear* editor James Moseley, others in the UFO field at the time derisively referred to Aho as "Major A-Hole." In this regard, Tim Beckley recalled hosting

Otis T. Carr displaying a scale model of the OTC-X1 to Long John Nebel (Sam Vandivert)

a UFO conference at which Aho was a featured speaker. When Aho ran over time and ignored cues to vacate the podium, Beckley came up from behind and gently tapped him on the shoulder in an attempt to give Aho the hook. In response, Aho spun around and flipped Beckley the bird, then continued on unabated with his presentation.

In 1959, Aho formed a partnership with Otis T. Carr, a self-described Nicholas Tesla protégé who claimed to have discovered a hitherto unknown propulsion system, the Utron Electrical Accumulator. Carr announced he was busy at work developing a terrestrial spacecraft—known officially as "The OTC-X1 Circular Foil Craft"—the design of which would be saucer-shaped and carry a crew consisting of he and his pal Major Aho of the "Air Force Reserves."

Carr and Aho traveled across the country visiting flying saucer clubs soliciting donations for the OTC-X1, which they planned to launch into outer space on April 19, 1959 at the Frontier City amusement park in Oklahoma City, Oklahoma. Leading up to the event, Carr appeared on Long John Nebel's *Party Line* and invited him to attend the historic OTC-X1 blast-off. A few days before this historic launch, Long John traveled to Oklahoma City and after a little sleuthing was able to track down the OTC-X1's secret location at a warehouse on the outskirts of town. Long John repeatedly pounded on the door of the warehouse until at last he was met by a rather hulking figure who informed him that the site was "classified." After a spirited back and forth, Long John was able to persuade his way inside the "lab" to view the OTC-X1, which resembled more a pile of unconnected parts than a functioning spaceship. As for the whereabouts of Commander Carr, rumor had it he'd been overtaken by a mysterious throat ailment that rendered him unable to speak.

Come launch day, Carr was a no-show and Aho—left holding the proverbial bag—announced that the OTC-X1's maiden voyage had been indefinitely postponed due to "technical difficulties" associated with a "mercury leak." The next day, Long John tracked down Carr at the local Mercy Hospital where he discovered the saucer scientist in his night dress, chatting up an attractive candy-striper about the wonders of the OTC-X1 and his prowess as a spaceship pilot. Long John surprised him with "Hello, Otis" and Carr abruptly fell forward on to his bed in exaggerated gasps of pain.[2]

Afterwards, Carr was convicted of swindling investors with his phony flying saucer and sentenced to six months. No charges were brought against Aho, who was viewed as an unwitting dupe in the scam. Not long after the OTC-X1 debacle, Aho was on a solo lecture tour when he found himself committed to the mental ward at Bellevue Hospital,

Ralph Ring at the Retro UFO Convention - Landers, California, 2008 (Photo credit: Adam Gorightly)

as documented in "Wayne Aho Falls Victim to the Men in White Coats" an article published in the UFO periodical *S.P.A.C.E.* The author of this article, one Nobert F. Gariety, was a John Birch Society member who claimed that Aho had been railroaded and thrown into the nuthouse by the International Jewish Banking Conspiracy (or something of that sort) due to his involvement in the OTC-X1 debacle.

In recent years, a fellow named Ralph Ring surfaced with claims he was part of the crew that worked with Otis Carr and that he (Ring) piloted an OTC-X1 test flight that traveled ten miles to arrive at its destination instantaneously. According to Ring, Carr was about to introduce the OTC-X1 to the public when the Feds raided his lab and destroyed everything in it to suppress the OTC-X1 because it was powered by 'free energy'—and we all know how much the Feds hate free energy. Ring also claims that he helped Jacques Cousteau develop the aqualung, although recent evidence suggests that it was actually a song by Jethro Tull.

1. Aho, Wayne. 1972. *Mojave Desert Experience*. Seattle: New Age Foundation.
2. Flammonde, Paris. 1971. *The Age of Flying Saucers*. New York: Hawthorn.

The mysterious Cedric Allingham (*Flying Saucer From Mars*)

ALLINGHAM, CEDRIC (born 1922 in Bombay?)

Cedric Allingham allegedly witnessed a flying saucer land near Lossiemouth, Scotland, on February 18, 1954. Allingham took a photo of the ship's pilot as evidence of this otherworldly encounter which appeared in his book, *Flying Saucer from Mars: An Eyewitness Account of the Landing of a Martian* (1955) that included a statement by a fisherman named James Duncan who corroborated Allingham's account. Afterwards, Allingham made only one public appearance then mysteriously disappeared.

A decade later, journalist Robert Chapman attempted to contact Duncan but was unable to locate him. Allingham proved equally elusive, and when the publishers of *Flying Saucer from Mars* were approached as to his whereabouts, they claimed Allingham had died while receiving medical treatment at a sanitarium in Switzerland. These discoveries led many to suspect that Allingham—and the supposed witness, James Duncan—never actually existed.

It's now been fairly well established that "Cedric Allingham" was the literary construct of Sir Patrick Moore (1923–2012). An astronomer, television personality, author and musician, Moore never publically admitted his involvement in the hoax, although it was an open secret between his close friends that he'd masterminded the ruse along with his friend Peter Davies, the "Martian" in a conveniently blurred photograph.[1] Davies also masqueraded as the author standing by a telescope in the frontispiece of *Flying Saucer from Mars* with the caption: "An informal photograph of Mr. Cedric Allingham, with his 10-inch reflecting telescope."[2]

During the 1950s, Moore hosted the BBC program *Panorama* and among the guests he interviewed were George Adamski and his *Flying Saucers Have Landed* co-author, Desmond Leslie. As it turns out, Moore and Leslie were old chums, having served together in the RAF during World War II. Moore later admitted that he and Leslie "enjoyed playing practical jokes."

1. Clark, Jerome. 2000. *Extraordinary Encounters: An Encyclopedia of Extraterrestrials and Otherworldly Beings.* Santa Barbara, CA: ABC-CLIO.
2. Clarke, David and Roberts, Andy. 2007. *Flying Saucerers: A Social History of UFOlogy.* London: Alternative Albion.

Carl Anderson (Photo credit: Joe Fex/APE-X Research)

ANDERSON, CARL (1913–1980)

Carl Anderson's first purported UFO encounter occurred on April 4, 1954, while camping in Desert Hot Springs, California. On the night in question, Anderson, his wife Stella and their two kids, Bobby and Betty Ann (names straight out of a *Leave it to Beaver* episode) were startled from slumber with the sudden dematerialization of their tent after which they were paralyzed by a beam of light:

> We did not know at the time just how long we remained in this paralyzed condition while we continued to watch and listen. We could now hear voices mumbling in a low tone, but could not tell, however, if the conversation was in English, as the sounds were very faint.

> We do not know whether or not any people alighted from this craft. We did not see any. But we did hear voices. After what seemed like hours we began to hear a slight humming sound like a generator running.

> A low droning, pulsating hum. The dim glow surrounding the saucer slowly took on an orange cast, then a bright red color. It glowed like a huge ball of red fire. Then it started to rise straight up, very slowly at first, then faster and faster as it got higher and higher. The red light changed to a brilliant bluish white. Then slowly the tent began to reappear and once more we were aware of its presence. As the tent became a reality we were once more free to move about. We now realized that we had been paralyzed for our own good. It was not meant for us to go near or touch this wonderful craft from another world.[1]

On the evening of June 27, 1958, Anderson was taking a stroll in Fullerton, California, when a Martian named Kumar appeared out of nowhere, offered him a lit cigarette, then lit another for

Cover of Carl Anderson's *Two Nights To Remember*

himself. After exchanging pleasantries, Kumar said he had to be going but would soon return with a squadron of rescue ships to evacuate "enlightened" humans in advance of the forthcoming atomic war. Kumar then pressed a button on his belt and disappeared into thin air.

Over the next few years, Kumar visited Anderson and on those occasions levitated and performed other Jesus-type feats. On one visit, Kumar brought along an "adorable" seven foot tall Venusian princess named Nirvana, who served the men a sparkling elixir from crystal goblets.

Anderson's final meeting with Kumar occurred on May 4, 1963, when he was taken aboard a spacecraft and given a demonstration of its propulsion system. At this time, according to Anderson, he was instructed to travel to Germany to share this Martian technology with German scientists.

Although one of the lesser known contactees in the U.S., for some reason Anderson became a hit in Europe and his book *Two Nights To Remember* was translated by a Swedish publisher. Anderson and fellow Contactee Reinhold Schmidt were featured speakers at the Fourth International UFO Congress on October 22th–24, 1960 in Wiesbaden, Germany, which evidently allowed him the opportunity to share Kumar's Martian technology with German scientists attending the event, including famed physicist and space flight pioneer, Dr. Hermann Oberth. According to some accounts, Oberth was less than thrilled to share the stage with the likes of Anderson and Schmidt, whom he considered a couple of quacks.

1. Anderson, Carl A. 1956. *Two Nights To Remember*. Los Angeles: New Age Publishing Co.

Orfeo Angelucci at Giant Rock (Joe Fex/APE-X Research)

ANGELUCCI, ORFEO (1912–1993)

Orfeo Angelucci's first purported UFO encounter occurred on August 4, 1946, during the course of an amateur scientific experiment he conducted involving the release of "Navy-type balloons" into the upper atmosphere. Although unsuccessful, Angelucci's experiment apparently attracted a flying saucer that streaked across the sky, the first of his many sightings to follow.

On May 23, 1952, Orfeo was driving home from work (at Lockheed Aircraft in Burbank, California) when he observed a red glow in the sky. At some point the object slowed down until it was nearly motionless, hovering over a field; it ejected two smaller green orbs that landed near Orfeo's car. The larger, red object, then departed.

"Don't be afraid, we are friends," the orbs telepathically transmitted, advising Orfeo to "drink from the crystal cup you will find on the fender of your car." Orfeo described this strange elixir as "the most delicious beverage [he] had ever tasted."

The orbs transmogrified into a three-dimensional television set that projected images of a man and woman from another planet who were "the ultimate of perfection." Orfeo's ETs friends issued a dire warning that if mankind didn't clean up its act and fast then Earth (the "home of sorrows") would be doomed to imminent destruction in the faraway year of 1986. They also cautioned about getting too hung up on material attachments and that to be truly free we humans needed to transcend the limits of physical reality. Nut and bolt craft—the space people informed Orfeo—weren't really needed for space travel; the only reason for manifesting flying saucers—which happened to travel at the speed of light!—was to allow Earth's people to see them. "The speed of light is the speed of truth," they explained, further confounding Orfeo. If that wasn't perplexing enough, Orfeo was informed that the saucer ships were powered by tapping into the cosmic magnetic force, which was another name for "synthetic brains." Orfeo was eventually treated to a voyage around the cosmos and baptized "in the true light of the worlds eternal." On subsequent starship trips he visited an unnamed planet where he met Jesus of Nazareth. "This is the beginning of the New Age," outer space Jesus told him.

Orfeo Angelucci (left) with Daniel Fry at Giant Rock (Joe Fex/APE-X Research)

One afternoon—as he was at home lying on his sofa—Orfeo fell into a trance and was transported to a strange, new world. As he floated astrally around a grand chamber room, Orfeo looked down on his formerly frail and sickly body to discover it had been transformed into an Adonis-looking fellow in a gold and white toga. As Orfeo's astral eyes wandered about the room, the sound of distant thunder suddenly erupted, as then a chamber door opened and out sauntered a golden-haired gal named Lyra who addressed Orfeo as 'Neptune.' (Apparently Orfeo was Neptune from a previous incarnation.) Shortly after, Orfeo (Neptune) and Lyra were joined by a golden-haired boy named Orion who explained that long ago on Earth there had been a devastating battle between some good guys against some bad guys and that the bad guys ultimately won the war and then made everything, well...bad. The leader of the bad guy bunch was revealed to be Lucifer, who—according to Orfeo's extraterrestrial pals—was still living on Earth, but currently keeping a low profile. Later on, Orfeo had a chance for some one-on-one time with Lyra, and they shared a "mystical communion."

Angelucci's encounters evoked surreal, sometimes hallucinatory imagery. One such incident occurred at Tiny's Diner in Twenty-Nine Palms, California where a space brother named Adam offered Orfeo an "oyster white pellet" which he plopped in a glass of water like a psychedelic

Pepto-Bismol. After the pill plopped and fizzed, it created an amber colored nectar— "a very rare champagne"—that emitted a pleasant, intoxicating fragrance. After downing his intergalactic cocktail, Orfeo felt as if transported into "some radiant star system." Later in this adventure, celestial music emerged from the glass of nectar and Orfeo beheld a tiny woman dancing inside with long golden hair, brilliant emerald eyes, her lovely body barely concealed by a translucent silken robe. Orfeo described the expression on her face as an "eternity among the angels."[1]

According to Jim Moseley, Angelucci had been confined at one time to a mental institution, which might explain the seemingly surreal states described in *The Secret of the Saucers* (1955). Of course, if half of what Angelucci witnessed was in any way real, it would have caused even the most sober-minded among us to question our sanity. Angelucci has been regarded as one of the more lyrical voices of the Contactee Movement, described by Carl Jung as the perfect example of the "individuation process...plainly depicted...an unconscious, symbolical form."

Like so many in the contactee scene, Angelucci slowly faded from public view as the decades passed, only to reemerge in the late 1980s when he appeared in a PBS documentary called *California Saucers* and revealed a new spin on his previous otherworldly encounters: "What I think happened was that I dreamed a lot of my experiences which came back through my subconscious in visions."

1. Nebel, Long John. 1961. *The Way Out World*. Prentice-Hall, Inc. (p. 42-43).

Cynthia Appleton and her half Venusian son, Matthew

APPLETON, CYNTHIA (born ca. 1930)

On November 18, 1957, British housewife Cynthia Appleton witnessed a blonde-haired Venusian materialize in her home in Birmingham, England. Outfitted with a domed helmet and metallic jumpsuit, the otherworldly visitor telepathically voiced his concerns that we Earthlings were going about space travel all wrong: "Your scientists are pulling against the greatest force of gravity by going straight up—you should travel with a sideways attitude." The Venusian then opened his arms and a television set of sorts appeared, projecting three dimensional images of miniature flying saucers.[1] Appleton commented: "These spaceships were like nothing I have ever seen in my life before. They seemed to take off and hovered in space for two or three seconds, went off to the left, then they went very quickly to the right." After a few minutes, the holographic TV screen suddenly disappeared along with the Venusian who had held it in his arms.[2]

On January 7, 1958, the blonde-haired Nordic fellow (sans domed helmet) returned, preceded by a burst of light. This time the Venusian brought along his 'Superior' and the two informed Appleton that 'special brainwaves' facilitated their communications. Later appearances featured the two Venusians decked out in business suits and homburg hats, arriving in a car instead of a silver spaceship. Among the secrets revealed by the pair was that time did not exist, and that the cure for cancer involved changing the vibrational rate of atoms at a sub-atomic level. Appleton told the Venusians they were wasting their time imparting such weighty information to a simple housewife who could barely keep up with what they were saying.

On May 10, 1959, Appleton's story took a turn for the weird (if that's at all possible) when she reported to the press that "I'm going to have a baby from Venus." Appleton was first alerted to this Venusian bun in the oven in September 1958, the revelation coming—of course—from her Venusian friends. Whatever the case, Appleton retained no memory of ever being engaged in flagrante delicto with either of her otherworldly visitors, so perhaps we can chalk up her apparent amnesia to missing time. The Venusians also predicted that the child would be named Matthew and have blond hair, weigh 7 lbs 3 oz, and at age fourteen would become "the leader of men." True to these Venusian predictions, the baby boy did indeed have blond hair, weighed exactly as noted and, with all this being so, was appropriately named Matthew.

Afterwards, Appleton, her son Matthew, and the rest of her family withdrew from public view. If Matthew Appleton actually did become the leader of men, he has done so in a covert manner, directing his Earthling minions from behind a cloak of secrecy.[3]

1. Duplantier,Gene, ed. "Saucers, Space & Science Magazine." January 1958, No. 2.

2. Clarke, David and Roberts, Andy. 2007. *Flying Saucerers: A Social History of UFOlogy.* London: Alternative Albion.

3. Leek, Martyn. 2003. "The riddle of Brum's alien baby; 44 YEARS ON: WHERE IS BOY FROM VENUS?" *The Birmingham Post.*

Kenneth Arnold

ARNOLD, KENNETH (1915–1984)

While not considered a contactee in the classic sense, this list would be remiss if we failed to acknowledge Kenneth Arnold's lasting influence on ufology. Perhaps more than any other single event, his June 24, 1947 sighting of "nine gleaming objects" over Mount Rainier in Washington State was the rocket that launched the modern era of UFOs.

An experienced pilot with over 9,000 hours of flight time, Arnold's sighting added an air of legitimacy to what was considered by many at the time as the playing field of crackpots and hoaxers. Although the term "flying saucer" has been widely attributed to Arnold, he actually described several "chevron-shaped" objects that moved like "saucers skipping across water."

In the spring of 1948, an account of Arnold's sighting, "I Did See The Flying Discs!" was published in the premier issue of Ray Palmer's *Fate* magazine, which further catapulted the story into the public's imagination. Arnold was among a handful of early UFO field investigators, much of his activities sponsored by Palmer. These investigations included Samuel Eaton Thompson's March 28, 1950 encounter in Centralia, Washington with a contingent of nude Venusians, as well as the famed Maury Island Incident that predated Arnold's own sighting by three days.

Although he has long been characterized as a conservative business man and sober experiencer of the UFO phenomenon, recent revelations suggest a high weirdness component to Arnold's sightings. According to the May 2014 edition of Mike Clelland's *Hidden Experience* blog, Arnold's daughter, Kim, related that her father, "...went on to see a number of other UFOs throughout his life, he reported that UFOs could read his mind, he and his family saw floating orbs in their home, he claimed his phone was tapped, he was threatened by the military to keep quiet about what he knew and he was fascinated with synchronicities. He came to see these events as happening to him for a reason and he eventually saw the whole thing as a spiritual experience. [Arnold] also came to believe that the UFO phenomenon might represent some kind of connection between the living and the dead...."

In *Strange Mysteries of Time and Space* (1959), UFO researcher Harold T. Wilkins wrote that

Arnold had been "visited by unseen entities" whom he "believed to be pilots of these weird disks. They were invisible..."

Further reading

Arnold, Kenneth and Palmer, Ray. 1952. *The Coming of the Saucers*. Wisconsin: Privately published.

Bessie Arthur, "The Space Lady of Colorado Springs" (Joe Fex/APE-X Research)

ARTHUR, BESSIE (aka "The Space Lady of Colorado Springs")

While vacationing in Santa Monica, California, in 1937, Bessie Arthur was out for an evening stroll when a bright star approached at an astounding rate of speed. The star zigzagged around before it stopped and then turned into a "large floating bubble" carrying a "Lady of the Stars." Bessie was led up a stairway of light into the hovering bubble ship and the Lady of the Stars said: "I am Aura Rhanes, this is Al Padgett (the man on my right bowed), and this is Bernard Kaiser."

Aura, it turned out, was the captain of the ship, which came from planet Clarion where it was said to be so peaceful they had no need for policemen and were in such outstanding health that there were no hospitals or medicine—even though they occasionally smoked cigarettes. The purpose of their visit was to bring peace and better ways of living to the people of Earth. As Aura explained: "The trouble of the earth people largely lies in their terrific greediness. Through their greediness they are led into various forms of craftiness to satisfy their greed. But how they make me laugh!"[1]

1. Arthur, Bessie. "A Visit with the Space People in 1937." *Mystic Magazine*, February 1955.

Doris Levesque representing Ashtar Command at the Giant Rock Convention (Joe Fex/APE-X Research)

ASHTAR COMMAND

Although George Van Tassel was supposedly the first human to channel space commander Ashtar, his legacy would continue to thrive over the years through a host of contactee channelers that included Trevor James Constable and Rev. Robert Short.

Ashtar's influence spread out to a space brother alliance known as "Ashtar Command" that in the mid-1950s started beaming cosmic messages to Doris Levesque who lived in Joshua Tree, California. In 1957, Levesque founded *White Star*, an organization devoted to spreading the good space brother word, including the publication of the *White Star Illuminator* newsletter. According to *Melton's Encyclopedia Of American Religions*:

> Levesque teaches that the earth is in a transition period created by the atomic age. Cataclysm is to be avoided by moving away from the destruction of nature. Universal laws, especially that of divine love, must be expressed. Love is the prime motivating force in the universe, which is organized on the principles of density and substance. Man evolves by assuming more density, which vibrates at high rates. Life on all planets is at different points of evolution. A key evolutionary concept is light, which is said to be created by vibration traveling in substance, and evolution to higher spiritual levels accompanies the presence of more light. Followers are encouraged to meditate and to visualize the coming of the light into situations where it is needed.

Following in Levesque's footsteps, a lady named Thelma B. Terrell struck up her own conversations with Ashtar Command in 1980. Terrell adopted the name of Tuella and in *Project World Evacuation* (1982) laid out Ashtar Command's plan to evacuate Earth just as soon as the axis starts tilting any day now. Along with several other books published in the 1980s, Tuella sent out a newsletter called *Ashtar's Golden Circle*. For more information on the axis tilting you can contact Tuella at P.O. Box 328, Clarksdale, Arizona 86324.

Guy and Edna Ballard

BALLARD, GUY (1878–1939)

In 1930, Guy Ballard experienced a vision while hiking Mount Shasta when the Count of Saint Germain appeared and offered him a cup of "pure electronic essence." Ballard was enveloped by "a White Flame which formed a circle about fifty feet in diameter" and then whisked away with Saint Germain on an astral voyage, visiting—among other locales—the buried cities of the Amazon, Yellowstone National Park and the Grand Tetons. Beneath the Tetons—in a gold-laden retreat—Ballard and Saint Germain encountered twelve Venusian masters (also known as "The Lords of the Flame.") Ballard's account depicted his Venusian friends as the same golden-haired Nordic types who would later hook up with George Adamski. After the Venusians performed a set of music, a large mirror was rolled out featuring wondrous images broadcast directly from Venus.[1]

Inspired by these Venusian images, Ballard and his wife Edna launched a religious order called I AM. The love offerings soon poured in, and the Ballard's built a looming tabernacle in downtown Los Angeles from the top of which a blazing neon light flashed word to all of the mighty I AM presence.

Like so many of the early contactees, Ballard was gifted with the apparent ability to channel his golden-haired Venusian friends, including the "Tall Master of Venus" who referred to Guy and Edna as "the most precious beings on the face of this Earth today." Other Venusians channeled by Ballard included a fellow named Sananda, known more commonly on our planet as Jesus Christ.

After Guy Ballard's death in 1939, dame Edna took over the channeling duties and kept the messages from Sananda rolling until her own ascension to the great beyond in 1971.

1. Rasmussen, Cecilia, January 25, 1998. "From L.A. Sprang Cult of I AM", *The Los Angeles Times*.

Further reading

Ballard, Guy. 1934. *Unveiled Mysteries* (written under the pen name of Godfré Ray King), Saint Germain Press.

Gray Barker (Gray Barker Collection, Clarksburg-Harrison Public Library)

BARKER, GRAY (1925–1984)

West Virginia native Gray Barker's entrée into the wooly world of ufology kicked off in September 1952 when he traveled to Braxton County, West Virginia to investigate reports of the Flatwoods Monster, a purported creature associated with a UFO flap that occurred during the period.

Afterwards, Barker launched his own newsletter, *The Saucerian*, and a publishing house under the same name. Through *Saucerian Press*, Barker brought many of the early contactee stories to a wider audience and was instrumental in introducing the Men in Black (MIB) mythos into popular culture with *They Knew Too Much About Flying Saucers* (1956), a recounting of Albert Bender's unsettling MIB experiences, as well as a number of other early alleged MIB encounters.

Albert Bender's initial account depicted MIBs as secretive government spooks sent to strike fear into the hearts of UFO witnesses who "knew too much." By the time Barker got his hands on the story, he embellished Bender's MIBs with strange speaking patterns and odd colored skin, suggestive of unearthly origins. UFO researcher Allen Greenfield has classified Barker as more of a folklorist than a straight nut and bolt UFO investigator.

Barker was fond of passing along rumors that doppelgängers of certain ufologists were making the rounds of UFO conferences (including the doppelgängers of John Keel and Jim Moseley), the implication being that these darkly clad characters were masquerading in a mischievous manner to infiltrate and undermine the UFO research community.

Barker was also a poet, and perhaps his most biting commentary on ufology appears in the poem, *"UFO Is A Bucket Of Shit"*:

> *UFO is a bucket of shit*
> *Its followers: perverts, monomaniacs, dipsomaniacs*
> *Artists of the fast buck*
> *True believers, objective believers, new age believers*

Keyhoe believers

Shushed by the three men
Or masturbated by space men

UFO is a bucket of shit

The A.F. investigated UFOs
And issued a report
Couched in polite language
Which translated, means:

"UFO is a bucket of shit"

Meade Layne is a bucket of shit
Lex Mebane is a bucket of shit
James W. Moseley is a bucket of shit
Richard Ogden is a bucket of shit
Ray Palmer is a bucket of shit

And I sit here writing
While the shit drips down my face
In great rivulets

Barker and Jim Moseley gained infamy for playing pranks on unsuspecting saucer buffs. The most notable of these was pulled on George Adamski with what became infamously known as the Straith Letter Hoax, a party that got started in December 1957 when Barker gained access to batch of absconded State Department stationery courtesy of an anonymous friend whose father served in the government. During a weekend of heavy boozing, Barker and Moseley concocted the Straith Letter (on the aforementioned absconded State Department stationary), in addition to several other spurious communiqués, addressing them to different personalities on the saucer scene. The letter in question—signed by R.E. Straith, a member of the State Department's "Cultural Exchange Committee"—informed Adamski that his 1952 sighting in Desert Center, California had been confirmed by government officials, and encouraged Prof. Adamski to visit their D.C. offices whenever he was in town.

Adamski all but wet his pants over this phony State Department endorsement, trotting out the Straith Letter at every opportunity to support his claims of ET contact. This prompted an investigation by the *real* State Department and FBI, who ordered Adamski to stop promoting this cockamamie letter as it was an obvious hoax and there was no such department as the "Cultural Exchange Committee." Of course this didn't dissuade Adamski, who claimed that the government was trying to suppress the Straith Letter from the public.

At some point the Feds grew to suspect that Barker was behind the Straith Letter, and they questioned both he and Moseley on a number of occasions, although each denied involvement. Barker— worried that he was going to end up doing hard time at Leavenworth—destroyed the typewriter on which the Straith Letter was composed and buried its remains in wet cement at a

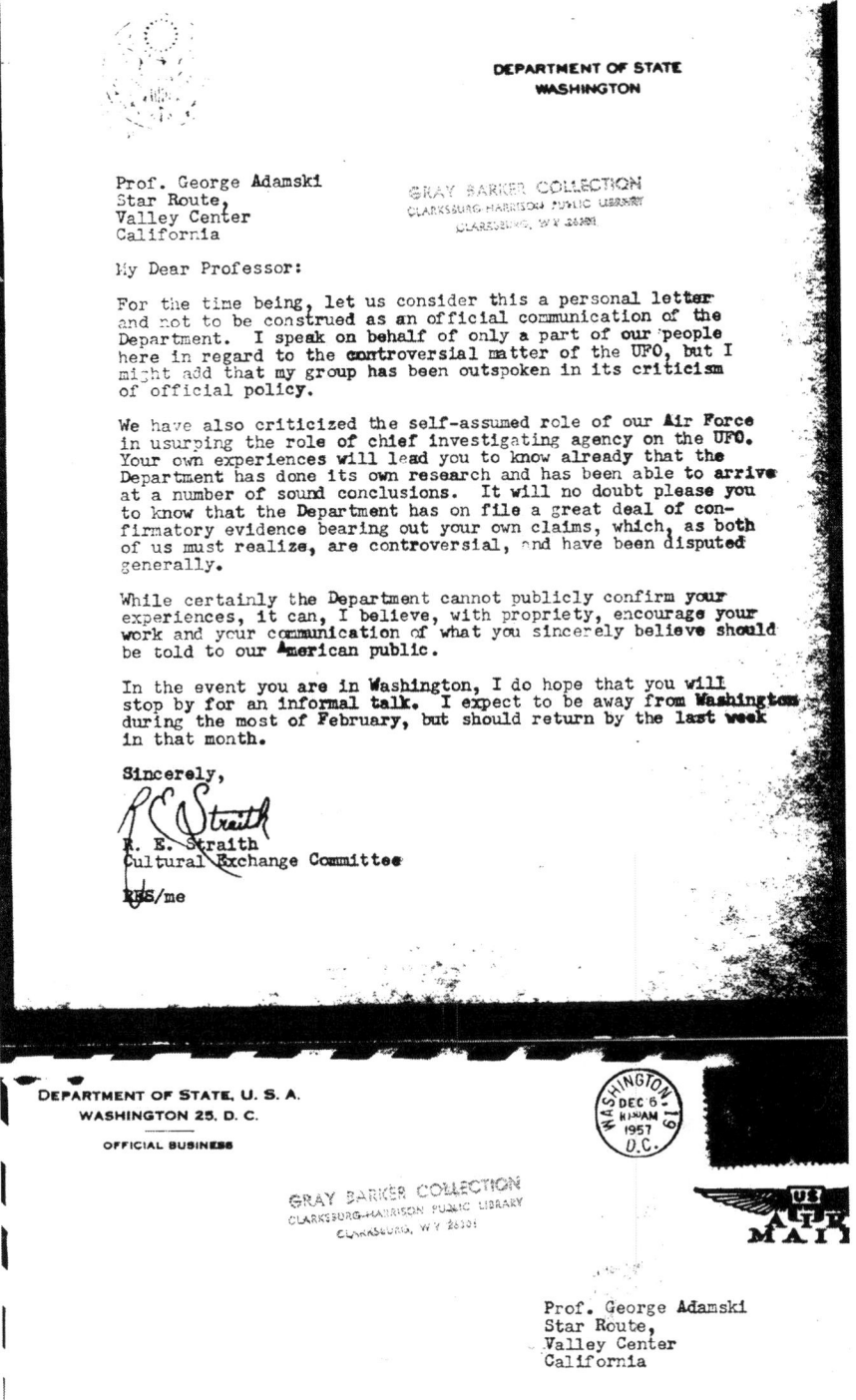

The infamous Straith Letter
(Gray Barker Collection, Clarksburg-Harrison Public Library)

construction site in his hometown of Clarksburg, West Virginia. The Feds—unable to uncover any tangible evidence linking Barker to the letter—eventually dropped the case, probably viewing it as a rather harmless stunt. Following Barker's death, Jim Moseley came clean about his involvement with the Straith Letter hoax in a 1985 issue of *Saucer Smear*.[1]

Another memorable Barker/Moseley prank occurred in 1966 when the two concocted the "Lost Creek, West Virginia, UFO film" which basically consisted of attaching a miniature flying saucer to a fishing pole line, dangling it around and filming its wondrous orbit. Moseley later used this fake film during college lecture gigs to astound and amaze his audiences, presenting it as authentic UFO footage.

In an August 2007 interview, long-time UFO researcher Allen Greenfield revealed another stunning example of Barker/Moseley mischief:

Greenfield: I got the idea sometime in the late 1960s/early '70s to do a periodic city wide skywatch where I would simply advertise in the local newspaper...and I would get hundreds of calls...At that time I had an office devoted to ufology and was basically doing UFO work full time and I was getting more calls than I could really handle as you can expect in a city (New York) that was then about a million people. And in the middle of this I get this really weird phone call with a mechanical sounding voice...Now this was in the 1960s, ya know, when it wasn't so easy to manufacture these machine type voices, and the voice said: "YOU WILL DISCONTINUE THIS PROJECT OR REAP THE RESULTS!" and then it made some very weird beepbeepbeepbeep sounds. About halfway through that I had switched on a tape recorder and was recording it and I played it back for people and I said, "That was a really strange thing: we had some sightings and I also got a very strange phone call." About two years later, Moseley got a quizzical look on his face, looked at me like I was insane, and he said, "You still haven't figured out that that was Gray and me with our equipment in West Virginia?

Gorightly: That's very interesting because John Keel received those type of phone calls.

Greenfield: *He certainly did.*[2]

1. Moseley, James & Pflock, Karl. 2002. *Shockingly Close To The Truth: Confessions of a Grave-Robbing Ufologist*. New York: Prometheus Books.
2. Adam Gorightly's *Untamed Dimensions* podcast, August 2007.

Michael X. aka Michael Barton (Joe Fex/APE-X Research)

Barton, Michael (1937–2003)

In the mid-1950s, Michael Barton took a pilgrimage to Giant Rock. Inspired by George Van Tassel's apparent ability to channel ETs, Barton embraced the notion that the universe is composed of "mind stuff" that can transmit thought vibrations. On the historic night of May 22, 1955—his gaze fixed determinedly on Venus—Barton projected a "vibratory beam of light" and, using what he called "space telepathy," broadcast the following interstellar message:

MICHAEL OF EARTH CALLING VENUS. COME IN VENUS. COME IN VENUS. OVER.

Soon after, a melodious-voiced Venusian informed Barton that he'd received his communication via "Telethot." Thus began a dialogue between the two recounted in *Flying Saucer Revelations* (1957) in which Barton's Venusian informant shared such enlightening nuggets:

> The mystic purpose of all created human intelligence is to actively express love, which
> is the stabilizing power that harmonizes the impelling power of "will." This brings about
> a balance – and is the primary law of the entire Cosmos...

Although he occasionally lectured at meetings of Daniel Fry's *Understanding*, Barton was a bit of a recluse who adopted the pen name Michael X. to conceal his identity. Through his vanity press, *Futura*, Barton published a series of flying saucer pamphlets, many of which portrayed the space brothers as all sweetness and light. In addition to standard contactee faire, Barton dabbled in some of the more heretical areas of ufology with titles like *We Want You: Is Hitler Alive?* (1969), one of the very first books covering the Nazi-UFO angle. It was around this time that things started getting a little weird for the X-Man.

During one of his meditations, Barton received a mental message to meet at a secluded spot in the

Mojave Desert for a face-to-face with his otherworldly contacts so they could lay some "important information" on him. After arriving at the desert rendezvous point, Barton sat waiting his car when he noticed a glint of something in the distance and assumed it was the ET saucer arriving. As he walked toward the object, a sudden sense of dread overtook Barton and an inner voice instructed him to retreat post haste.

Just before he turned around to high-tail it, Barton caught a glimpse of someone partially concealed in the underbrush lowering a rifle, which he now realized was the object that had glimmered in the sunlight. Afterwards, Barton speculated that some Illuminati like secret society had somehow hijacked his telepathic transmissions in order to set up the ambush. Not long after, Barton left ufology in fear of his life to become a UPS driver.

In the early 2000s, Tim Beckley tracked down Barton in regards to republishing some of his old *Futura* books and Barton consented with the caveat that his Nazi-UFO titles be excluded from the mix. To this end it could be speculated that the perceived threat against his life—which prompted Barton's sudden ufological departure—was somehow related to Hitler's flying saucers in Antarctica![1]

1. Beckley, Timothy Green. 2016. *Nazi UFO Time Travelers: Do We Owe The Future To The Fuhrer?* New Brunswick, NJ: Inner Light Publications.

GREETING TO ALL
FROM M.I.N.D.

Wes and Jo-Nell Bateman at Giant Rock (Joe Fex/APE-X Research)

BATEMAN, WESLEY (1920–2009)

In 1963, Wes Bateman—a self-described "Telepath for the Confederation of Worlds"—initiated communications with an extraterrestrial brain trust known as "Outer State." Soon after, he and his wife Jo-Nell founded Mental Investigations of New Dimensions (M.I.N.D.) based out of their bungalow in Hollywood, California.

M.I.N.D.'s main mission was to announce that mass saucer landings were forthcoming and to prepare mankind for this eventual ET-human hookup. The Batemans appeared on radio and TV programs where they predicted specific times and places where the flying saucers would appear. Some of these predictions apparently came true—at least according to signed witness statements produced by the Batemans.

During the mid-1960s—according to Bateman—he became a major source of inspiration for the producers of *Star Trek*, and in particular Gene L. Coon, who along with other *Star Trek* writers attended Bateman's UFO lectures and cribbed ideas he discussed such as wormholes and warp drives (not to mention the "Prime Directive") and incorporated these concepts into the *Star Trek* television series.[1]

1. *The Jerry Pippin Show.* "Wes Bateman Memorial, 3-11-2009."

Further reading

Bateman, Wes. 1993. *Knowledge From The Stars*. Light Technology Publications.

Bob Beck (left) with Max Miller of Flying Saucers International (Joe Fex/APE-X Research)

BECK, ROBERT "BOB" (1925–2002)

In 1948, Bob Beck started his own photographic-audiovisual firm, *Color Control Color Laboratories Company* that designed special lighting techniques used for a number of MGM productions like *An American in Paris* and *Show Boat*. In the 1960s, Beck was responsible for the groundbreaking special effects featured in Roger Corman's psychedelic epic *The Trip*.

Along the way, Beck befriended George Van Tassel, attending several Giant Rock Conventions and other UFO events in California, photographing the contactees in attendance. (Many of these photos appear exclusively in this book.) Van Tassel's work in "cellular rejuvenation" dovetailed with similar interests shared by Beck related to alternative health cures produced by electromagnetism. To this end, Beck was involved—at least in an advisory capacity—with the construction of Van Tassel's Integratron.

Nowadays—on podcasts and radio shows that cater to the conspiracy/Patriot/anti-NWO crowd—you're liable to hear any number of advertisements touting electromagnetic health cures. Most of these devices—in one form or another—were originally developed by Beck who, in turn, was influenced by the pioneering work of cutting-edge inventors like Georges Lakhovsky, Royal Rife and Nikola Tesla.

In 1979, Beck launched *Bek Tek*, a company manufacturing "psychotronic medicine" machines, one of which was the *Brain Tuner* that was said to balance the electrical activity of the two hemispheres of the brain—and when that happens apparently all types of positive health benefits result. Beck incorporated his Brain Tuner and other techniques into what he later branded as the "Beck Protocol" that, among other things, could allegedly cure AIDS and other chronic illnesses through something known as "blood electrification." It was through this protocol that Beck purportedly cured himself of cancer and grew back all the hair he had lost during chemotherapy.

In 1990, Beck developed the first colloidal silver ion generator for in-home use, which is another curative substance you can hear all about on Jeff Rense, Alex Jones and other internet used car salesmen who peddle such wares. Due to these and other endeavors, Beck claimed he was incarcerated "many times by orders of the FDA."

Albert Bender posing beside a portrait of an MIB (Gray Barker Collection, Clarksburg-Harrison Public Library)

Bender, Albert (1921–2016)

During the early 1950s, Albert Bender oversaw the International Flying Saucer Bureau (IFSB), a civilian research group based out of Bridgeport, Connecticut, with a worldwide membership of 1500. In conjunction with the IFSB, Bender published *Space Review*, a newsletter dedicated to the latest saucer happenings.

In March 1953, the IFSB conducted a group mental telepathy experiment ("Contact Day") to establish ET contact by transmitting the following mental message:

THE MESSAGE
(To Be Memorized)

Calling occupants of interplanetary craft. Calling occupants of interplanetary craft that have been observing our planet EARTH. We of IFSB wish to make contact with you. We are your friends, and would like you to make an appearance here on EARTH. Your presence before us will be welcomed with the utmost friendship. We will do all in our power to promote mutual understanding between your people and the people of EARTH. Please come in peace and help us in our EARTHLY problems. Give us some sign that you have received our message. Be responsible for creating a miracle here on our planet to wake up the ignorant ones to reality. Let us hear from you. We are your friends. (End of message.)

In early September 1953—in what would have been the October issue of *Space Review*—Bender planned to announce the solution of the flying saucer mystery, but before he could do so was visited by three mysterious Men-in-Black (MIBs) who spooked him into silence. Bender delivered the following portentous message in *Space Review* for his fellow IFSB members to ponder:

STATEMENT OF IMPORTANCE

The mystery of the flying saucers is no longer a mystery. The source is already known, but any information about this is being withheld by orders from a higher source. We would like to print the full story in *Space Review*, but because of the nature of the information we are sorry that we have been advised in the negative. We advise those engaged in saucer work to please be very cautious.

Bender ceased publication of *Space Review*, closed down IFSB, and retired from ufology. He later revealed to close associates that the solution to the "mystery" was that the U.S.A. would soon fall victim to a massive flying saucer attack! However, this attack was not interplanetary, but actually originated from the Earth's polar regions. Due to this dangerous knowledge, Bender was ostensibly hushed up, one of the very first victims of the legendary "Silencers" who have haunted UFO lore ever since. Others have speculated that Bender cooked up the whole caper as a convenient excuse to exit ufology, as the pressures of overseeing IFSB had become too much, perhaps even leading to a psychological meltdown.

It was Bender's purported MIB encounter which reignited attention to a phenomenon that's almost as old as time itself. These tales of creepy black garbed men go back eons and have long been associated with the sinister doings of witches, warlocks, and other things that go boo in the night. Upon closer examination, it appears that Bender's MIB experiences may have had more to do with his long standing interest in the occult rather than some sort of secret government backlash in response to flying saucer investigations. Due to his peculiar interests, Bender transformed an upstairs room in his stepfather's house into what he called his "chamber of horrors."[1] He painted the walls with depictions of grotesque scenes from the works of Shelley, Stoker and Poe and adorned it with "macabre items such as artificial human skulls, shrunken heads, bats, spiders, snakes." At the same time, Bender was "reading books on black magic, occult subjects, and other similar works...[he] even tried to hold some séances." In recent years, UFO researcher and occult historian Allen Greenfield discovered—among some old photos of Bender's "chamber of horrors"—that in one corner of the room an altar had been erected, ostensibly used for ritual magic. From this, it could be conjectured, Bender's occult dabblings might have awakened some ancient demons that paid him a visit.

In *Flying Saucers and the Three Men* (1963), Bender recounted his visit by the three mysterious men, whom he says whisked him away to planet Kazik. It was there that he was taken to a room where three exceptionally attractive women "dressed in tight white uniforms" removed his clothing and, as Bender recalled:

My body suddenly became rigid and I could not move a single muscle...I became

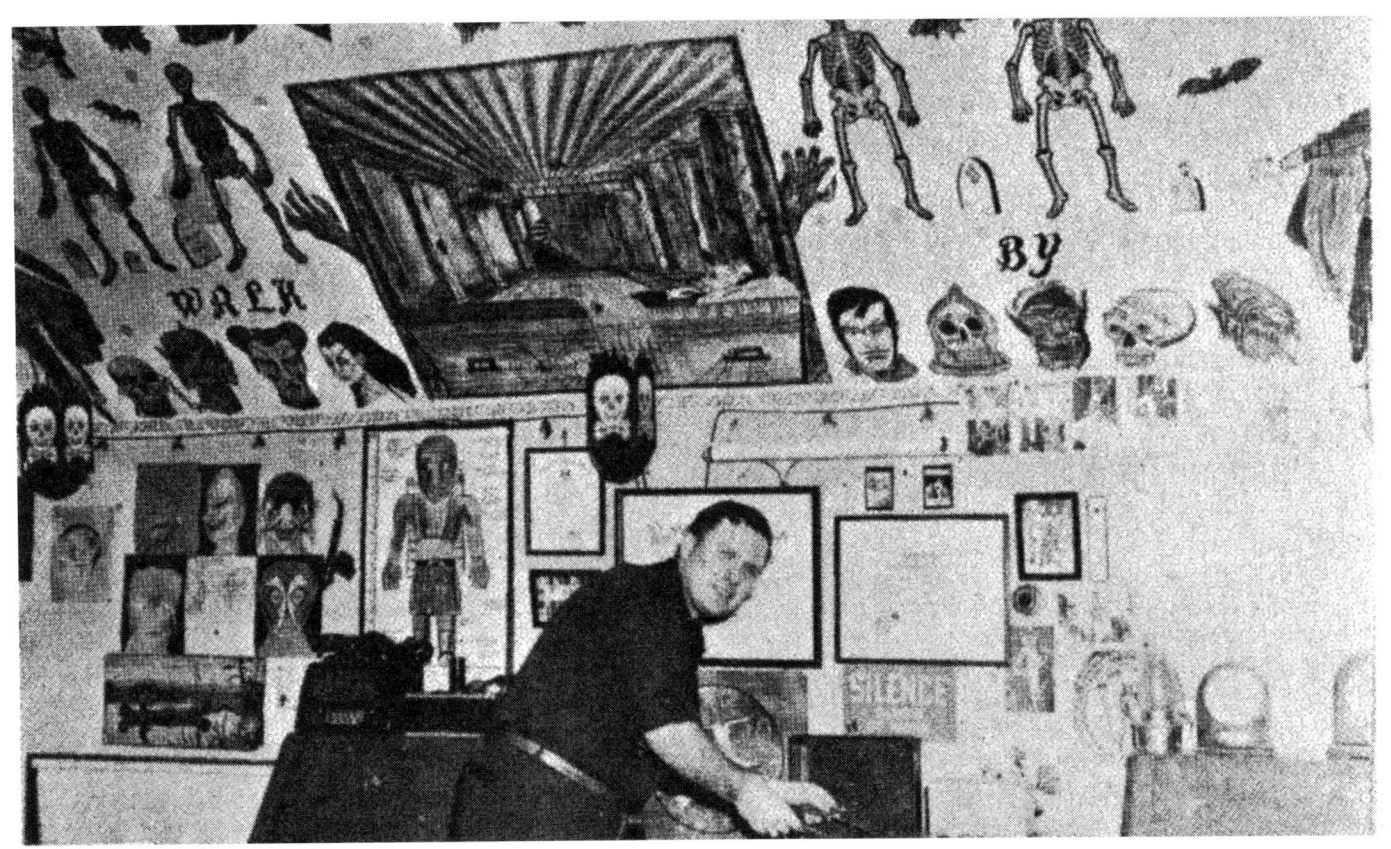

Albert Bender in his "chamber of horrors"

frightened...my fright changed to embarrassment as I felt their hands begin to remove my clothing. I could do nothing to stop them, for I was stiff as a board. With great efficacy they removed every piece of my clothing, leaving me naked as the day I was born...[they produced] a vile containing a liquid which they poured over my body. Then the three messaged the liquid into my skin. As they did so my body became warm as if heat were being applied. They messaged every part of my body without exception...

Bender emerged briefly from his self-imposed ufological exile with an 'appearance' at what was the largest and best attended UFO Convention in U.S. history in New York City on June 24, 1967, called, appropriately enough, "The Big Flying Saucer Show." However—due to unspecified fears for his safety—Bender sent a tape recording that was played to a packed house of wide-eyed attendees. In it, he reminisced about the history of the IFSB, his chilling MIB encounters, in addition to a number of recent contactee-type experiences which were going to be part of a new book Gray Barker planned to publish. Barker later described Bender's forthcoming book as "not good enough to do anything with."

1. Clark, Jerome. 1992. *The Emergence of a Phenomenon: UFOs from the Beginning through 1959 - The UFO Encyclopedia - Volume 2*. Detroit: Omnigraphics, Inc. (pp. 153-155).

Erika Bertschinger

Bertschinger, Erika (born ca. 1929)

In 1973, Erika Bertschinger fell off a horse and landed on her head, after which she realized she was the reincarnation of the Blessed Virgin Mary.[1] Not long after, Bertschinger began conversing with a whole host of disembodied beings, many of them biblical figures that included Jesus, who—it turns out—was an ET.

In 1980, Bertschinger changed her name to Ureilla and founded a religious order (or what some termed a cult) called Fiat Lux headquartered in Germany's Black Forest. Fiat Lux (Latin for "Let There Be Light") subscribed to the belief that World War III would kick off in 1998 followed by a Nazi flying saucer invasion that would bring about Armageddon. While all this commotion was going on, Bertschinger and her bunch would be transported up by a "Big Beam" into an awaiting mothership as Earth was being cleansed of all human evil and afterwards restored to a pre-Adam and Eve paradise. After all was right again, the Fiat Luxers would then return to start over again—overseen, of course, by Jesus Christ, the ET.[2]

Unfortunately—or at least unfortunately for Bertschinger's bunch—Armageddon didn't go down quite as planned, if you recall 1998, and shortly after Fiat Lux went underground, contemplating their next move on the world's stage. Since then, Fiat Lux has experienced occasional run-ins with the law regarding tax evasion and the sale of medicinal elixirs containing alleged healing properties. Convinced that "www" equates to "666," Fiat Lux does not maintain a website or email address, so if you want to find out more you'll have to travel to Germany.

1. Johnson, Ken, 2012. *Cults and the Trinity*.
2. Lewis, James R. Lewis. 2004. *Oxford Handbook of New Religious Movements*. New York: Oxford University Press, (p. 425).

BERNEY, HAROLD (1898–1967)

At the time of his prison release in December 1945, Harold Berney had a rap sheet stretching back nearly 30 years that included theft, embezzlement and securities fraud. For a while, it seems, Berney pursued the straight and narrow, holding down the job of sign painter until around 1953 when he started a fraudulent business called the Aberney Corporation, a venture supposedly to produce television antennas. Berney roped in a couple of investors, one of whom was later identified as Pauline Goebel, who also served as Berney's secretary in the venture.

In the fall of 1954, Berney informed Miss Goebel that—due to his illustrious position as CEO of the Aberney Corporation—he and executives from Westinghouse had been summoned by government officials to attend a top secret meeting at a military base in Texas. It was there that Berney was led aboard a flying saucer where a disembodied voice informed him that he'd "been elected as a representative of the Earth to the planet Venus." After a brief conversation, the voice became a visible blue glow that suddenly changed into the shape of a human being who introduced himself as a 600-year-old Venusian prince named Uccelles. Prince Uccelles explained that he wished to establish a relationship with the U.S. government and provide a vast array of secret technologies that could be used for the betterment of our planet.

Afterwards, Berney traveled to Venus on a two-mile-long starship and upon arrival discovered a thriving interplanetary mecca of advanced governments and futuristic cities where everyone got along just fine "thank you" and war was a concept that the Venusians had never even dreamt of. In fact, gold was so abundant that the Venusians used it "in manufacturing plumbing fixtures" just like at Trump Tower. With the assistance of Miss Goebel's typing skills, Berney's experiences were chronicled in an unpublished manuscript entitled *Two Weeks On Venus*.

After he returned from Venus, Berney announced that he was working in coordination with an east coast firm to manufacture some of these Venusian technological wonders. This included something called the "Modulator" that employed "magnetic flux" to produce "free energy"—which is always a good thing—unless of course it's a scam to bilk gullible investors out of their life's savings. According to Berney, the Modulator could "lift and gently lower a million tons in a split second. It could propel aircraft and spacecraft at the speed of light—or keep them motionless in the sky…and produce energy potential far greater than anything that atomic energy can produce!"

Berney began selling stock in this super-secret business venture, the details of which were known only to selected White House officials…and those lucky enough to be let in on the deal. Things were moving steadily forward (supposedly) until November 1956 when Berney's wife Dorothy received a letter from Prince Uccelles informing her that—while on a recent trip to Venus—her husband had died and, because he was considered such a big-shot, his body was lying in state there. However, Mrs. Berney wasn't buying the dead-on-Venus bit and assumed that her conniving hubby had simply used this ruse as a pretense for desertion.

Shortly after Berney pulled his disappearing act, the FBI got wise to his activities—Venusian and otherwise—and arrested the erstwhile space traveler in March 1957 on charges of wire fraud and interstate transport of stolen goods. Berney—who bilked investors to the tune of $58K—was convicted in December 1957 and sentenced to prison for a term of twenty months to five years.[1]

---

1. "Two Weeks on Venus." *Time Magazine*, Monday, Apr. 15, 1957.

Truman Betherum at the 1961 Giant Rock Convention (Joe Fex/APE-X Research)

Bethurum, Truman (1898–1969)

One evening in July of 1952, Truman Bethurum—a heavy equipment mechanic working on a project near the California/Nevada border—pulled off the side of the road to catch some quick shut-eye when he was startled from sleep by several small olive-skinned beings gathered around the cab of his pick-up truck. "Our homes are our castles in a faraway land," Bethurum's new found friends informed him. Meanwhile a silver saucer 300 feet in diameter spun overhead.

"Have you a captain?" Bethurum inquired, rubbing the sleep from his bedazzled eyes.

"Surest thing you know," one of the olive-skinned ETs replied and invited Bethurum aboard their ship (which they called a "scow").[1] In short order, Bethurum found himself in the presence of the ship's captain, a gorgeous gal named Aura Rhanes. As Bethurum waxed in *Aboard A Flying Saucer* (1954): "Little did I suspect that their captain would turn out to be a woman—and what a woman!"

Bethurum described Aura as "tops in shapeliness and beauty" with a complexion that was "a beautiful olive and roses" causing him to stare dumbfounded, unable to form a sentence. "Speak up, friend," Captain Rhanes implored Bethurum. "You're not hexed!"

Aura and her crew spoke perfect English—in rhyming couplets, no less—and hailed from Clarion, a planet permanently hidden behind Earth's moon. According to the Claronites, their home was straight out of some Utopian paradise where such things as divorce, smoking tobacco, drinking liquor, and other such evil earthly pursuits didn't exist. (Boring!) On account of all this wholesome living, Clarionites lived to be around a thousand years old and could levitate at will. They were also tops in scientific technology and had developed a machine called the Retroscope that allowed them to see any place in the universe at any time in history.

The Clarionite "scow" was constructed of "the finest Martian steel." The crew members dressed like Greyhound bus drivers, except for our adorable Captain Rhanes, who sported a radiant red skirt, black velvet short sleeve blouse and black beret with red trim like some kind of space age beatnik. For general amusement, the Claronites passed the time—during the course of their cosmic travels—

Aura Rhanes (Illustration by Carol Ann Rodriguez)

playing polkas and square dancing. On a more serious note, Captain Rhanes informed Bethurum that if mankind didn't quit squabbling amongst themselves, they would never be able to achieve space flight. She also had a flair for the dramatic: "I expect to be around for 1,000 years, but the water in your deserts will mostly be tears." Sad!

Following his initial contact with Captain Aura and her crew of Greyhound bus drivers, Bethurum returned to his hotel room and wrote this historic note: "If I am found dead in my bed, it will be because my heart has stopped from the terrible excitement induced by seeing and going aboard a flying saucer!"

Over a three month period, Aura visited Truman on eleven occasions, sometimes materializing in his bedroom, much to the chagrin of Bethurum's wife, Mary, who later cited the comely space captain in her divorce petition.

Bethurum enjoyed another shot at marital bliss in 1960, although unfortunately it wasn't with shapely Aura, but a weathered old gal named Alvira Roberts, their nuptials taking place on the podium at the Giant Rock Spacecraft Convention.

During one of Aura's later materializations, she instructed Bethurum to gather around himself some friends—particularly those with greenbacks—and establish the "Sanctuary of Thought," a cosmically inspired commune dedicated to "peace and brotherly love" based out of Prescott, Arizona. It was here Bethurum sold his books and delivered services as a "spiritual advisor."

The last time Bethurum beheld his curvaceous space captain was in the wee hours of August 27, 1952 at an all-night roadside diner in Glendale, Nevada:

> Bethurum was enjoying a late night snack of pie and coffee with Whitey Edwards... when he felt an elbow in his side. Edwards gestured eagerly toward the lunch counter, where a small man was seated next to a tiny woman wearing a black and red beret, a black, velvety blouse, and a brilliant red pleated skirt... It had to be Aura Rhanes and one of her crewmen!

Bethurum looked, and confirmed Edwards' suspicion. Would he like to be introduced? Edwards, strangely put off by the presence of the celestial visitors, refused and began gathering his things to leave.

"If you do," Bethurum cautioned, "stand near the door so you can see what they get into and which way they go when they come out."

Then he approached his extraterrestrial friends. "I beg your pardon, Lady, but haven't we met before?"

No, she insisted to each of his repeated requests for recognition, no, no. He turned to pay his check, and the pair were gone. He rushed outside and demanded Whitey Edwards' report – where had they gone?

"Honest, Truman," his friend responded, "Not a blessed soul passed through that door until you came out."

1. Nebel, Long John. 1961. *The Way Out World*. Prentice-Hall, Inc. (p. 36).

Marjorie Cameron at Giant Rock in late 1950s (Photo by her second husband, Sherry the Shadowman)

CAMERON, MARJORIE (1922–1995)

Much has been written regarding the brief but curious partnership between pioneering rocket scientist Jack Parsons and Scientology founder L. Ron Hubbard, including a magick ritual the two men performed in 1946 called the Babalon Working, the intent of which was to conjure a child in the ethereal realm that would be called down and directed into the womb of a female volunteer. When born, this magickal child would incarnate the forces of Babalon and become the Scarlet Woman of Revelations, symbolizing the dawning of the Age of Horus, the coming new eon.

Jack Parsons received explicit directions from the Great Beast himself, Aleister Crowley, on a ceremony to summon the female participant for the Babalon Working. Not long after performing this Crowleyean ritual, a lightning bolt purportedly cracked outside of Parsons' home at 1003 South Orange Grove in Pasadena, California, and seemingly out of nowhere Cameron materialized on his doorstep, a striking figure of unusual beauty with fiery red hair. Appearing disheveled, and unaware of how she'd landed on Parsons' doorstep, the two soon fell into each other's arms, spending the next couple of weeks in the sack getting to know each other on a more intimate basis.[1] Conversely, Cameron's description of how she and Jack first hooked up was disappointingly more prosaic, but however their first meeting actually went down, the two began a torrid love affair that ultimately consummated in marriage in October 1946.

From the outset of their relationship, the specter of flying saucers surrounded Parsons and Cameron's relationship. While sitting in the garden at Parsons' mansion one day, Cameron witnessed a silver cigar shaped UFO hovering silently overhead. When she related this sighting to Parsons, he considered it a sign that she was the chosen one with whom to conduct the Babalon Working.[2]

Parsons' life ended with a monumental bang on June 17, 1952 when he blew himself to smithereens while mixing explosives at his home lab. There are those who suspect that the explosion was no mere accident, and that foul play was involved. Other speculation includes the theory that Parsons was attempting to conjure into existence an elemental being by way of an "homunculus" experiment—an experiment that evidently backfired in a big way. Crowley protégé Kenneth Grant suggested that Cameron—during the course of the Babalon Working—became possessed by malevolent ETs and this somehow led to his demise.

Shortly after Jack Parsons' death, a swarm of UFOs reportedly buzzed the White House, the Capitol and Pentagon. These were sightings apparently confirmed by photographs, radar and pilot testimony, putting the nation on alert. When Cameron read about this event in the newspapers, she considered it a cosmic acknowledgement of Parsons' passing from the Earth plane to higher levels of consciousness. According to Cameron's friend, artist Allen Midgette, "UFOs provided Cameron with a transdimensional link to Jack [Parsons]."

In the late 1950s/early '60s, Cameron moved to Pioneertown, California, just a stone's throw from Giant Rock and befriended George Van Tassel. Inspired by the Integratron, Cameron had plans to build a Temple of Thelema on her ranch property that would consist of five interconnecting pods on stilts, serving as a beacon to draw in exotic energies, earthly and otherwise.

According to a poet friend named Aya:

> Cameron had her visions out there. And she was going through all that spiritual messaging, and even seeing saucer sightings, and just feeling the energy of the ships and lights following you out there, that was just part of what she was searching for. It had to do with time travel and getting into the other dimension thing, which we're so sure is there, but you don't know how to reach it.

1. Kansa, Spencer. 2014. *Wormwood Star: The Magickal Life of Marjorie Cameron.* Mandrake.
2. Carter, John, 2000. *Sex and Rockets: The Occult World of Jack Parsons.* Port Townsend, WA: Feral House.

Michael Cecil (*Round Trip To Hell on a Flying Saucer*)

CECIL, MICHAEL

In August 1952, Michael Cecil witnessed a strange vehicle hovering low and noiseless in the skies over Bakersfield, California. Through the v-shaped windows of the craft, Cecil observed two men at the controls dressed in "odd-looking head gear and uniforms." The craft projected a 3-D holographic image of a "phantom city" and after completing this peculiar aerial display, it performed a u-turn then slowly sailed away into the night.

A few days later, Cecil witnessed a second sighting of a speedier sort of spaceship that he described as "a silver plate object bristling in the sky." To Cecil, these sightings seemed to be a demonstration of some sort, perhaps preparing him for the later satanic strangeness to unfold.

In mid-October, a couple of curious (and apparently otherworldly) visitors appeared at Cecil's auto shop, maintaining a presence there over the next several weeks, fading in and out like spectres, which only he could see. Dressed in tunic-like outfits with hoods and moccasins, the two men didn't really have much to say, but what they did say was delivered telepathically. Even though he was startled by their sudden appearance, Cecil noted that the men seemed "nice" and had light beams coming out of their eyes. On one occasion, he was able to observe green bubbles inside their bodies. They also smiled a lot and possessed "remarkable minds."

Cecil's strange experience culminated with an apparent flying saucer trip to Hell; an experience he didn't consider a physical reality, as his body was still at his Bakersfield auto shop. During the course of the trip he would occasionally snap out of his trance to answer the phone, or complete some other task. However, once the task was completed, Cecil would again resume his flying saucer trip that—although apparently transpiring in mental space—seemed totally real.

Planet Hell, it turns out, lived up to its reputation, featuring a burning lake in which the dead in their coffins were cast, only to emerge as tormented souls on fire, screaming in flesh searing agony. Cecil figured he was doomed to this same fiery fate until Jesus miraculously appeared in a white beam of light and delivered him back to his auto shop, a round trip that apparently transpired over the course of four days, although the clock on his wall indicated he'd been gone for only four hours.

Further reading

Cecil, Michael. 1955. *Round Trip To Hell on a Flying Saucer*. New York: Vantage.

HELLO!
My Name Is

HARMONY GROVE
1960 SPACECRAFT
CONVENTION

Lee Childers aka Prince NEasom (Joe Fex/APE-X Research)

CHILDERS, LEE (1922–1982)

Lee Childers was treated to his first spaceship trip in 1955 courtesy of extraterrestrial Commander Marcosan. This included a stop-over on Mars—revealed to be a "dead planet"—in addition to a jaunt to the moon, which featured cities that could be raised or lowered in and out of moon craters. Commander Marcosan's spaceship—which traveled at the astounding speed of 250,000 miles an hour—caused Childers to become so space-sick that one of the crew members (an 8 foot tall fellow) held him out a porthole to allow him to throw up. All in all, Childers was taken on a total of twenty-one such trips, which he claimed to be a space-faring record. On one such voyage Childers rode in a spaceship that was 100 miles in diameter called TREJEDOM.

Childers burst on to the ufological scene in a big way in December 1958 when a saucer club called the Bureau of UFO Research and Analysis (BUFORA) arranged a press conference in New York City where Childers announced to the world that—in addition to being a baker from Detroit, Michigan—he was also a 250 year old interplanetary traveler (otherwise known as Prince NEasom from the Royal Family of Planet Tythan.)

At his press conference, Childers unveiled a rejuvenation machine which had allegedly brought him back from death on three separate occasions, each after tangling with some unruly Men-In-Black who kept killing Prince NEasom on account of his efforts to alert mankind that we're doomed for nuclear annihilation if we didn't heed the space brother's dire warnings.

Accompanying Childers were a couple of female assistants, Beth Docker and Fannie Lowrey. It was later revealed that Childers had ditched his wife and five children for the tender charms of Miss Docker, who in time adopted the name "Princess NEgonna."

During the same weekend of his press conference, Childers—along with his female posse—appeared on Long John Nebel's *Party Line* and before going on-air predicted that a fleet of flying saucers would show up on cue and rebroadcast the program to a worldwide audience using advanced saucer technology.

Lee Childers and Beth Docker at Giant Rock (Joe Fex/APE-X Research)

Nebel—famous for accommodating all manner of kooks—found Childers' claims so preposterous that he kicked Prince NEasom and his crew off the airwaves just a few minutes into the show, the first and only time that Long John had used the hook on a guest. Needless to say, the fleet of predicted saucers were a no-show.

Even George Van Tassel—who hardly ever had a harsh word for his fellow contactees—denounced Childers as a fraud on the grounds that he had bad teeth, something Van Tassel considered an impossibility for someone purported to be a true interplanetary traveler.[1]

1. Moseley, James & Pflock, Karl. 2002. *Shockingly Close To The Truth: Confessions of a Grave-Robbing Ufologist.* New York: Prometheus Books.

Trevor James Constable behind the controls of his cloudbuster (*The Cosmic Pulse of Life*)

CONSTABLE, TREVOR JAMES (1925–2016)

Trevor James Constable was one of George Van Tassel's earliest visitors at Giant Rock and due to this influence began channeling Ashtar, a name that turns up time and again throughout UFO lore. Unlike other Ashtar iterations, the version with whom Constable maintained telepathic contact was an Etherian from the fourth dimension, also known as the Realms of Schare. By and large, the Etherians were a benevolent bunch, but through their teachings Constable learned also of evil ETs visiting Earth whom he called "The Dark Ones."

The Etherians—and the flying saucers they spun in on, Ashtar explained—exist all around us, and sometimes even pass through us, although in most cases we aren't able to see them, which explains their tendency to blink in and out of materiality, and why they often take on corporeal form to accommodate what humans expect to see, including nut and bolt craft that are created on a temporary basis to facilitate these human interactions.

In the summer of 1957, Constable began using infra-red film to photograph what he described as "critters"; entities or spaceships (perhaps they were one and the same) that were invisible—or at least could not be viewed by "normal" eyes.[1] What the infrared film allowed Constable to do was peek beyond the curtain, so to speak, and tune into a bandwidth not normally accessed by human perception. The "critters," or space creatures, in Constable's photographs appeared as a wide range of strange things, some of which were similar to flying saucer shapes, while other photos revealed amoeba-like entities. Constable used a version Wilhelm Reich's Cloudbuster to pull these creatures into the atmosphere, or into the infrared spectrum, enabling him to photograph them.

Even within the wooly world of ufology, Constable's theories bordered on heretical. Because of this—and to shelter his professional career as a military historian—he initially flew under the radar using the pseudonym of "T. James" for his first book *Spacemen Friends and Foes* (1956), and then later "Trevor James" for *They Live In The Sky!* (1958). Eventually—as he became more comfortable promoting these ideas—he used his full name Trevor James Constable for his magnum opus, *The*

Cosmic Pulse of Life (1976).

1. Clark, Jerome. 1992. *The Emergence of a Phenomenon: UFOs from the Beginning through 1959 - The UFO Encyclopedia - Volume 2*. Detroit: Omnigraphics, Inc. (p.876).

Lee Crandall (*The Venusians*)

CRANDALL, LEE (born ca. 1927)

Southern California native Lee Crandall was the first human ever to visit Venus...according to Lee Crandall. This momentous occasion occurred on August 31, 1954 when he was treated to the requisite spaceship trip...but we're getting ahead of ourselves. Let's begin at the beginning.

Crandall's outstanding Venusian adventure began one summer day in sunny L.A. (June 10, 1954 to be exact) as he was hurrying to catch a bus and bumped into a tall man in a brown suit. Crandall profusely apologized to the brown-suited fellow who then proceeded to vanished into thin air.[1]

Crandall's next encounter with the incredible disappearing man occurred on June 30th when to his "utter amazement there in the doorway stood the tall man in brown. For at least three minutes, he stood there, smiling, then turned at an angle and with a faint whizz sound, vanish again from my sight. By now I began to doubt my own sanity!"

A couple weeks later, the brown suited fellow materialized at Crandall's workplace and this time actually said something: "Mr. Crandall, I'd like to talk to you outside." The gist of the conversation was that he—the brown suited mystery man—wanted to be Crandall's friend. Oh, and incidentally, he was from Venus. When Crandall displayed disbelief, the alleged Venusian stated, "Believe me it is so, and trust in my friendship." With those words, another vanishing act occurred.

On August 17th, Crandall was awakened in the middle of the night by his doorbell. When he asked who the hell it was calling at such an ungodly hour, a calm, mellow voice replied: "This is your friend, Lee." Crandall opened the door to discover another similarly brown suited stranger—a handsome fellow around thirty five years of age named Brother Bocco—who explained that he'd come on behalf of Brother Taho (the other brown suited disappearing guy.) Bocco informed Crandall that his mission was to deliver him to Venus! However, Crandall wasn't too keen at that particular moment to travel all the way to Venus in the middle of the night, so he declined the offer and Brother Bocco predictably vanished.

Crandall's next encounter occurred on August 27th when Brother Bocco showed up on his doorstep and brought along a scout ship that hovered outside "throwing light in delicate pastel shades, so soft were the upshooting rays that they could only be compared to raised feathers or to petals of an ethereal flower." Once again the spaceship trip was offered. This time Crandall accepted the invitation and left a note for his parents that said: "Folks, gone to Venus. All is well. Lee."

Their scout ship landed near a majestic white temple where a large crowd of brown-suited Venusian men had assembled, many of whom were kneeling in prayer. The sea of brown suits parted, as Bocco and Taho led Crandall to an alter where "three important men" performed some sort of Venusian baptism placing Lee's hand in "a white downy substance they called water." The three men explained that they were all about Universal Peace and that Crandall would be their "active agent for this Great Universal Endeavor of Understanding, which would soon be revealed."

A month after his initial Venusian adventure, Crandall was visited by Brother Bocco who invited him for a return trip. En route they passed through a series of "hemispheres," one of which consisted of "hundreds of beautiful feminine creatures, all blondes, all clothed in white trailing garments, floating in a swimming position…"

While on a "show me" trip, Crandall's Venusian hosts brought to his "attention large barrels full of feathery like material. They said this was what the ship was made of. This material would be processed and molded into shapes with their hands, then magnetized. They said that magnetism was the propelling energy providing motion for these strange feathery mechanisms…After a complete tour of this strange laboratory we left and once again re-entered the ship, this time dropping below the first plane I had landed on, to a lower plane. This is where the women live. Thousands of them were gathered there assembled in a large open space for the purpose of looking at a man from Earth…They were all around thirty-five years of age, had long brown hair, beautiful eyes, olive skin, large mouth and very full lips. They were simply beautiful creatures…all dressed in white ankle-length garments, long sleeves, with no jewels or make-up…Their leader was introduced to me Sister Sistrano. In very good English she welcomed me on behalf of the group and five of them came forward to greet me, bowing their heads. The leader said that the music I would now hear would come from the humming in unison of these five performers, blending in the most wonderful harmony of vibrant subdued sounds. These continuous vibrations were encircling the planet in one sonorous wave…After bidding these beautiful creatures farewell, we again boarded our ship and moved back down to what I shall call the middle plane of the planet…"

Crandall's account (published in a booklet called *The Venusians*) included exhaustive (and achingly ponderous) details of Venusian physiology. At the time, Crandall was studying to become a chiropractor, and so apparently felt the need to share his vast knowledge of human *and* Venusian anatomy with his readership.

In a 2003 post at *UFO Updates*, the sometimes contrary contactee Ray Stanford noted that "Lee

Crandall delivered a half-used bar of Ivory Soap (with white chicken feathers pressed into it) to his publishers and told them it was a spare piece of Brother Bocco's Venusian spaceship made of "... magnetized white dove feathers, given in consolation of your spines not being sufficiently crystallized as to enable you to see and approach the spaceship personally..."[2]

1. http://gratisenergi.se/crandall.htm
2. http://ufoupdateslist.com/2003/aug/m09-004.shtml

Fred Crisman, "the most informed man in the United States on UFOs"

CRISMAN, FRED (1919–1975)

On June 21, 1947, a timber salvage worker named Harold Dahl—in the company of his teen-age son and dog—were out on a boat in Puget Sound, Washington (near Maury Island) when "six very large donut-shaped machines" appeared in the sky. One of the donut ships began laboring when another of its companions descended and touched the laboring craft as if to repair it, after which it "spewed out" molten fragments—later referred to as "slag"—that rained down on Dahl's workboat, killing his poor pooch and severely scorching his son's arm (supposedly). After ejecting this slag spew, the craft rejoined its fellow donut ships and zoomed off at a high rate of speed. Dahl gathered up some of the slag fragments and returned to the harbor to give his supervisor the lowdown.

Dahl's supervisor, in this case, happened to be one of the more curious characters in the annals of ufology, a fellow named Fred Crisman who also played a role in certain JFK assassination conspiracy theories. Not long after Dahl's sighting, a mysterious Man in Black paid him a visit, perhaps the first recorded instance of MIB activity in the Modern Era of UFOs. (Maybe.) The MIB—appropriately driving a black sedan—explained that he knew all about Dahl's donut ship sighting, adding that:"Silence is the best thing for you and your family. You have seen what you ought not to have seen!"

On June 23rd, Crisman purportedly visited the site of the donut ship sighting to collect some slag samples and at that time photographed more donut ships that circled around the harbor before disappearing into a cloud. In early July, Crisman contacted Ray Palmer of *Fate* magazine in an attempt to further advance the Maury Island story, sending along some sample's of the slag. In response, Palmer recruited Kenneth Arnold to investigate Dahl and Crisman's claims, and write up a report.

A year prior to the Maury Island incident, Crisman contacted Palmer claiming that during World War II he and another soldier had engaged in a firefight with the Deros (those very same evil subterranean creatures described by Richard Shaver in the pages of *Amazing Stories*) and his companion soldier had been shot with a ray gun that left a dime sized hole in his hand. But that wasn't all: Crisman offered to travel to a cave in Texas he knew about to recover some ancient Dero machinery if Palmer was willing to pony up $500 for expenses. Palmer wisely declined Crisman's proposition.

On July 29th, Kenneth Arnold flew to Tacoma to interview Crisman and Dahl. Upon arrival—and aware of a shortage of hotel rooms in town—he started calling around and was at first unsuccessful in securing accommodations. Arnold's last resort was the most expensive hotel in town, the Winthrop, and when he called there the front desk confirmed that a room was already reserved in his name. When Arnold informed the hotel desk clerk he hadn't made a reservation—and that it was probably another person by the same name—he was told that the reservation was indeed booked for a Mr. Kenneth Arnold of Boise, Idaho. Later that day, Arnold interviewed Dahl and Crisman. Uncertain as to the veracity of their claims, on the following morning—July 30th—Arnold called in his friend, Captain E.J. Smith (Big Smithy)—a pilot with United Airlines based out of Seattle—to assist in the investigation.

That evening, Arnold received a phone call from UPI reporter Ted Morella, who said he'd received information from a "crackpot" who repeated a full account of Arnold's investigation, which Morella recited verbatim. This led Arnold to suspect that his room had been bugged and that his reservation had been surreptitiously arranged to place him in a location where his activities could be monitored. Throughout the day, Arnold and Big Smithy had been dogged by another local reporter, Paul Lantz, who was attempting to get the inside scoop.

Throughout the course of his investigation, Arnold attempted to keep it on the down-low, and the only ones he knew who were aware of his activities were Palmer, Big Smithy, Crisman, and Dahl. Because of this, Arnold grew to suspect that Paul Lantz had been tipped off by either Crisman or Dahl in an attempt to promote their story. Concerned that he was being set up by a pair of hucksters, Arnold put in a call to his Air Force contacts—Lt. Frank Brown and Captain William Davidson—inviting them to join the investigation. The officers accepted Arnold's invite and flew to Tacoma that same day, but after questioning Crisman and Dahl they were apparently unimpressed with the men's story.

Crisman and Dahl invited the officers for a boat trip out to Maury Island, but Brown and Davidson declined, stating they had to return early the next morning to California. As a parting gift, the officers were given a carton containing some of the slag fragments. Arnold and Big Smithy, however, agreed to the Maury Island trip which ultimately turned out to be a bust. Crisman and Dahl were unable able to start the engine of their boat, which seemed like a convenient excuse to call off the trip.

Shortly after take-off—in the early hours of August 1st—one of the engines of the B-52 transporting Brown and Davidson caught fire and went down in flames, killing both men, the first official crash of an Air Force plane. The next afternoon, the *Tacoma Times* featured a most curious headline: SABOTAGE HINTED IN CRASH OF ARMY BOMBER AT KELSO. The news article, written by Paul Lantz, reported that the B-52 "had been sabotaged 'or shot down' to prevent shipment of flying disc fragments..." and "that the ill-fated craft had been carrying 'classified material.'" One can assume that Fred Crisman had a hand in spinning this story, which—if such was the case—seemed like a tasteless publicity stunt. To this end, many suspect that Crisman cooked up the whole Maury Island affair out of whole cloth, the intent of which was to sell it to Ray Palmer and cash in on the sudden saucer craze sweeping the nation. This would support the theory that it was Crisman, under an assumed identity, who contacted reporter Morella to leak details of Arnold's investigation, and that Arnold's room at the Winthrop had not actually been bugged—it was simply Crisman (affecting an anonymous identity) repeating what he'd overheard to Morella.

The aftermath of the Maury Island incident proved equally unsettling. Paul Lantz—one of the reporters covering the story—died within six months of the investigation from undetermined causes. Not long after, Harold Dahl disappeared, apparently motivated to skip town due to the shortened life span of others connected to the case. Around this time, Crisman—a WWII vet—was reactivated for duty and assigned to Alaska, which suggested to some that the Feds had swooped in and spirited him away as a means of quashing further Maury Island investigations.

On Arnold's flight home, the apparent veil of doom hanging over Maury Island reared its head when he lost power to the engine of his airplane. Fortunately, Arnold was able to land safely in Boise, although he did need a new set of undergarments. Shaken by these events, Arnold dropped the Maury Island case, as he felt no tangible evidence had emerged during the investigation, not to mention the uneasy feeling that Crisman and Dahl had been trying to pull a fast one.

In a 1958 issue of Ray Palmer's *Flying Saucer* magazine, Crisman (using the pseudonym of Eldon Everett) briefly re-emerged to re-promote his Maury Island yarn, in addition to other saucer encounters he'd supposedly experienced in the ensuing years. Afterwards, Crisman kept a low profile on the subject until again resurfacing, however briefly, in 1967 at the Northwest UFO Space Convention in Seattle (sponsored by Daniel Fry's *Understanding*) where he recounted the Maury Island Incident and claimed that he still had the photos of the slag spewing donut ships, but for whatever reasons decided not to display them at the event, nor have these photos ever surfaced—if, in fact, they actually ever existed.

Crisman became associated with another sketchy saucer enthusiast named Thomas Beckham, and the two men organized the First (and last!) Midwest UFO Conference in Omaha, Nebraska on August 12th, 1967. Among the speakers Crisman lined up for the event was our old friend Major Wayne Aho, although for some inexplicable reason the elusive Mr. Crisman was a no-show.[1]

In early 1968, Crisman (using the pseudonym of Fred Lee) sent a letter to Lucius Farish of the

Parapsychology Research Group informing him that, "Mr. Crisman is probably the most informed man in the United States on UFOs and also one of the hardest to find—as the FBI has learned several times!"[2]

Crisman became a short-lived suspect in New Orleans District Attorney Jim Garrison's JFK assassination investigation, identified by conspiracy sleuths as one of the three mystery tramps who were presumably up to no good in Dealey Plaza. These allegations against Crisman were later debunked in 1977 by the House Select Committee on Assassinations who determined that—on November 22nd, 1963—Crisman had been filling in as a substitute teacher at Rainer Union High School in Rainer, Oregon, his whereabouts corroborated in affidavits provided by three teachers in attendance that day: Marva Harris, Norma Chase and Stanley Peerloom.[3]

1. Thomas, Kenn, 1999. *Maury Island UFO: The Crisman Conspiracy*. Lilburn, GA: IllumiNet Press.
2. Gulyas, Aaron John. 2015. *The Paranormal and the Paranoid Lanham*, Maryland: Rowman & Littlefield.(pp. 30–31).
3. Report of the Select Committee on Assassinations of the U.S. House of Representatives. 1979. (p. 92).

Woody Derenberger

Derenberger, Woodrow "Woody" (1916–1990)

Woody Derenberger's life took a turn for the weird in the early morning hours of November 2, 1966, while driving Interstate 77 near Parkersburg, West Virginia—and you can probably guess what happened next.

A spaceship resembling a huge "kerosene lamp" appeared, causing Woody to pull off on the shoulder of the road, after which a man in shiny trousers exited the craft, walk up to him and requested that Woody roll down the window of his Ford Econovan. Mr. Shiny Pants telepathically assured Woody that he meant no harm—only much happiness—and communicated his name as Indrid Cold. Woody later reported that Indrid—who referred to himself as a "searcher"—possessed a nice tan and looked no different than the average person you'd meet strolling down the street. After a few minutes of conversation, Indrid said he'd be seeing him again and then hopped aboard his spacecraft and away he went.

The local Parkersburg media quickly caught wind of Woody's story and he consented to an interview the next day at television station WTAP. Other media outlets and local law enforcement met with Woody at this time—including a U.S. Air Force official—and the general consensus was that Woody seemed to be on the up and up.

Not long after Woody's sighting (of the man in the kerosene lamp craft with the shiny blue pants) people in the same neck of those West Virginia woods reported the appearance of an apparent bird-like creature with blood red eyes. This, of course, was an entity later to become known as the Mothman who many suspect was somehow related to a number of other UFO sightings that occurred in West Virginia during this period.

On November 4th, Woody was driving back from Ohio when he started receiving telepathic transmissions from Mr. Cold calling in from planet Lanulos. Cold cautioned Woody to slow his roll and drive carefully because he didn't want to be responsible for Woody wrapping his Econovan around a telephone pole while receiving these telepathic transmissions. Among other words of wisdom Mr.

Cold shared was that time on Lanulos was unlike time on Earth, and that Lanulosians strutted their stuff in the buff, on a sort of outer space nudist colony.

Eventually, Indrid—along with his spaceship's navigator, Carl Ardo—visited Woody and his family at Derenberger's home, a story chronicled in *Visitors From Lanulos* (1971).

FERGUSON, WILLIAM (1900–1967)

A self-professed "Adept at the art of relaxation," William Ferguson used the term "absolute relaxation" to describe his astral projection (or out-of-body) experiences, which included voyages to the sixth and seventh dimensions.[1]

In 1938, Ferguson relaxed his way to Mars and met with Khauga who just happened to be the chief Uniphysicist of the Solar System.[2] According to Ferguson, he was the very first Earthman to visit Mars and because of this there was "great rejoicing" among his new-found Martian friends.

While hanging with Khauga, Ferguson was treated to a tour of the red planet, which he soon discovered was a virtual paradise. Saith Khauga:

> How do you like our city, or living spaces, as we call them? They form a great network all over the planet, your astronomers call them canals. For two thousand years we have lived in these enclosed living spaces. We have our cities and countrysides all enclosed, and maintain a constant temperature of 76 degrees. Our vegetation grows continuously. We have made our own weather. The enclosures are tremendous electro-magnetic force fields created by our Uniphysicists.

> In our expedition to the Earth, we intend to release large quantities of expanded elements on the surface of your planet, which will, in turn, speed up the expansion of the elements you are working with. We have waited for this time in the Earth's development to step in and help our sister Planet Earth. If your scientists will listen to the truth, and stop pursuing selfish interests, and obeying the dictates of the combines, they can have an oasis in the deserts and an abundance of every usable thing man can imagine.

Inspired by his amazing Martian adventures, Ferguson founded the *Cosmic Circle of Fellowship*,

...a religious organization of the sovereign State of Illinois, under the complete guidance of Celestial and Immortal Beings from Outer Space. The messenger of these space beings is William Ferguson of the Planet Earth, and other Priests and Priestesses, who have been and will be, elevated to the Priesthood of the Cosmic Circle of Fellowship...

We worship only the Alpha and the Omega, who are the First Cause, (Everliving). We adore many Celestials and Immortals, who are working with us and guiding us. We invite all people of the Planet Earth to join us in fellowship and the worship of Alpha and Omega.[3]

Khauga instructed Ferguson to construct a device called the Zerret Applicator that could supposedly cure everything from gout to lumbago. This wonder device (selling for the low, low price of $50!) was made of plastic with nifty blue and white vertical stripes. When you held it in your hands, it emitted z-rays, "a force unknown to science." (At least the part about "unknown to science" was true.) According to the Zerret Applicator instruction manual:

When you hold the Applicator, it works on your life current, expanding the atoms of the same. As this takes place, it expands all atoms of your being. Expansion of your atoms produces what is commonly called relaxation.

After receiving complaints about the Zerret Applicator, the FDA brought the hammer down on Ferguson, claiming he'd misbranded the Zerret Applicator as a cure-all—when it was really a cure for nothing. Ferguson was sentenced to two years in prison for medical fraud and the FDA even went so far as to create a PSA featuring actor Raymond Massey with a stern Zerret Applicator rebuke:

I'm Raymond Massey and I have a special message for senior citizens. Today's doctors, drugs, and medical devices truly work medical miracles for the young and old alike, but there are some as phony as a three dollar bill, like this Zerret Applicator, for example, which has claimed to cure arthritis with Z–Rays... *There are no z-rays!*

1. Ferguson, William. 1937. *Relax First*. Bronson-Canode.
2. Clark, Jerome. 2000. *Extraordinary Encounters: An Encyclopedia of Extraterrestrials and Otherworldly Beings*. Santa Barbara, CA: ABC-CLIO. (p. 143).
3. Lewis, James R. (ed.),1995. *The Gods Have Landed: New Religions from Other Worlds*. State University of New York Press.

Left to right: Aleuti Francesca, Major Wayne Aho, Kenn Thomas, Rev. Robert Short, Guy Kirkwood, and Shirley Short at the 1998 UFO Congress (Photo credit: Nick Redfern)

FRANCIS, MARIANNE (aka Aleuti Francesca)

Originally from London, England, Marianne Francis relocated to Southern California in the late 1950s where she discovered something called Tele-Thought that allowed her to establish interstellar communications with the space brothers.

Marianne had been a "sensitive" all her life, but her sensitivity significantly spiked when—with the aid of her husband, physicist Ken Kellar—she began using a contraption called a Light Beam to focus her Tele-Thought transmissions at a mothership identified as XY7 of Saturn Command.[1]

In the early 1960s, Marianne and Ken—inspired by messages from their Saturnian friends—founded the Santa Barbara Space Craft Research Society where they hosted lectures with prominent figures on the California saucer scene. In 1975, Marianne legally changed her name to Aleuti Francesca per instructions from on high. In 1966, she and her hubby Ken moved to a "mountain vortex" in White City, Oregon and started the Solar Light Retreat. Unsurprisingly, the type of seminars one would expect to attend there were of the typical New Age variety, like the Earth is currently going through a cleansing, the end result of which will herald the beginning of a Golden Age of Light.

1. Melton, Gordon J., 2009. *Melton's Encyclopedia Of American Religions.*

Daniel Fry in the underground room at Giant Rock (Joe Fex/APE-X Research)

FRY, DANIEL (1908–1992)

While working as an explosives technician at White Sands Proving Ground in Alamogordo, New Mexico, Daniel Fry went out for an evening stroll on July 4, 1950 and witnessed an "oblate spheroid" come to a silent landing. Intrigued by the strange craft, Fry passed his hand over the exterior to test its temperature, and a telepathic voice rang out: "Better not touch the hull, pal, it's still hot!"

After exchanging telepathic pleasantries with an ET named A-lan (pronounced "a-lawn")—who remotely piloted the "oblate spheroid" from a Mothership located 900 miles above Earth—Fry was taken for a quick show-me trip to New York and back in an astounding 30 minutes, traveling 8000 miles an hour. (Pretty fast even for a saucer!)

In the weeks to follow, Fry was treated to additional trips as A-lan supplied him with a stunning array of knowledge on such subjects as advanced physics and the hidden history of Earth. Afterwards, A-lan appointed Fry as the Earthling representative to carry forth the space brother message that "Understanding is the key to peace and happiness."[1] Good to know.

After having all this Universal Wisdom dropped on him, Fry decided to expand his knowledge base even more by receiving a "Doctorate of Cosmism" from Saint Andrew College, a mail order outfit located in London, England. Fry later remarked that he was "recognized by many as the best informed scientist in the world on the subject of space and space travel."

In 1955, Fry founded *Understanding Inc.* based out of El Monte, California, a flying saucer club that in the years to come would expand to a nationwide network of 43 "study groups" consisting of 1500 members. These different study groups hosted lectures overseen by Dr. Fry (as he started calling himself) who traveled around the country on the largesse of his starry-eyed supporters, many of them elderly women who were smitten with the dashing Dr. Fry.[2]

From 1956 through 1979, Fry published a monthly newsletter, *Understanding*, and was prominent on the saucer lecture circuit, as well as a familiar figure at George Van Tassel's Giant Rock Spacecraft Conventions.

In 1974, Understanding Inc. was gifted fifty-five acres of land including eight buildings in Tonopah, Arizona, by one of Fry's many female admirers, Mrs. Enid Smith. A couple years later, Fry moved to the Tonopah property and established his permanent base of operations there. Not long after, an arson fire destroyed the *Understanding Inc.* library and other buildings on the property. This event—in combination with dwindling membership rolls—signaled the beginning of the end for Dr. Fry's ufological empire.

1. Fry, Daniel. 1954. *The White Sands Incident*. Los Angeles: New Age Publishing Co.
2. Moseley, James & Pflock, Karl. 2002. *Shockingly Close To The Truth: Confessions of a Grave-Robbing Ufologist*. New York: Prometheus Books.

Gavin Girvan at Giant Rock (Joe Fex/APE-X Research)

GIRVIN, CALVIN (1926-2005)

Calvin Girvin experienced a series of dreams where he traveled to Venus and met with Cryxtan and Ashtar who clued him in to the hidden history of humankind and how long, long ago their Venusian forefathers colonized Earth and brought along a bunch of Venusian ape women slaves to perform manual labor.

At some point during their colonization, the homesick and horny Venusian men engaged in sex (otherwise known as bestiality!) with the ape women and as a result created "hu-mans." After the history lesson was over, Cryxtan recruited Girvan to work for Venus as a benevolent spy of sorts, and the plan they cooked up was that Girvan would seek employment with the U.S. Air Force and—after landing a position—he'd somehow gain access to classified flying saucer files, then pass this intelligence on to his Venusians handlers. (Why the Venusians needed information about the very same secret saucers they themselves were piloting is unclear.)

According to Girvan, he was able to secure employment as an Air Force food server at the Pentagon. On September 16, 1952—while traveling from Maryland to Washington, DC for his first day of work—a "scout ship" swooped down, picked up Girvin and gave him a lift to a nearby mothership. After a short briefing on his upcoming assignment, Girvin's Venusian friends then beamed him back to Earth just in time for his first day on the job.

During his Pentagon stint, Girvin availed himself of every opportunity to bring up the topic of flying saucers with Air Force officials while dishing out their gruel. One can assume that Girvin's commanding officers grew to suspect he was a bit daft, or perhaps suspected him of being a spy—or maybe he just flat out got on their nerves—which might explain why he was soon after reassigned to Hawaii.

Further reading

Girvin, Calvin. 1958. *The Night Has a Thousand Saucers*. El Monte, California: Understanding Publishing Co.

Nodrog at the Welasco Flea Market circa 1985 (Photo credit: Douglas Curran)

GORDON, ORVILLE T. (aka O.T. Nodrog)

In the 1930s, Orville T. Gordon started a lumberyard in Welasco, Texas that remained in operation until the early 1960s when he shut down the business due to an ongoing feud with local government over unpaid taxes. In 1963, Orville purportedly came into contact with a group of extraterrestrials who—after witnessing how humankind was despoiling the Earth—got a bit miffed and informed him of their plans to bring about Armageddon to teach the sinners a lesson. To prepare for the forthcoming apocalyptic flood, Orville founded a group (which some have termed a cult) called Outer Dimensional Forces and changed his name to O.T. Nodrog. (Nodrog is Gordon spelled backwards.)

In his efforts to immanentize the eschaton, Gordon (now Nodrog) constructed a UFO landing strip at his erstwhile lumberyard and christened it the "Armageddon Time Ark Base." It was here, presumably, the space brothers would swoop down at the appointed hour and spirit away Nodrog and his crew.

With all that being said, a perusal of ODF literature seems to suggest that Nodrog and his group are the actual ETs (or at least ET channelers) and the Armageddon Time Ark Base, of which they rant, is an invisible flying saucer hidden on Nodrog's property that will be employed in the End Times (with Nodrog in the role of Noah.) Or something like that. In addition to selling berries and honey at the Welasco flea market, Nodrog offered seats for sale on his UFO and an ostensible ticket out at the appointed hour.

The United States (in ODF-speak) is known as the "Manasseh Complex," a reference to one of the Lost Tribes of Israel that once inhabited North America before it went to seed on account of corrupt government agencies and other evil-doers. "Time Station Earth" embodies only three and a half dimensions, whereas the Armageddon Time Ark is a fifth-dimensional construct tuned to a higher vibratory level. If you want to become more confused, ODF maintains a website at www.atabase.com which includes the revelation that AIDS is the "Armageddon disease."

Douglas Curran's *In Advance of the Landing: Folk Concepts of Outer Space* (1986) chronicled an episode that occurred in June 1976 when Nodrog sent a package of materials to John Schuessler, a NASA space shuttle engineer and founding member of the Mutual UFO Network (MUFON). The package included blueprints for a spaceship propelled by "5 D.O. Power!" and a list of charges Nodrog had brought against MUFON in the name of Commander Yahshua Hamashiia of the Positive Section of Outer Dimensional Forces. To conclude his long winded diatribe, Nodrog offered Schuessler an opportunity to surrender at the Armageddon Time Ark Base on July 4, 1976.

Schuessler decided to ignore Nodrog's missive and a month later received another package postmarked: "A.T.A. Base, Manasseh Free Territory, Manasseh complex, Area 6, Armageddon Valley." Among the contents of Nodrog's next rant, these ominous words stood out: "War Crime 7-A Decree of Judgment!" in addition to an edict that found Schuessler and MUFON guilty of suppressing the ODF's Armageddon Time Ark Base operation.

Unnerved by the threatening tone, Schuessler brought Nodrog's letters to the attention of the FBI. Around this same time, a fellow named Merlon Lingenfelter and his family joined ODF and moved into the Armageddon Time Ark compound. Merlon—it so happens—was a right wing extremist aligned with the Christian Identity Movement and the anti-gov group, Posse Comitatus. In addition to a seething hatred for the International Jewish Banking Conspiracy, Lingenfelter was also skilled at rigging up explosives, which would come in handy as the ODF grew increasingly hostile toward local government.

By the late '70s, Welasco townsfolk had grown less than enamored with Nodrog's apocalyptic lumberyard which was viewed as a massive eyesore holding back development. Part of this planned development included an expressway that would run through a section of Nodrog's land. There were also plans for a new shopping center adjacent to the expressway that would include a Walmart. To this end, Walmart attempted to purchase the land, but Nodrog told them to go pound sand. Through legal wrangling, local officials condemned this portion of Nodrog's property as a public safety hazard and awarded him compensation for the land grab, which was then deposited in his name at a local bank—but Nodrog was having no part of the Zionist pay-off and refused the money!

Things came to a head on February 25, 1985 when a pipe bomb exploded in a car parked in front of a Sherwin-Williams paint store managed by Welasco mayor, Hector Farias. The individual who planted the bomb confused another car for the one owned by Farias and fortunately no one was injured. That same day, a threatening letter courtesy of the ODF arrived at Weslaco City Hall. Afterwards, security was beefed up at the facility in anticipation of more ODF mischief.

On July 16, 1985, ATF agents raided the ODF compound, seizing a cache of illegal firearms. During a search of the premises, beehives were discovered in the living quarters and there was no evidence of indoor plumbing. (Apparently, the City of Weslaco had cut off Nodrog's water supply at some point due to his failure to pay property taxes.)[1] In the aftermath of the raid, Weslaco City Hall received so many prank calls that for "two weeks, city officials stopped answering their phones."

In March 1986, ODF member Mark Alan Lingenfelter was brought to trial for the bungled pipe bomb caper and was represented in court by his father, Merlon, who informed *The Brownsville Herald*: "Your President, all supporting Bloodsuckers of the United States, plus all Bloodsuckers of Canada and Mexico, have been duly served and convicted in the Outer Dimensional Forces Foursquare Court at Alternate Base, of Triple High Treason!" (Yes, you read that right: Triple High Treason.)

During the course of the trial, U.S. District Judge Ricardo Hinojosa dismissed himself from the proceedings on account of a series of threatening letters he received from defendant Lingenfelter who had been held in contempt of court after several outbursts. The jury found Lingenfelter guilty and he was sentenced to 10 years in prison.

As for Nodrog, he hasn't been seen since the late 1990s and many locals assume that his physical body is buried somewhere on the ODF compound while his spirit resides in the fifth dimension.

1. Eduardo Martinez's *Pharr From Heaven* blog.

Maria Graciette at the 1966 Giant Rock Convention with her psychic box (Joe Fex/APE-X Research)

GRACIETTE, MARIA

A Los Angeles-based contactee with purported psychic powers, Maria Graciette billed herself as a countess and former Miss Portugal. A true renaissance lady of the new age, Graciette authored *Astrology and Your Sex Life* (1965) and recorded an LP called *Astrology, Know the Language of the Stars*.

As Graciette told *The San Bernardino County Sun*:

> Since I was a little girl, I've been able to see auras around people. When I was very young, my teacher gave me a mysterious box and told me never to lose it. I've had the box for a long, long time!

> I had always used it in my studio to store things. It was by accident that I discovered the mysterious power of the box. I had thrown some pictures in the box and when I took them out I could see auras around the figures in the image. I have always been able to see auras in photographs, but now it seems to me that it is much easier to read the auras in an image when it has been placed in the box...I do not know what it is, I cannot explain it but when I write a statement on a sheet of paper and put it in the box, the statement is always true.[1]

Graciette was a guest speaker at the 1966 Giant Rock Interplanetary Spacecraft Convention in addition to a number of other '60s saucer happenings such as Daniel Fry's Understanding Conventions. At the "Understandorama" in Harmony Grove, California, in November 1964, Graciette hosted a forum called "My experiences aboard a spaceship"—although we could find little in the way of specifics regarding Graciette's purported UFO contactee experience.

Throughout the '70s, '80s and '90s, Graciette made a series of psychic predictions that often found their way into the pages of *The National Enquirer*. Here are some highlights:

*A UFO base, thousands of years old, would be found deep in the Mexican desert.

*Vice President Quayle, attending a World Series game, would impulsively interfere with a play.

*A meteorite would crash into the White House Rose Garden, placing President and Mrs. Bush at risk from radiation.

*Actor Tom Cruise would lose his hair due to a stress-related illness.

As for her title of Miss Portugal—and of being some sort of "Countess"—the excellent Mexican UFO website "Marcianitos Verdes" could find no evidence to back up these claims and suspected that Graciette had constructed them out of whole cloth.[2]

1. "ESP, UFO experts at Psychic Fair", *The San Bernardino County Sun*, San Bernardino, California, November 24, 1974.
2. http://marcianitosverdes.haaan.com/2017/11/maria-graciette-elliott-la-miss-portugal-que-se-convirti-en-contactada-2/

Gabriel Green at Giant Rock, October 1966 (Joe Fex/APE-X Research)

GREEN, GABRIEL (1924–2001)

In 1957, Southern California native Gabriel "Gabe" Green encountered UFO occupants from the planet Korender. Inspired by his otherworldly interactions, Green founded the Amalgamated Flying Saucer Clubs of America, Inc. (AFSCA). During its heyday, AFSCA boasted 2,500 members worldwide and published a newsletter, *Flying Saucers International.*

Throughout the 1960s, Green organized a series of UFO conferences in Los Angeles that featured prominent contactees. At the 1960 AFSCA convention, Green launched his candidacy for President on the *Universal Flying Saucer Party* ticket, encouraged in these efforts by Rentan from Alpha Centauri. ("Abe in 1860. Gabe in 1960!")[1]

Identifying himself as "The Space People's Choice", Green's next political bid came in 1962 for the California State Senate. Although unsuccessful, he reportedly received 113,205 votes, including an endorsement from Nobel Peace Prize winner Linus Pauling. Green made a second Presidential bid in 1972, recruiting fellow contactee Daniel Fry as his running mate on the political platform of "United Universal World Economics."

Gabe and his wife Helen were familiar figures at the Giant Rock Spacecraft Conventions, often decked out in matching otherworldly attire. Helen passed away suddenly in 1970 and afterwards Gabe received otherworldly transmissions to the effect that her spirit had been transported to a Mothership orbiting the Earth.

A broken hearted Gabe spent the remainder of his life attempting to establish interplanetary contact with his dearly departed, but to no avail. In a perfect universe, the two are now reunited aboard that Great Mothership in the Sky following Gabe's passing in 2001.

1. Flammonde, Paris. 1971. *The Age of Flying Saucers*. New York: Hawthorn. (p. 144).

Further reading

Green, Gabriel. 1967. *Let's Face Facts about Flying Saucers*. New York: Popular Library.

Charles Hickson (left) and Calvin Parker

HICKSON, CHARLES (1921–2011)

Charles Hickson was involved in what UFO historian Jerome Clark called "the second most famous UFO abduction case in history." But why include Hickson in a list of contactees? What many do not know is that Hickson claimed three subsequent encounters with extraterrestrial intelligences after his iconic experience with Calvin Parker on October 11, 1973, and believed that he had established some sort of contact with the beings who originally abducted him. One of the experiences even involved several members of his family, which makes things a little more difficult to dismiss.

On the evening of October 11, 1973, Hickson and workmate Parker were fishing off a pier near the shipyard where they were both employed in Pascagoula, Mississippi. Around 9 p.m. they both heard "a buzzing sound" and turned around to see an oval-shaped object with what looked like windows and blue lights near its top resting in a clearing (or hovering over the water in some accounts) about 30 to 40 yards away. They both later said they observed three figures that acted like robots exit the craft and advance towards them. Although they didn't have the language or awareness to describe them, they resembled Native American Kachinas, with conical protrusions where noses and ears would be, and "hands" that resembled mittens or claws. The things also had greyish skin that was wrinkled in horizontal rows. They grabbed the two men and dragged them into the object.

Inside, they were separated while Hickson endured an examination by some sort of "electric eye" that ran up and down his body. Parker said that he fainted throughout most of the episode and didn't remember very much. Hickson later said that a voice in his head told him, "We are peaceful. We meant you no harm."[1]

Other witnesses in the area later described strange lighted, flying objects as well at around the same time. Hickson and Parker went to see the local sheriff, who isolated them in a bugged room in order to see if they might be lying. There was no real evidence that revealed that they did not believe their story. The resulting publicity caused Parker to have a nervous breakdown, and Hickson and his family and co-workers quickly grew weary of the constant presence of reporters and other

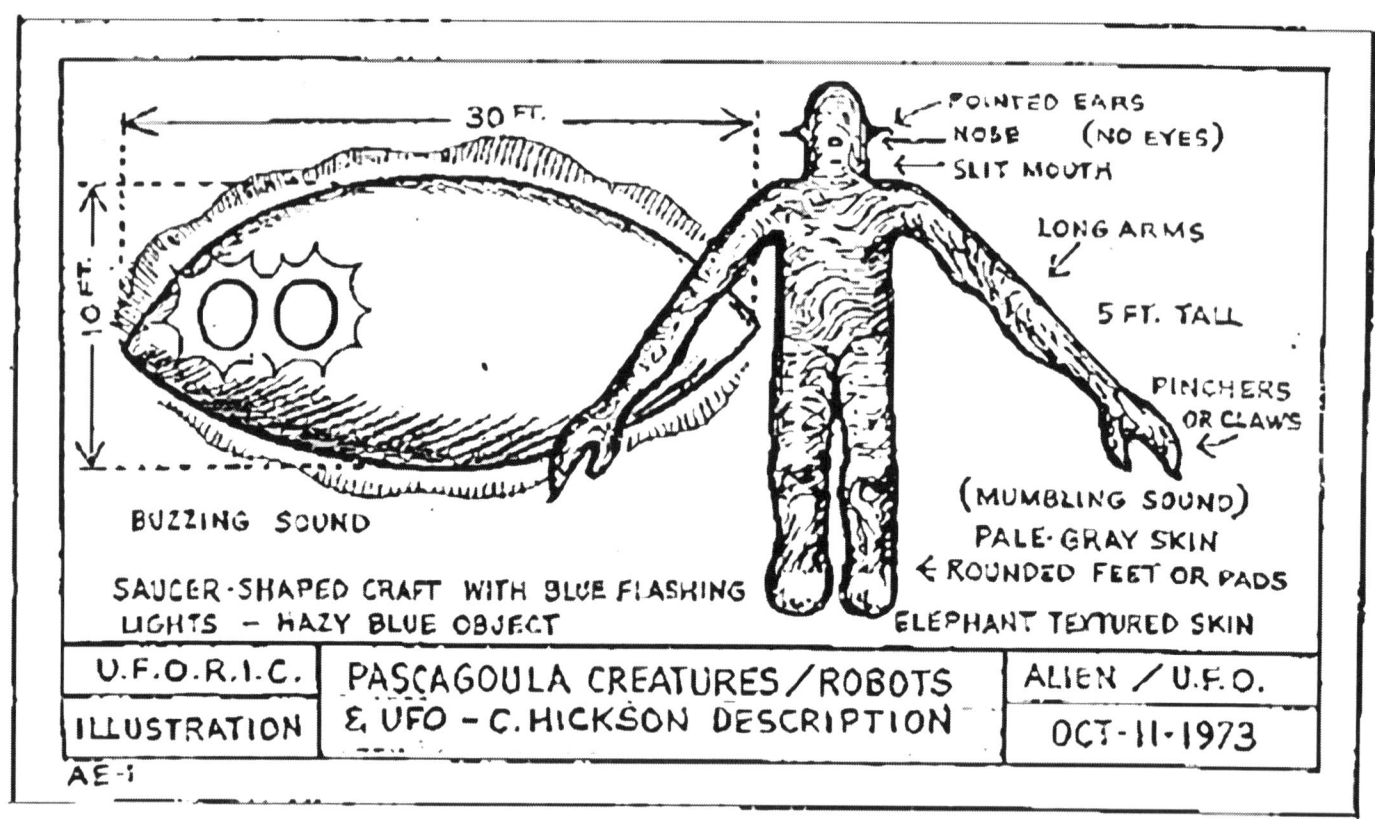

Illustration of the Pascagoula creature and the UFO it rode in on (UFO Research Institute of Canada)

curious people.

Within a month of the event, UFO researcher Allan Hendry spoke to Calvin Parker, who he says claimed that the experience left him with the ability to "bend metal objects like paper clips in sealed jars 'just like Uri Geller.'"[2] Parker then went into a self-imposed news blackout and didn't speak publicly about the experience for over 40 years.

In January of the next year, still hounded by the publicity, Hickson escaped for a day of solitary hunting for small game on a private tree farm managed by a friend. In his 1983 book, *UFO Contact at Pascagoula,* co-written with Michigan college professor William Mendez, he observed that "squirrels make a very fine stew," so with this assurance, his wife Blanche packed him a lunch and his son-in-law dropped him off. Hickson was sitting under a tree when he recalled that "it dawned on me that I hadn't seen any movement at all around me—not even any birds, that seemed real strange." He looked up to see the same object he had witnessed three months earlier hovering in a clearing about 75 yards away. A voice in his head (or what he referred to as a "radio") said "We mean you no harm. We mean no one any harm. You may communicate with us later. You have endured. You have been chosen. There is no need for fear. We will communicate soon." Under hypnosis over two years later, he said one other thought had been sent to him: "We will return."[3]

The month after his tree farm incident, Hickson said he received another message from his space contacts. Under hypnosis, he recalled hearing a dog barking at night behind his apartment. He went outside to see what was the matter and got the feeling that there was "something around" him. Hickson said that he received another message that night, but was nervous about discussing it. He later said that the message this time was "You must tell the world we mean no harm. Your world needs help. We will help in the future before it's too late. You are not prepared to understand yet. We will return again soon."[4]

True to their word, whatever it was that was hanging around Charles Hickson made a dramatic appearance on May 12 of 1974. He was driving back from a Mother's Day family gathering with seven other family members on a lonely road through a scrub pine forest in southern Mississippi when someone in the car noticed a light pacing them through the trees. In a few moments, a large object that was "about one hundred feet" in diameter and with "a row of windows completely across it" stopped and hovered over the highway about 100 yards away. Hickson's son-in-law stopped the car. There was chaos in the car as his wife held him tight and screamed for him not to get out. In a few seconds, he heard the "radio" in his mind. "Go. There will be another time. Another place." was the message this time.[5]

Although he continued to talk freely about his experience for the remainder of his life, as far as we know, there was no return before Charles Hickson passed away on September 9, 2011.

1. Clark, Jerome. 1998. "Pascagoula Abduction Case" in *The UFO Encyclopedia: The Phenomenon from the Beginning, Vol. 2, L-Z.* Omigraphics, Inc. (p. 715).
2. Hendry, Allan. 1979. *The UFO Handbook.* Doubleday and Company. (p. 137-38).
3. Hickson, Charles, and Mendez, William. 1979. *UFO Contact at Pascagoula.* Wendelle C. Stevens (p. 169).
4. Clark. (p. 718).
5. Hickson and Mendez. (p. 190).

Dana Howard at Giant Rock (Joe Fex/APE-X Research)

HOWARD, DANA (1895–1974)

In 1939, Dana Howard was communing with nature one day when her attention was drawn to a gnarled, old tree where she discovered, leaning against its trunk, a beautiful golden-haired lady with "a strange mystic light flooding her dark, prophetic eyes."

"Do not be afraid, Girl of Earth" intoned the golden-haired gal. "Let the doors of your mind open and distant planets will speak in poetry and songs."[1]

After uttering those immortal words, a gem-studded spaceship honked its celestial horn and lowered "an almost invisible 'ladder' that extended from the ship to the earth." The golden haired lady climbed up the ladder into the spaceship and that was the last Dana saw of her—at least for another decade.

On April 29, 1955, Howard attended a séance at the Church of Divine Light in Los Angeles during which a psychic medium named Reverend Bertie Lilly Candler materialized an 8-foot-tall blonde woman, who was the very same golden haired beauty Dana had previously encountered. "I am Diana. I come from Venus."

Diana of Venus apparently re-materialized on the earth plane with the implicit purpose of establishing contact with Miss Howard. This led to a long and fruitful relationship between Howard and her Venusian gal-pal, eventually setting the stage for Dana's subsequent travels to Venus via "teleportation" where she tied the knot with a Venusian fellow named Lelando and raised a family there.

Venus—in Howard's estimation—was like a higher plane of consciousness aiding the spiritual development of humankind, and Dana's role in the grand scheme of things was as an ambassador to promote higher Venusian awareness to the people of Earth.

1. Howard, Dana. 1955. *Diane, She Came From Venus*. London: Regency.

Further reading

Howard, Dana. 1954. *My Flight to Venus*, San Gabriel, CA: Willing Publishing Company.
Howard, Dana. 1959. *Up Rainbow Hill*. Los Angeles, CA: Llewellyn.

Barbara Hudson

Hudson, Barbara (born ca. 1940)

In 1955, fifteen-year-old Barbara Hudson witnessed a tall man enter her bedroom in the early morning hours. He sent light beams from his eyes into hers, inducing a trance state. This mystery man extended his hand and asked Barbara to follow. Trusting soul that she was, Hudson accepted the tall man's hand who led her into the living room where a gray mist had formed. Hudson soon found herself in what appeared to be an elevator that transported her up to a room with "many instruments and multicolored lights." One wall of the room featured an image of Earth on a screen surrounded by more tall people seated around control panels. Afterwards, Barbara was treated to a meal comprised only of fruits, and then back down the elevator, through the living room's gray mist, she returned to bed.

At the Giant Rock Conventions of the 1960s (and other ufological outings), Hudson became a running mate of sorts with Gray Barker and Jim Moseley, forming a trio that average middle America probably viewed with a certain degree of curiosity: Two hard drinking white male Ufologist-Pranksters—one gay and one straight—in the company of a young, attractive African-American woman who claimed she belonged to a secret organization called "The Group." According to Gray Barker, Hudson "radiated both a dainty femininity and a certain sexiness" amid an "aura of mystery."[1]

Barker helped foster this mysterious aura with his claim that he observed Hudson's doppelgänger at the 1970 Giant Rock Convention, although one could attribute such tales to Barker's penchant to stretch the truth or, conversely, from seeing double after a few too many nips of demon alcohol.

Hudson's entrée into the '60s saucer scene began when three mysterious men (presumably in black) showed up at her apartment in New York City one evening and informed her that she'd been chosen to become a member of a secretive outfit involved with UFOs. The three mystery men drove Hudson to a remote stretch of Long Island, along the way treating her to a demonstration of exotic ET gadgets. When they arrived at the secluded Long Island compound, Hudson was introduced to other members of "The Group," a secret alliance of humans and ETs who had joined forces to reveal

Jim Moseley at Giant Rock, 1961
(Joe Fex/APE-X Research)

the startling truth of the flying saucer mystery!

"The Group" was responsible for Hudson's involvement with the UFO conference scene, and in fact directed her to attend one of Jim Moseley's conventions so they could "keep an eye on things." According to Tim Beckley, Moseley's interest in Hudson was not only UFO related, but the two enjoyed a romantic relationship. Hudson—along with Barker, Moseley and Beckley—traveled to Point Pleasant during the Mothman craze, and some of her activities there are chronicled in Barker's *The Silver Bridge* (1970).

Tim Beckley heard many of Hudson's stories firsthand and felt that she related them with conviction, although—as Beckley informed your humble authors—there was no way to verify her claims, all which added to Hudson's "aura of mystery."

1. Barker, Gray. 1976. *Gray Barker At Giant Rock*. Clarksburg, WV: Saucerian Books.

PLANE VANISHES IN MYSTERY

Wife Fears Hubby in Flying Saucer Kidnap

BY CHARLES RIDGWAY, Mirror Staff Reporter

Two missing electricians may have been kidnaped by interplanetary invaders in a flying saucer, fears Mrs. Wilbur J. Wilkinson of 1933½ LeMoyne Ave., wife of one of the missing men.

The two flying saucer fans, Wilkinson and Karl Hunrath of 2315 S Flower St., took off in a rented airplane from Gardena Airport last Wednesday with a three-hour gas supply.

Despite a widespread search, no trace of the plane or its occupants has been seen.

Wilkinson's wife told The Mirror today that Hunrath was an avid believer in flying saucers. He and Wilkinson believed the end of the earth was nearing, and that strange little men from the planet "Maser" were ready to invade.

Hunt Saucer

Hunrath claimed to know the whereabouts of a flying saucer recently landed. Wilkinson's den, in their rented hillside home, is lined with flying saucer pictures, weird signs and formulas, which his wife says were supposed to be the new interplanetary language.

"Of course, I don't quite go for all the flying saucer talk, but Karl had convinced Wilbur they actually existed," Mrs. Wilkinson related.

"He had tape recordings of conversations with men from other planets who landed here in saucers."

She also pointed to messages tacked on Wilkinson's walls, supposedly received by radio from the interplanetary visitors. One was from a "Prince Reggs of the planet Maser."

The Wilkinsons, who have three children, Patricia, 12; Judith, 5, and John, 2, moved here from Racine, Wis., June 28. Wilbur is employed by Hoffman Radio Corp., where he was recently promoted to be in charge of the inspection department, Mrs. Wilkinson said.

The 38-year-old electrician has a den full of electronic equipment, radios and tape recorders.

"He was planning to go into the recording business," his tearful wife told The Mirror.

"He really didn't seem too interested in flying saucers except when Karl Hunrath came around. Karl was the one who talked us into coming to California because he said he could actually show a flying saucer to Wilbur."

Deputy sheriffs took a dim view of the "saucer kidnaping."

They warned Mrs. Wilkinson the two missing men

Turn to Page 30

WILBUR J. WILKINSON
One of missing men.

—MIRRORFOTOS

FROM OUTER SPACE?
These weird symbols and words were found on wall of Wilkinson's home. Some have English words penciled lightly beneath. In upper photo, "Lesh-tal," next to last line, is translated "Create Life." Lower, second line, "Xenph-man" has scribbled under it: "Poseid Returning." Third from bottom, "Josh-tau-marin," is translated: "Births give cataclysms."

Udal - Hoo - Dau

E-i-l

Kal - Mo - Kal

Iso - Tok - Mal

Lo'sh - Lal

Mogal - Moo - Mah

Xenph - man

Man - Man - Woo - Foo - Tin - Mah

Josh - tau - marin

Marmal

Ragif - Karo - m

HUNRATH, KARL

In the monumental ufological year of 1952, Karl Hunrath caught the saucer bug and constructed a machine called "Bosco." (Yes, that's what he actually called it.) Encased in a mysterious black box, Bosco was said to duplicate the magnetic field of UFOs and could ostensibly call them down.

In early 1953, Hunrath quit his job in Racine, Wisconsin and traveled to California where he hooked up with George Adamski and gave him the lowdown on how Bosco not only attracted flying saucers, but could also produce enough free energy to provide all the electricity needed to power Palomar Gardens.[1]

The only problem was that Bosco was stored in Wisconsin and Hunrath was going to have his co-inventor, Wilbur "Jack" Wilkinson, bring it out to California, so there was going to be a little delay on all the free energy soon to flow Adamski's way. All of this Bosco business seemed all right with Professor Adamski until—during a Palomar Gardens wine drinking fest—Hunrath went off the rails about how Bosco could disable flying saucers, causing them to land against their will, and potentially even crash.[2]

Why Hunrath wished to bring down the kindly space brothers is anybody's guess, but this business about crashing saucers so alarmed the good professor that he told Hunrath to get the hell off his property—that there'd be no disabling flying saucers if he had anything to say about it—and take that infernal Bosco with him! Part of Adamski's concern was that if Bosco could bring down UFOs then it could most likely mess with military aircraft as well, to which Hunrath replied: "WHO CARES? WE WANT THE SAUCERS!"[3]

After witnessing this heated exchange, one of the professor's followers, Lucy McGinnis, notified the authorities that Hunrath's black box thingy could potentially disable military aircraft! Not long after, both the FBI and Air Force Office of Special Investigations (AFOSI) paid a visit to Palomar Gardens to question Adamski on the matter. In response, the professor informed them, in no uncertain terms, that his former colleague (Hunrath) had gone off the deep end and was quite possibly possessed by otherworldly demons.

Before his relationship with Adamski soured, Hunrath—along with George Hunt Williamson and fellow saucer enthusiast, Jerrold Baker—formed the short-lived "Adamski Foundation," an organization dedicated to preserving the works of the good professor.

In August 1953, Bosco co-inventor Wilbur Wilkinson joined Hunrath who, it appears, had fallen under the spell of George Hunt Williamson and his ability to channel entities from across the galaxy. During this period, Hunrath, Wilkinson, and Baker spent considerable time at Williamson's home in Prescott, Arizona, where Williamson had set up a pseudo-scientific laboratory. To this end, an odd variety of ET contact methods were used that included short-wave radio, telepathy, use of an Ouija board as well as the ingestion of mescaline that allowed the men to enter altered states and ostensibly enhance their otherworldly communications.[4]

At this time, the men adopted space brother names: Hunrath was Firkon, Wilkinson was Ramu, Williamson was Mark III, and Baker was Markon. Whether the men actually believed they were aliens, or channels for aliens, or whatever their intent was, isn't entirely clear, but some of these very same alien names (Firkon and Ramu) later appeared in Adamski's book *Inside the Spaceships*.[5]

That summer, Hunrath and Wilkerson relocated to Los Angeles to seek employment in order to fund their many flying saucer investigations, landing jobs as electricians. Wilkinson moved his family into a rented home near Echo Park, while Hunrath found accommodations at a rooming house in downtown Los Angeles.

On November 10th, 1953, Hunrath phoned Hollywood ufologist Manon Darlaine, alerting her that he and Wilkinson were planning to meet up the next day with a landed saucer and invited her to tag along. Manon politely declined, fearing the men weren't operating with a full set of dilithium crystals.

The next day, Hunrath and Wilkinson rented a small plane from the now defunct Gardena Valley Airport, and with three hours of fuel flew off into the great unknown, never to be seen again. For some reason, the men neglected to file a flight plan, which made subsequent search and rescue efforts all the more challenging.

Hunrath—who was at the controls of the plane—was not an experienced pilot, and only a week prior to their flight had taken a refresher course. It was rumored that the men planned to fly in the direction of Prescott, Arizona, a flight line which would have taken them over the remote Southern California desert mountains where it was presumed they crashed.

Following their disappearance, a *Los Angeles Mirror* article featured the alarming title *PLANE VANISHES IN MYSTERY: Wife Fears Hubby in Flying Saucer Kidnapping* in which Mrs. J. Wilkinson of 1933 ½ LeMoyne Ave. stated that her husband might have been nabbed by "interplanetary invaders in a flying saucer." Mrs. Wilkinson described her husband Wilbur as an "avid believer in flying saucers" and that he and Hunrath "believed the end of earth was nearing and that strange little men from the planet 'Maser' were ready to invade." Mrs. Wilkinson took the *Mirror* reporter on a tour of her husband's "den" which was lined with "flying saucer pictures, weird signs, and formulas..." One of the messages on the wall was from "Prince Reggs of the planet Maser."

Afterwards, reports surfaced that the FBI had looked into the case and came to suspect that the missing men may have high-tailed it to Mexico due to certain illicit activities unrelated to UFOs or Bosco.[6]

1. Barker, Gray. 1965. *Gray Barker's Book of Saucers*. Clarksburg, WV: Saucerian Books. (p. 36).

2. Moseley, James. 1971. *The Wright Field Story*. Clarksburg, WV: Saucerian Books. (p. 24).

3. Barker, Gray. 1965. *Gray Barker's Book of Saucers*. (p. 36).

4. Redfern, Nick. 2014. *Close Encounters of the Fatal Kind*. New Page Books. (p. 62).

5. Moseley, James. 1971. *The Wright Field Story*. Clarksburg, WV: Saucerian Books. (p. 25).

6. Moseley, James & Karl Pflock. 2002. *Shockingly Close To The Truth: Confessions of a Grave-Robbing Ufologist*. New York: Prometheus Books.

David Huggins (Photo credit: Farah Yurdozu)

Huggins, David (born ca. 1943)

While the focus of this book is on contactees as opposed to abductees, David Huggins seems to fall into both camps. Huggins' initial experience could be considered an abduction experience, but as his experiences progressed, they reflected more of the positive spin encountered by the old school contactees.

In 1951—at the tender age of eight—Huggins claimed he was taken aboard a UFO and received the requisite electronic nose implant, a procedure that was apparently quite painful and brought the young lad to tears. Huggins was comforted at this time by one of the UFO occupants, a female ET named Crescent, whom he later married.

Huggins claimed sexual intimacy not only with Crescent, but with several ET females—none of whom had names—so he went ahead and named them himself. One of the creatures—who resembled a praying mantis—was named "Hmmm" due to the sounds she made during sex. The apparent purpose of all of these sexual encounters was to produce as many human-alien hybrids as possible to populate the galaxy. The latest account was that Huggins had sired over sixty ET children.

According to UFO researcher, Farah Yurdozu:

> David's story of otherworldly relationships and worldly personal turmoil is part of the folkloric traditions of many cultures stretching back to ancient times, and it fulfills a pattern that many see as evidence of alien contact millennia in the past. For example, in the jinn legends of Turkey, children are "taken" to another dimension by the nighttime visitors of great metaphysical power, the jinns. Later in life, many jinn contactees tell of having ongoing sexual and sometimes emotional relationships with jinns, which often produce hybrid offspring.

> David's relationships with Crescent also brings to mind the ancient incubus-succubus

female demons who visit sleeping humans and have sex with them were first mentioned in Sumerian texts. These interdimensional beings were represented as gods and demons who were not able to conceive children. They needed human genetic material to continue their own race by having hybrid babies from Earth men and women.

Huggins contact with these alien ladies (or succubi, as the case may be) continued over several decades, a story told in *Love In An Alien Purgatory: The Life and Fantastic Art of David Huggins*, which features many of his unusual ET-inspired portraits. In addition, Huggins has authored a stage play entitled "UFO" that tells the story of his dalliances with the fairer ET sex.

Further reading

Yurdozu, Farah, 2009. *An Alien Purgatory: The Life and Fantastic Art of David Huggins*, Anomalist Books.

Ida Kannenberg

KANNENBERG, IDA (1914–2010)

In 1940—while traveling through the California desert, where a lot of saucer sightings always seem to happen—Ida Kannenberg was invited aboard a UFO with the understanding that the occupants needed a sample of her blood to take back to their home planet to cure some type of interplanetary health crisis.

Ida later discovered that her ET contacts were using the pretext about needing her blood as a means to surreptitiously implant her with a communication device that was later activated in 1968 when time travelers from Atlantis started filling her head with a vast array of mind-blowing data.

Kannenberg also met up with Bigfoot along the way, a story she related in *My Brother Is a Hairy Man: An Extraterrestrial View on Bigfoot and Human Genesis* (2013).

Further reading

Kannenberg, Ida M., 2007. *Time Travelers from Atlantis: The Collected Essays of Ida M. Kannenberg*. Experiencers eBooks.

George King (Joe Fex/APE-X Research)

KING, GEORGE (1919–1997)

In May 1954, an ethereal voice popped into the head of London cab driver George King: "Prepare yourself! You are to become the voice of the Interplanetary Parliament!" Eight days after King received this vital information, an unidentified (supposedly world famous) swami materialized at his flat and treated King to a crash course in tantric yoga which apparently enabled him to gain vast knowledge regarding the secrets of the universe.

The aforementioned unnamed (world famous) swami instructed King to form an organization that would help the planet get its act together. To accomplish this feat, King was required to establish telepathic contact with Master Aetherius from Venus who would steer him in the right direction. In 1955, King founded the Aetherius Society and according to the group's newsletter, *The Cosmic Voice*: "The orientation of the Aetherius Society is a spiritual one, since it is definitely known that the mission of the Flying Saucers and their crews to Earth is a spiritual mission."

Other Venusians soon came telepathically calling—in addition to a legion of assorted cosmic masters (including Jesus)—enlisting King into something called the Great White Brotherhood. Although it sounded like a Klu Klux Klan chapter, the Great White Brotherhood was actually a group of ascended master good guys (ala Theosophy) that have been engaged since time immemorial in a war against a legion of black magicians whose ultimate aim is to enslave the human race. Not good.

To battle against this subversion, King designed what became known as "prayer batteries" that store up to 700 hours of "spiritual energy" (for a whopping 10,000 years!) that can be held in reserve and later put to use in making the Universe a safer place.

Not all of George King's interplanetary interactions were of the telepathic type. In his classic tome, *You Are Responsible!* (1961), King recounted a trip to Mars (actually to one of the moons of Mars, if you want to split hairs) where he haphazardly entered a room he apparently didn't belong in and red lights started flashing (Warning! Warning!) Soon King found himself in the crosshairs of a shoot-first-ask-questions-later ray gun wielding dwarf from another planet. After being blasted by the dwarf and sustaining life threatening injuries, King was able to psychically propel himself back to London and—with the aid of some "excellent spiritual healers" —return to optimum health in no time flat.

On a return trip to Mars (not just one of the moons of Mars, but actually Mars this time), King was invited to attend the Martian General Assembly where a somber discussion ensued regarding a mysterious asteroid that posed a threat to the red planet—and Earth as well!—and, in fact, this asteroid was the same place where King had encountered the ray gun wielding dwarf in the room he shouldn't have been in. Apparently, a Martian scout ship had been sent to investigate the asteroid (or moon, or whatever you want to call it) and ended up being destroyed. Long story short, the Martians agreed that they needed some sort of retaliatory response to this evil dwarf asteroid, and King volunteered his services since he already had insider knowledge on the subject of evil dwarfs and the asteroid they rode in on.

As part of this tactical operation, King recruited his telepathic Venusian friends and along with the Martians formed an Earth/Mars/Venus alliance that destroyed the evil asteroid and the ray gun-wielding dwarfs along with it. Unfortunately, 174 Martians died during the course of the conflict, but Earth was saved (and that's all that really counts.)[1]

Despite all of these interplanetary heroics, George King was later taken to task by TV star Jackie Gleason on an episode of Long John Nebel's *Party Line*:

GLEASON: How are you?

KING: Very well, thank you.

GLEASON: Are these people from outer space friends of yours?

KING: I believe that they are friends of mine, yes.

GLEASON: Could you call upon them for assistance? For instance, if you were in some sort of legal difficulty, embracing some part of their recognition of you, would they come to your aid?

KING: Under those circumstances, they would help, yes.

GLEASON: If I were, for instance, to say to you that you are a bare-faced liar, now you know you could sue me for libel, right?

Aetherius battery charging session, 1985 (Photo credit: Douglas Curran)

KING: Yes, yes.

GLEASON: Now you think you could get any legal assistance from them in a case like this?

KING: No, I don't.

GLEASON: Why?

KING: Why should they help?

GLEASON: Well, you're championing their cause.

KING: No, No I'm not. I'm trying to give a spiritual message, which I believe to be good for all people...

GLEASON: Why do we need a spiritual message from someone in a flying saucer? Don't we have enough from Christ, Buddha, Moses, men like that?

KING: Do we live by those teachings?

GLEASON: I do.

KING: You do? Then you're the first Christian I've ever seen.

GLEASON: You mean that no one lives by the laws of Buddha, Christ, or...

KING: I never met anyone.

GLEASON: By the way, do you know that every time you are uncertain when you say something, you cough? Do you know what that means psychologically? In other words, you cough every time you tell a lie.

KING: Do I?

GLEASON: Now George, look at the juicy opportunity you have. Here's a guy that you're talking to that's got a lot of dough. You can sue me for maybe a million dollars, and maybe get it. All you have to do to get it is to bring one of your friends from Mars to OK this thing. And then you win.

KING: I've already answered this question. There isn't a man on Earth who could do this.

GLEASON: In other words, you have absolutely no proof from these people whom you are championing? You have absolutely no backing from anybody in outer space for what you say?

KING: Just a moment please. Just one minute.

GLEASON: I'm waiting, and cough a little bit.

KING: I shall put this phone down in a moment.

GLEASON: Yes?

KING: I'm a guest here, you see.

GLEASON: Not in my house, you're not a guest. I think you're a phony!

KING: C L I C K ! !²

Gleason's dressing down of George King notwithstanding, the Aetherius Society continues to flourish, which is evident to anyone who has attended one of their Operation Prayer Power battery-charging sessions that "combine dynamic prayer, Tibetan mantra, and the science of radionics" as a "potent new tool against disease and suffering on earth." According to Aetherius Society propaganda:

For two hours, (Aetherius members) join together in a powerful ritual, using dynamic prayer, eastern mantra, and mystic mudras. The Energy they invoke is collected and stored in a radionic battery. These charging sessions continue week after week, filling each battery with thousands of hours of Prayer Energy.

Whenever there is a disaster on Earth in need of Spiritual Energy, such as a hurricane, earthquake or war, this store of uplifting healing energy can be released almost immediately through a Spiritual Energy Radiator. This radionic device can discharge a battery in a fraction of the time it took to charge it. This concentrated Prayer Energy is then manipulated by cooperating Masters to the area in need.

Since we started this Mission in 1973, we have had astounding successes aiding victims of catastrophes and other natural disasters.

OPERATION PRAYER POWER charging sessions are open to anyone who is willing to expend the necessary effort to learn and practice the Holy mantras used as a powerful way to help humanity.

1. Gulyas, Aaron John. 2013. *Extraterrestrials and the American Zeitgeist: Alien Contact Tales Since the 1950s.* McFarland.
2. Nebel, Long John. 1961. *The Way Out World.* Prentice-Hall, Inc. (p. 52).

Elizabeth Klarer

KLARER, ELIZABETH (1910–1994)

After reading George Adamski's *Flying Saucers Have Landed*, South African Elizabeth Klarer suddenly recalled a series of telepathic transmissions she began receiving in childhood from a fellow named Akon from a planet called Meton.

Thus began a series of steamy sexual encounters that allegedly kicked off in 1956 when Klarer managed to call down a flying saucer that transported her to Meton where she hooked up with her long-time telepathic friend and the two got to know one another on a more intimate basis. "Sex for them [the Metonites]," Klarer wrote, "is a most beautiful thing." Akon informed Klarer that his race needed new blood and that's the reason he'd selected her for "breeding experiments." (Wink-wink.) As Klarer later recalled:

> I surrendered in ecstasy to the magic of his love making, our bodies merging in magnetic
> union as the divine essence of our spirits became one and I found the true meaning of
> love in mating with a man from another planet.[1]

This human-alien hookup ultimately resulted in Klarer getting knocked up by Akon and conceiving a hybrid son named Ayling. According to Klarer, her tryst with Akon—and Ayling's subsequent birth—took all of four months, after which she returned to Earth.

1. Klarer, Elizabeth. 1980. *Beyond the Light Barrier*. South Africa: Howard Timmins.

Dino Kraspedon

KRASPEDON, DINO (1920–1985)

In November 1952, Dino Kraspedon was taken aboard a flying saucer and given an hour-long show-me tour by the ship's captain, who informed him he had to get back to whatever planet he was from but would soon return. Five months later, the flying saucer captain did indeed return, showing up at Dino's doorstep and pretending to be a Jehovah's Witness so as to not alarm his wife.

Dino met with his flying saucer captain—who it turns out hailed from a "satellite of Jupiter"—on five separate occasions. *My Contact With Flying Saucers* (1959) recounts their many conversations, which included amazing revelations on "matter and energy" that—although earth shattering—came across as rather dry monologues when presented, as they were, in a Q & A format.

One of these startling revelations was that another sun would soon be entering our solar system as a red star then would turn into a blue star (as red stars are often wont to do) and that *our* sun—and this new sun—would counterbalance each other and rotate around the center of the galaxy. The take-home of all this, one can assume, is we would then have two suns in our solar system, which is probably better than one.

Dino's flying saucer captain also revealed the secrets of anti-gravity, which is what apparently powered their saucer, yet he begged Dino to not share these secrets because he feared that if this information fell into the wrong hands (i.e. humankind) it would then be used to devious ends.

The space brothers, unsurprisingly, wanted mankind to became more peaceful, and follow the space brother way, which was all love and light, much like so many other space brother messages of the day—and of course Dino was down with this.

Dino's flying saucer captain made several predictions—many of which proved incredibly accurate—including the assassinations of Robert F. Kennedy and Martin Luther King. Dino also accurately predicted (once again courtesy of his ET friends) a series of robberies, bombings, and murders that occurred in Brazil in late August 1968.

Later, Dino's real-life alter-ego Aladino Felix was arrested as the leader of the gang that perpetrated these crimes—which explained how his ET friends had so accurately predicted the future. At that time, Felix informed authorities that he was "an ambassador to the earth from Venus" and that "My friends from space will come here and free me and avenge my arrest. You can look for tragic consequences to humanity when the flying saucers invade this planet!"

In 1971, Felix was sentenced to five years in prison (later reduced to 8 months) then shortly after was transferred to a mental health facility.

Ralph Lael

LAEL, RALPH (1909–1978)

Strange legends abound around Brown Mountain—located in North Carolina on the Pisgah National Forest—with stories about "great balls of fire rising and bursting above the top of the mountain."

In *The Brown Mountain Lights* (1965), Ralph Lael recounted his expeditions to this mysterious mountain and how he established mental contact with "ghost lights." In particular, a 1961 encounter when the lights guided Lael to a large rock, out of which a door suddenly opened, leading into a secret alien cave and a room with walls of solid crystal that were as "clear as glass." A voice spoke to him—apparently from Venus—and in short order Lael found himself on a spaceship bound for the stars.

After landing on Venus—a planet made entirely of pure crystal—Lael was introduced to a couple of Venusians who informed him they were descendants of the planet Pewam, one of whom was an attractive lady named Noma dressed only in a skimpy bra and panties. Noma took Lael to a private room and you can guess the rest.

After getting those formalities out of the way, Lael was introduced to a seven-foot-tall fellow named Heath. As always seems to be the case, the Venusians voiced concerns about Earth's inhabitants blowing themselves up. To illustrate his point, Heath turned on a massive flat screen TV that presented real time imagery of the Cuban missile crisis then going down—with Heath providing running commentary on the situation—noting that Pewam had fallen upon a similar fate, having gone kablooey when the Pewamians started playing around with dangerous technologies, as seen in a series of newsreels documenting Pewam's destruction—which is exactly where we Earthlings were headed unless we got off our atomic bomb kick.

When the demonstration was over, Lael was returned to Earth via the secret alien cave, and while being led back through the mountain by a "glowing sphere," he came across a mummified humanoid creature with a large round head and spindly arms. When Ralph asked who the dead mummy was, the "glowing sphere" was a bit vague, saying it was some type of ET species and that Lael was free

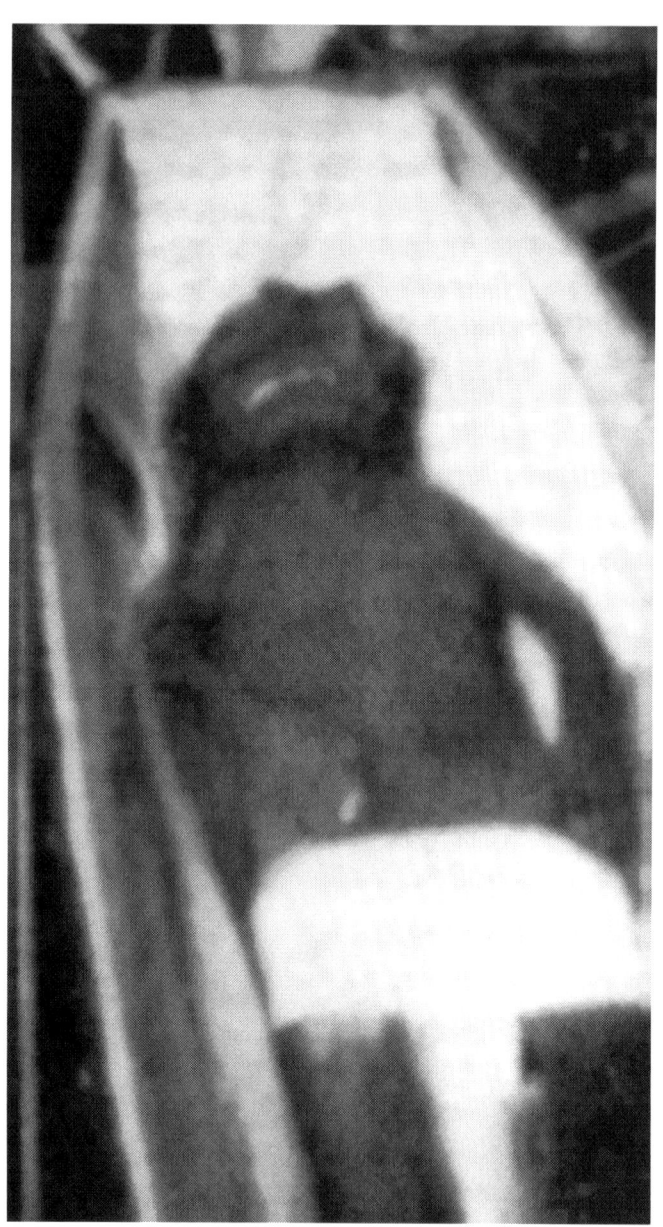

Ralph Lael's alien mummy

to take it home with him, as it would serve as evidence to his fellow humans of his amazing Venusian adventure.

Lael opened the "Outer Space Rock Shop Museum" located near Brown Mountain that featured rock displays as well as the alien mummy in a glass-covered casket. Following his death, Lael's museum was demolished and the 'Space Mummy' mysteriously disappeared, although it's unknown at this time whether the Men in Black were involved in the heist.

Charles and Lillian Laughead with John Otto at Giant Rock (Joe Fex/APE-X Research)

Laughead, Charles (1910–1980)

In June 1954, Dr. Charles Laughead (pronounced law-head) and his wife Lillian fell under the sway of Chicago housewife and psychic medium Dorothy Martin, who at the time was receiving direct Venusian communications from "The Elder Brother." When word got out about Martin—and her apparent ability to channel otherworldly entities—a group formed around her called "The Seekers." Along with Martin, Dr. Laughead assumed a leadership role in the group and it got progressively crazier from there.

In mid-December 1954, Laughead was dismissed from his position at Michigan State College after administrators received complaints that he was spreading flying saucer propaganda on campus. Soon after, Laughead grabbed headlines when he predicted a forthcoming cataclysmic flood that would occur on December 21st and wipe Oak Park, Illinois, off the map. Afterwards, the deluge would spread across the continental U.S. and submerge the West Coast. However, there would be a few positive spin-offs from this deluge, one of which would presumably raise and reveal the lost continent of Lemuria from the ocean depths.

Laughead's source, of course, was Dorothy Martin, who had received her startling Lemurian revelations from an ET conglomerate known as "The Guardians" (from the planet Clarion.) One of the more provocative newspaper headlines covering the story announced: "PROPHECY FROM PLANET CLARION. CALL TO CITY: FLEE THAT FLOOD. IT'LL SWAMP US ON DEC. 21, OUTER SPACE TELLS SUBURBANITE." (Best. Headline. Ever.)

This, in turn, caused an uproar among the Oak Park locals, who were wondering if Dorothy Martin and her fellow "Seekers" were just plain batty—or if there really was something to her apocalyptic pronouncements. Whatever the case, members of The Seekers apparently weren't too concerned about the forthcoming deluge as they'd been informed that a flying saucer would come to their rescue right before the flood and whisk them away to Clarion for Christmas.

The Seekers were instructed to remove all metal objects from their bodies prior to blast-off—

including zippers, bra straps, metal clasps, bobby pins, and belt buckles—to prevent them from being burnt to a crisp because apparently this can happen to humans with metal on their persons when taking flying saucer trips. (Of course, this might have been a cheap ploy on the part of certain amorous Clarionites to get the gullible Earthlings to slip into their skivvies.)

Unsurprisingly, December 21th came and went without the much anticipated saucer pickup and cataclysmic flood. A recounting of this strange saga is chronicled in *When Prophecy Fails: A Social and Psychological Study of a Modern Group That Predicted the Destruction of the World* (1956), a first-hand account by sociologist Leon Festinger, who infiltrated Martin's group. In *When Prophecy Fails*, Laughead is identified as "Dr. Thomas Armstrong" and his wife Lillian as "Daisy". Charles Laughead later earned the dubious nickname of Dr. Doomsday in certain ufological circles on account of his role in the Seekers saga.

After the receiving negative publicity for the failed predictions, The Seekers disbanded, although it wasn't long before Charles and Lillian were following the guidance of a another psychic medium named Rose Phillips who predicted a flying saucer landing that also never happened, this one scheduled for East Lansing, Michigan, in May 1955.

After wearing out their welcome in Oak Park and East Lansing, Charles and Lillian traveled westward to be in the orbit of the burgeoning Southern California Contactee Movement. In 1955, Charles was a guest speaker at the second annual Giant Rock Interplanetary Spacecraft Convention, rubbing elbows with other such stalwarts of the saucer scene as George Adamski and George Van Tassel.

During this period, the Laugheads relocated to Whipple, Arizona, just a stone's throw from Prescott, AZ, home of contactee George Hunt Williamson, whom Laughead had met and befriended during a lecture Williamson delivered to the Detroit Saucer Club in December 1954. They were soon joined by their old friend Dorothy Martin (now going by the name of "Sister Thedra") who had recently landed there after a swift exit from the Windy City suburbs. During channeling sessions (transcribed by Lillian Laughead), the Sister Thedra/Williamson trance channeling tag team was contacted by "Brother Philip" who directed the group to travel to Peru in "search for ancient lost cities and records in the vast unexplored area east of the Andean range."[1]

The quest began in early December 1956, as the Laugheads, Sister Thedra and Williamson, along with his wife Betty, traveled in Peru and set up a flying saucer commune near Lake Titicaca known as the Abbey of the Seven Rays. In March, they were joined by Williamson's pal, John McCoy, in addition to fellow saucer seekers Ray and Rex Stanford. However, the Stanford brothers soon fell out of favor with Williamson, and he later referred to them as "the incompatible ones."

The Abbey of the Seven Rays fizzled out by the summer of 1957 and the Laugheads returned to the U.S. to continue their flying saucer exploits on more familiar turf. That same year, the Laugheads published George Hunt Williamson's *Book of Transcripts* and Lillian Laughead was among those to whom Williamson dedicated his book *Other Tongues, Other Flesh* "for her contribution to the Lemurian interpretation of the tracks in the desert."

1. Zirger, Michel and Martinelli, Maurizio. 2016. *The Incredible Life of George Hunt Williamson: Mystical Journey: Itinerary of a Privileged UFO Witness*. Publisher: Verdechiaro Edizioni.

Meade Layne

LAYNE, MEADE (1882–1961)

Former English department head at Illinois Wesleyan University, Meade Layne left the academic world in the 1940s to pursue a career in parapsychology. In 1945, he founded Borderland Sciences Research Associates (BSRA), an "association of persons interested in 'borderland' facts and happenings... facts and events which orthodox or official science cannot or will not investigate."

To this end, Layne teamed up with psychic medium Mark Probert (the "Telegnostic from San Diego") in efforts to establish interstellar contact. Probert was among a handful of San Diegans who—while waiting to view a meteor shower on October 9th, 1946—observed the passage of a strange structure in the sky. With the craft still in view, Probert phoned Layne, who encouraged him to establish telepathic communication with this weird flying machine.[1]

After the sighting, Probert told a local reporter:

> The strange machine is called the Kareeta. It is attracted at this time because the earth is emitting a column of light which makes it easier to approach. The machine is powered by people possessing a very advanced knowledge of anti-gravity forces. It has 10,000 parts, a small but very powerful motor operating by electricity, and moving the wings, and an outer structure of light balsam wood, coated with an alloy. The people are nonaggressive and have been trying to contact the earth for many years. They have very light bodies. They fear to land, but would be willing to meet a committee of scientists at an isolated spot, or on a mountain top.[2]

Probert channeled The Inner Circle, a group of ascended masters who were in contact with entities known as the Ethereans who visited Earth in Ether Ships from the fourth dimension. The Ethereans—according to Probert—were able to "mat" and "demat" (materialize and dematerialize) as a means to enter and depart the Earth plane by lowering or raising their vibrational levels. Ether

Mark Probert summoning the masters

Ships, as would be expected, came from a place called Etheria which was "Along side, inside, outside of our world." All of this is explained (more or less!) in Meade Layne's *The Ether Ship Mystery And Its Solution* (1950).

Layne was among the first—if not the first—to propose the interdimensional theory when most contactees were content with Venusians sporting long, blond hair and mouthing syrupy New Age platitudes. It wasn't until a couple of decades later that the interdimensional theory started to gain traction from cutting edge ufologists like Jacques Vallee and John Keel.

1. Tumminia, Diana G., 2007. *Alien Worlds: Social and Religious Dimensions of Extraterrestrial Contact*. Syracuse University Press.

2. Layne, Meade. 1972. *The Coming of the Guardians*. BSRA.

Gloria Lee at the Cosmic Counsel Center in Los Angeles (Joe Fex/APE-X Research)

LEE, GLORIA (1926–1962)

A lady with classic good looks coupled with a classic martyr syndrome, Gloria Lee was among the more tragic figures to emerge from the Golden Age of Contactees. A former childhood actress, model, and airline stewardess, Lee began receiving communications in 1953 courtesy of an entity from Jupiter going by the initials of J.W.

1959 proved to be a very productive year for both Lee and J.W., which included the publication of *Why We Are Here!*, a channeled collaboration between the two that read much the same as other cosmic messenger books of the day, filled with a lot of universal wisdom and the Coming-Of-A-New-Age proclamations, although on a sadder note it predicted that England would be swept under the sea. That same year, Lee founded the Cosmon Research Foundation to further promote J.W.'s teachings, an organization that at its height reportedly boasted 2000 members.

Like many contactees of the era, Lee was a speaker at the Giant Rock Interplanetary Spacecraft Convention. During her presentation she shared J.W.'s words of wisdom that "Earthlings have misinterpreted the purpose of their sexual drives" and that marriage was a human conception that didn't exist on other planets, which allowed for greater sexual freedom throughout the cosmos. It was the dawning of the Age of Aquarius.

In the fall of 1962, Lee approached the United Nations with a plan for world peace that included construction of a space station, but officials rebuffed her. Steadfast in her resolve to bring peace and harmony to the galaxy, Lee took up residence in a Washington, D.C. hotel on September 13th and a short time later began a hunger fast to bring attention to her cause. As Lee informed journalists: "I've heard from J.W., and they're disturbed up there because of fighting in the world and the fact that nuclear bombs might upset their planets. The space people are going to invade the earth and establish a peace program. J.W. has ordered me to go on a fast for peace until he sends a 'light elevator' down to take me to Jupiter."

On December 3rd—sixty-six days into her fast—Lee fell into a coma and died at the tender age of 37, leaving behind a husband and two young children. As tragic as this story may sound, a short time later there was some good news from the spirit realm courtesy of psychic medium Nada-Yolanda (real name Pauline Sharpe): "Hello everybody, this is Gloria. Yes, it's really me. I'm really finding out how this thing works." What "this thing" was, we can only surmise—unless, of course, Gloria Lee's spirit was referring to J.W.'s "light elevator" having transported her to a far better place.[1]

Gloria Lee's messages from beyond were later compiled into a staggering five-volume set of books published by the Mark-Age Meta Center, Inc., a non-profit corporation based out of Miami, Florida, that was operated by the aforementioned Pauline Sharpe along with her companion and fellow channeler, Mark (aka Charles B. Gentzel.)[2]

1. Clark, Jerome. 2000. *Extraordinary Encounters: An Encyclopedia of Extraterrestrials and Otherworldly Beings*. Santa Barbara, CA: ABC-CLIO. (p. 133).
2. Flammonde, Paris. 1971. *The Age of Flying Saucers*. New York: Hawthorn. (p. 163).

LYUBEIN, SONYA (or Sonja Lyubesin)

Not a whole lot is known about Sonya Lyubein. Even the spelling of her name is a matter of some dispute. Former Adamski follower Laura Mundo identified her as Sonya Lyubein, while contactee Ray Stanford considered Mundo's spelling not quite right, but the best he could come up with was "Sonja Lyubesin"—which may not have been entirely accurate either. Warren Smith in *UFO Trek* (1976) also referred to her as Sonya Lyubein, so we'll just use that spelling to tell Sonya's story, which is just too saucy to exclude from these pages.

In 1956, Miss Lyubein visited Saturn and found the inhabitants there far more "sexually active" than we repressive Earthlings. During her sexy Saturnian stay, Lyubein purportedly hooked up with Orthon for a little bit of otherworldly bump and grind. During this period, Lyubein was a speaker at the Giant Rock Interplanetary Spacecraft Convention where she shared stories about "close encounters" with her swinging Saturnian lover.

In an "essay" entitled *Sex and the UFO*, Laura Mundo described Lyubein as a "promiscuous" young lady who allegedly attended an Australian orgy (in the company of another unidentified woman) that was arranged by free swinging Orthon and involved 32 other spacemen for whom—according to Mundo—the women performed "their sexual bidding." After hearing this story, George Adamski promptly invited Lyubein to come visit him at Palomar Gardens in order to further "mentor" her ufological career.

MARLO, DR. GEORGE

Leader of the St. Louis-based "UFO World Research," Dr. George Marlo claimed he traveled to the Inner Earth on a UFO (however that works) piloted by a couple Inner Earth dwellers named Sol-Mar and Zola, who lived in the city of Masars II, located below South Africa. According to Marlo's Inner Earth informants, Masars II was a perfect paradise that featured giant birds with 30-foot wingspans and people standing twelve feet tall!

Marlo also had contacts with UFO occupants outside the Inner Earth, and in January 1960 he sent out an announcement to a list of celebrities inviting them to be part of an actual (supposed) flying saucer ride from New York to Brazil. Marlo's celebrity invitee list included Jack Benny, Jack Paar, Arthur Godfrey, Art Linkletter, and Long John Nebel.

At some point, Gray Barker got in on the act, appearing on Long John's radio show to promote the forthcoming Brazilian saucer flight. Jackie Gleason called in on the "beeper line" and offered Barker a wager (of anywhere from $500 to $10,000) that the saucer trip would be a flop. Barker (who obviously never took Marlo seriously but wanted to come up with something sensational for that week's show) wisely declined Gleason's challenge. Just before the predicted saucer arrival, according to Marlo, the trip was cancelled due to threats from a certain government agent named "Mr. Z."

In the spring of 1963, a mysterious character named Alexander with an "odd, hard to place accent" was traveling around the country meeting with UFO researchers, one of whom was Dr. Marlo. Afterwards, Marlo informed Jim Moseley that

> I am finished with radio and T.V. appearances about UFO's [sic]. Will talk on other subjects, but this one is too dangerous for me. Since talking to Alexander, I know better now...I won't give out any information to the public that could and would cause panic. I can't give you any further details at this time, but may someday. Alexander wanted me to be a leader when they land the circular flying machines here on Earth. They have

other means of coming here too, or so he stated...Part of his plan was to confuse you...*I found myself talking to the air three times when he was with me.* He would disappear into the thin air on certain occasions when other people were around.[1]

1. Moseley, James. 1967. *Jim Moseley's Book of Saucer News.* Clarksburg, WV: Saucerian Books. (p. 45-46).

MARTIN, DAN

Dan Martin was driving on a remote Texas road in the early hours of August 1955 when he was overcome by numbness. Alarmed that he was experiencing a medical emergency, Martin pulled over to the shoulder of the road just as a "space locomotive" appeared. Through the windows of the craft, he observed two men at the controls who brought the "space locomotive" to a landing. Martin—having regained use of his limbs at this point—bounded out of his vehicle to investigate the strange craft just as a hatch opened up and out stepped a humanoid wearing a gas mask and goggles, which were soon removed to reveal an attractive woman in a striking silver suit. "Hello there, Mr. Martin," she said, to which Martin replied, "Hello, you."

Like Aura Rhanes, the young lady spoke perfect English, although she was from Mercury as opposed to the planet Clarion. When Martin asked her why she had been selected to talk to him—as opposed to the two fellows in the ship—the silver suited lady replied that she was the only one on board who spoke the human language. Martin quizzed her about Mercury being so close to the Sun that our scientists had determined life could not exist on such a hot and seemingly barren planet. At this, she smiled and replied, "Well, you see me. Am I alive?" With that, the silver suited gal had to skedaddle, but informed Martin that her people would return at a future date to share much more cosmic wisdom, and then hopped back into her space locomotive and chugged away.

On June 11, 1956, Martin was visited by an ET guy and gal who greeted him: "You are Mr. Martin, Dap O' Day." (Your authors aren't quite sure how this whole Dap O' Day business got started, although it appears to be an appellation the ETs bestowed upon Martin which he later incorporated into a personal emblem.) In short order, the ET guy and gal grasped Martin by his elbows and gently levitated him up into a giant vacuum thingy that sucked the trio up into the control room of a massive spaceship that featured a stunning array of buttons, levers, dials, and other blinking gizmos. His tour of the control room complete, Mr. Dap O' Day was escorted into an adjacent room by another alien guy and gal who appeared to be a couple. After taking a seat on a sofa, the ET gal insisted on rubbing her thighs against Martin's, which made him ill at ease and withdraw in "an act of modesty."

Following this awkward instance, Martin was informed that the spaceship was named Michiel and afterwards he spent some quality time hanging out with the captain of the ship who was also named Michiel. If that wasn't confusing enough, Martin learned that the spaceship "Michiel" was the literal Star of Bethlehem that announced the birth of baby Jesus. In addition, the spaceship Michiel had been involved in all manner of biblical events throughout the ages, such as causing Noah's Flood in addition to constructing the Great Pyramid of Giza.

To close out the evening, Captain Michiel treated Martin to a sumptuous dinner topped off by several bottles of fine, Mercurian wine. Life was good for Dap O' Day![1]

1. Martin, Dan. 1960. *The Watcher: Seven Hours Aboard a Space Ship.* Clarksburg, WV: Saucerian Books.

Dorothy Martin and Charles Laughead

MARTIN, DOROTHY (1900–1992)

In the late 1930s, Dorothy Martin attended a Theosophy lecture in New York City that sparked her interest in the occult and metaphysics. Martin later became a student of Dianetics and by the 1950s had steeped herself in many of the precursors that influenced the UFO contactee era, including *Oahspe* and Guy Ballard's I AM Movement.

In early 1953, Martin—then living in Oak Park, Illinois—had recently been diagnosed with cancer when one morning her life was forever changed:

> My whole arm felt warm right up to the shoulder...I had the feeling that someone was trying to get my attention. Without knowing why, I picked up a pencil and a pad that were lying on the table near my bed. My hand began to write in another handwriting...

Via automatic writing, Martin became the channel for the Elder Brother of Venus, who shared the following:

> I am always with you. The cares of the day cannot touch you. We will teach them that seek and are ready to follow in the light. I will take care of the details. Trust in us. Be patient and learn, for we are there preparing the work for you as a connoiter. That is an earthly liaison duty before I come. That will be soon.

Soon after, Martin started a group with Charles and Lillian Laughead called "The Seekers" and the messages became increasingly apocalyptic. Referred to as "Marian Keech" in Leon Festinger's *When Prophecy Fails*, Martin channeled a number of different entities such as "The Guardians" from Clarion, unspecified beings from Cerus, and—last but not least—the Elder Brother from Venus, who was apparently the reincarnation of Jesus Christ but was now going by the name of Sananda.

However, Martin was not the first to identify Jesus as the extraterrestrial Sananda; she probably picked up on this from her readings of Guy Ballard, who had years before made the acquaintance of Jesus/Sananda during his encounters with the Venusian Masters at Mount Shasta.

Martin subscribed to such publications as Meade Layne's *Round Robin* (the official bulletin of BSRA) and Gray Barker's *The Saucerian*, to which she fired off letters about the channeled messages she received from beyond. Barker, of course, egged Martin on, claiming his own curious encounters with representatives from Clarion, such as one story he shared with Martin about meeting a strange man at the post office who vanished into thin air. To this, one of Martin's ascended masters informed her that "the young man who contacted Gray Barker was our contact and had a message for him."

On December 17, 1954—a few days before the predicted flood that never happened—Martin received a phone call at "The Seekers" headquarters (which also doubled as her Oak Park home) from someone identifying themselves as Captain Video who notified her that a flying saucer would soon be landing and taking Martin and her crew away to a safer place in outer space. This phone call from Captain Video—an obvious practical joke—was nonetheless taken seriously by Martin and her flock, who started packing their bags in preparation for their forthcoming flying saucer flight. Captain Video—it so happens—was the lead character in a popular children's television series, but that didn't dissuade Martin and her followers from believing the saucer arrival was nigh.

Following her failed flood prediction, Martin mustered the troops one last time to sing Christmas carols in the hopes of summoning a saucer. This escalating circus created enough of an uproar that her neighbors filed police complaints in an attempt to get Martin and her bunch hauled away to the loony bin. As a result, Martin went into hiding and the following year resurfaced in Arizona where she became aligned with famed contactee George Hunt Williamson.

Martin (now using the name of Sister Thedra) and Williamson marshaled their forces into a two person trance channeling tag team and were instructed to travel to Peru to set up a flying saucer commune there called the Abbey of the Seven Rays. The Peru endeavor was pretty much a flop and Sister Thedra floundered there over the next several years until 1961, when Sananda instructed her to return to the U.S. First stop for Sister Thedra was the new age Mecca of Mount Shasta, California, an area rich in the lore of flying saucers and Lemurians. It was there in 1965 that Sister Thedra founded the Association of Sananda and Samat Kumara, and then in 1988 relocated her operation to Sedona, Arizona.

Living to the ripe old age of 92, Sister Thedra continued channeling assorted ascended masters until her death in 1992, which was quite remarkable given the fact that she'd been diagnosed with cancer way back in 1954. As for the Association of Sananda and Samat Kumara, it's still apparently in operation, based once again in Mount Shasta where Sister Thedra originally founded the organization.[1]

1. Tumminia, Diana G., editor. 2007. *Alien Worlds: Social and Religious Dimensions of Extraterrestrial Contact*. New York: Syracuse University Press. (p. 25-41).

MAYO, PAUL (1949–)

The little known UK case of Paul Mayo in the UK illustrates the phenomenon of UFO healings by supposed aliens, and a different, but surprisingly common sort of "contactee." Mayo suffered from a variety of pulmonary and breathing problems stemming from childhood exposure to mold and organophosphates. His doctor told him that he would not live past his 30s.

At age 29, Mayo was getting ready for breakfast one morning in November of 1978 when he looked up from where he was sitting on the bed to see:

> ...a "man" poke his head around the door. The man, who was five foot six in height and ordinary in appearance, entered the room silently and raised his palm in a waving gesture. It was at this point that Mayo realized he could not move. He was paralyzed where he sat at the edge of his bed. The stranger now began to "dissolve" before his eyes, leaving on an intricate outline of his nerves and blood vessels, which shone brilliantly, "like a million fibres of light."[1]

Mayo felt himself laying back on his bed and was soon surrounded by what looked like four men on either side of him, dressed in "tight fitting silver clothes." The last thing he remembered was being "ejected from his bed and literally floated through his bedroom wall."[2] When he came to about four hours later, he found his wife in the kitchen. She was apparently not surprised that it had taken Mayo over four hours to get ready for breakfast. She had eaten her food and left his meal on the table.

While they could not explain his lapse of normal consciousness, Mayo immediately discovered that he felt better than he had in years. His doctor later examined him and said that his recovery was "miraculous." Another strange aftereffect of the experience was that Mayo found he could not eat any meat. "The very act of bringing the meat to his mouth would make him feel instantly nauseous," although he was able to do so after many years, but only organically produced products and only in small amounts. He remains in excellent health even today.[3]

This was his first contact with what he could only describe as extraterrestrials who gave him no message to deliver to the world, no religious catechism, save that they were probably vegetarians.

Twice more, over ten years after the first experience, Mayo said he saw something or some things enter his bedroom. On these occasions, he perceived the beings more clearly, and described them as looking like what he thought of as towering Native American men with dark, weathered skin and "barrel chests" with waist-length silver hair. On their second visit, Mayo said a group of these beings picked him up and carried him through a "portal" in the wall to a bright light. When he emerged from the other side, he said he was in a vast field somewhere in what looked like the English countryside. There he saw others being carried in the same way towards scores of silvery flying saucers. His wife saw nothing of this, but has reported observing shadowy figures and even the ubiquitous grey alien skulking furtively about their home.[4]

1. Graham, Robbie. 2015. *Silver Screen Saucers.*White Crow Books. (p 123).
2. ibid, p. 124.
3. ibid, p. 124.
4. Graham, Robbie. Personal interview, January 8, 2008.

Gareth McCoy (Joe Fex/APE-X Research)

McCoy, John

John McCoy was among a group of early contactees that formed around George Hunt Williamson, among them Alfred Bailey, Lyman Streeter, Karl Hunrath, Wilbur Wilkinson and the Stanford brothers, Ray and Rex.

Like other members of this circle, McCoy was a psychic channeler and took part in short wave radio communications with the space brothers. McCoy operated his own publishing house, Essene Press, and his contributions to contactee literature include *They Shall Be Gathered Together* (1957) and *UFOs Confidential* (1958), co-authored with Williamson.

McCoy championed the theory that the International Banking Conspiracy made a deal with extraterrestrials to invade Earth, all part of some grand diabolical plan to create a global economic panic and allow the bankers to control the world. McCoy was also keen on the notion that artificial chemicals had been injected into the food supply to control and manipulate human behavior, in essence "poisoning our precious bodily fluids" a la General Jack D. Ripper in Stanley Kubrick's *Dr. Strangelove*.

According to a July 2, 1958 article in the *Long Beach Independent*, McCoy was going around making claims that a certain lady of his acquaintance possessed the power to call down flying saucers, and that this could be done "by appointment" in Joshua Tree, California, for those interested parties. The unnamed woman in question, in all likelihood, was McCoy's wife, Gareth.

John and Gareth were original members of Scientology, among the first one hundred Scientologists to attain the lofty status of Theta Clear, which presumably assisted in their saucer communications.[1]

McCoy was still active as a psychic channeler and publishing occult materials up until at least the mid-1990s.

1. https://androvillans.wordpress.com/2011/11/10/the-first-hundred-clears-what-went-wrong/

Bill Meier explaining the Pleadian flight path to Col. Wendelle Stevens circa mid 1970s (Joe Fex/APE-X Research)

MEIER, EDUARD ALBERT "BILLY" (1937–)

With fans like Shirley MacLaine, Eduard "Billy" Meier has become the modern poster-boy for UFO contact. Literally. One of his so-called "beamship" photos achieved immortality when the producers of *The X-Files* decided to use the image on the "I WANT TO BELIEVE" poster that adorns Fox Mulder's office on that wildly successful television show.

The "Billy" nickname was apparently bestowed on Meier by an American woman who thought his habit of dressing in cowboy garb made him look like Billy the Kid. Meier's hundreds of photos and films of his "beamships" from the Pleiades have been roundly criticized as fake, and in a few cases proved as fake, as well as the blurry images of his space babe contacts, some of which have proved to be old photos of the Goldiggers dance group, famous in the 1960s.

Meier says his first contact was when he was five years old. He said he learned to communicate with the saucer-drivers telepathically, and in 1944, when he was seven, he met "Sfath," an elder space brother who gave him a ride in his flying saucer. On his sixteenth birthday, Sfath's voice was replaced with (of course) a female voice calling herself "Asket," hailing from the DAL universe (a parallel reality).

After running away from home a few times, and joining the French Foreign Legion for a while, Asket told Meier to travel and gain life experience. He ended up in India in 1964 and gave an interview to the *New Delhi Statesman*, claiming that he had hundreds of UFO photos, but that he couldn't share them with anyone just yet.

Meier was the victim of a bus accident in Turkey in 1965, in which he lost most of his left arm. After recovering, Meier moved on to Greece where he met and eloped with a 17-year old girl named Kaliope Zafirerou. They somehow ended up in Pakistan and had a daughter who they named Gilgamesha. A son followed in 1969, and was christened Atlantis-Socrates.

They moved back to Meier's homeland, where he set up a metaphysical discussion group in 1974. The event which was to change the rest of his life (as if the adventures up to this point hadn't made some impression) came on January 28th of 1975, when he said a disc-shaped craft landed near him and a beautiful space woman stepped out. Meier said they talked for an hour and a half. The woman said her name was Semjase. She was to be the center of Meier's space-brother universe up to the present day. He calls his contacts the "Plejaren" since Semjase and the others told him they came from the Pleiades. A strange corollary to this issue is one of the fallen angels described in the Biblical book of Enoch was named "Shemyaza," which means, "He sees the name."[1]

In 1976, Adamski follower Lou Zinsstag and British Researcher Timothy Good visited UFO photo hoarder and former Air Force officer Wendelle Stevens, and told him about their favorable impressions of Meier. When Stevens and Meier finally met in October of 1977 and again in April of 1978, Meier impressed Stevens with his stories and gave him many photos to take back to Arizona. Along with a few colleagues (who had performed their own investigation of Meier's claims) Stevens formed Genesis III Productions Ltd. to showcase and exploit the Meier photos and material. They promised him a cut from the profits. Their first book, a large-format affair, was entitled *UFO... Contact From The Pleiades Vol. 1* and consisted of beautifully printed reproductions of some of the most impressive photos and descriptions of the supposedly exhaustive and scientific scrutiny that had been applied to Meier's claims and images. *Volume 2* was released in 1983.

To document and spread the word of the Plejaren, Meier formed the Freie Interessengemeinschaft für Grenzund Geisteswissenschaften und Ufologiestudien (FIGU) in the late 1970s. According to the Canadian FIGU website, the English translation is, the "Free Community of Interests for Border and Spiritual Sciences and Ufological Studies."[2] The foundation is still going strong and has attracted a new wave of supporters and devotees, the most vocal of which seems to be Michael Horn, who has been promoting himself to UFO-themed podcasts with come-ons such as:

> Hi, I suggest interviewing me, Michael Horn, the world's leading expert on UFOs, who represents the singularly authentic, scientifically proven, Billy Meier UFO case. While it's driving the amateurs, pseudo "experts" nuts in the sad UFO community, a good, critically thinking interviewer will not only perceive the authenticity of the Meier case but also question just...WHY it's been suppressed. Feel free to contact me: Michael Horn Authorized American Media Representative [for] The Billy Meier Contacts.[3]

A recent convert to the fold was UFO researcher Cheryl Costa, co-author of *UFO Sightings Desk Reference*, a recent book analyzing trends in UFO data who has tagged Meier's photos as her "smoking gun" proof of an alien presence because she observed flash frames in the Meier film footage that she claimed matches a similar flash in STS mission 48 footage of a strange "beam" that shot past the space shuttle.[4] This "flash" is also what is observed when a rotating film camera shutter has not yet reached the proper speed and overexposes a few frames. American Meier supporter Michael Horn has made the observation that some of the "mistakes" in Meier's footage are created by the Plejaren in order to give skeptics an "out" because "it would be too threatening to their belief systems."[5]

1. https://en.wikipedia.org/wiki/Samyaza
2. https://cafigu.org
3. Personal correspondence with the author.
4. https://www.syracusenewstimes.com/my-smoking-gun-ufo-proof/
5. Horn commentary: https://youtu.be/GpgF7pDx_zs

Howard and Connie Menger

MENGER, HOWARD (1922–2009)

"I am... Howard... Menger. The following statements which I shall make are... true facts." So begins Menger's 1957 record album "Authentic Music From Another Planet."[1] Along with only two published books (*From Outer Space to You* and *The High Bridge Incident*) this was enough to place Menger (pronounced "Mehn-jer") in the upper echelon of the 1950s contactees and assure him a lasting presence on the radio and lecture circuit.

Menger wrote and told of a beautiful space woman who apparently gave him feelings of a distinctly grown-up nature when he was only 10 years old, although he was careful to describe the encounters as very platonic. The woman would return later in life and cause him to leave his wife and family. In his first book, he described seeing her for the first time in a clearing in the woods near his childhood home:

> ...one day in 1932, when I was ten, I saw something even more beautiful than the surroundings. There, sitting on a rock by the brook, was the most exquisite woman my young eyes had ever beheld!
>
> The warm sunlight caught the highlights of her long golden hair as it cascaded around her face and shoulders. The curves of her lovely body were delicately contoured—revealed through the translucent material of clothing which reminded me of the habit of skiers.
>
> I halted in my tracks, and for a moment my breath stopped. I was not frightened, but an overwhelming wonderment froze me to the spot.
>
> She turned her head in my direction.

Even though very young, the feeling I received was unmistakable. It was a tremendous surge of warmth, love, and physical attraction which emanated from her to me.[2]

Menger enlisted in the Army during WWII. He served with a tank division and learned how to use a flamethrower to flush the enemy out of caves and buildings during the invasion of Okinawa. He related other contacts with space men and cosmic beauties throughout his tour of duty in the Pacific, whom he credited with saving his life a few times. They predicted that the Allies would win and also told him that things would get more interesting after the war with a warning: "If you think you're crazy NOW, Howard, wait until you see some of the other things that are going to happen to you!"[3]

He was honorably discharged in 1946 and moved to a farm near High Bridge, New Jersey. He ran a sign-painting business and tinkered with homemade inventions on his farm. Perhaps because of his electronic and mechanical interests, he was soon fascinated with flying saucers and in particular (although he denied it later) with George Adamski's book *The Flying Saucers Have Landed*, when he first read the title upon its release in 1953.

Feeling a desire to rekindle his contacts, he visited the spot where he had met his first alien love fourteen years before. Not surprisingly, she appeared again and told Menger that he had a job to do to help the Space People in their missions on Earth. He had to buy clothes for them (the women giggled and threw their Earth-bras away) and give haircuts to the men, who wore their hair long, like space hippies.

In September of 1956, Menger was invited aboard a "Venusian Scout Ship" and given a ride to the space people's home planet. During the journey, Menger said he was shown alien civilizations on other planets and vast structures on the moon. Soon after, he appeared on the Long John Nebel radio show with George Van Tassel and described his newfound space friends and their messages for mankind.

The encounters continued and intensified to the point that he eventually felt a strong compulsion to leave his wife for a space sister who he said resembled the woman who had aroused his interests when he was but a child. Although her name was Connie, he referred to her as "Marla Baxter" in his writings and on his record album. As required for contactee stardom, he released a book on his adventures, entitled *From Outer Space To You*, recounting his history with people from other worlds.

Menger held small saucer conventions on his property, featuring lectures on the reality and message of the space brothers. A series of famous photos depict a man that contactee Frank Stranges identified as Val Thor, his cosmic contact who often walked the corridors of the Pentagon. To date, no one has identified the man with the carefully coiffed pompadour. Attendees were also treated to figures dancing about in the woods on the property at night, although Menger said that the space people were not to be approached because they were shy.

Podcast host Gene Steinberg recalled that Menger appeared to backtrack on his claims after some of the contactee hysteria died down. Perhaps withering under the scrutiny of mainstream UFO study, he said that his shenanigans were all some sort of intelligence game:

> Now in the mid-1960s, I was working with Jim Moseley on *Saucer News*. Jim got a call from Menger, and we all hooked up for lunch at a restaurant across the street from the magazine's famous offices at 303 Fifth Avenue. Menger, despite being criticized extensively in the magazine, proved personable, and gave us some unexpected news. He said that he had begun to feel that his contacts were actually with government agents, who used him as part of a disinformation campaign.

> In later years, Menger was trying to sell plans for portable spacecraft and other stuff.

> I don't know what motivated him to make the claim of government participation. At the same time, I wouldn't be surprised if he told us the truth. Further, that other contactees of that era might have also been manipulated in that fashion. In the end, it made the UFO field look foolish to many people, and if that was the intent, it was a success.[4]

Ivan T. Sanderson, cryptozoologist and all-around investigator of the weird claimed he encountered equipment at Menger's farm that appeared to be labeled as the property of the U.S. Army. When Sanderson confronted him, Menger became agitated and angry and asked Sanderson to leave.[5]

In later years, Menger and his wife were occasionally featured at saucer conventions, but his star had faded, and he was looked upon as a relic of an earlier, more naïve era. Jim Moseley, researcher and chronicler of the UFO scene, recalled that Menger appeared at a Florida gathering in the 1990s along with Connie and one of his space-people-inspired contraptions. During a demonstration in a hotel, he plugged his invention into a wall socket and blew all the fuses in the facility.[6] Moseley also reported that Menger was apparently possessed of a furious temper when aroused, although this may have been due to his wartime experiences and possible PTSD.

He appears to have come to a sort of peace with his legacy at the time of his death in 2009.

1. Menger, Howard. 1957. *Authentic Music From Another Planet*. Slate Enterprises, Inc – LP-X211.
2. Menger, Howard, and Connie Menger. 1991. *The High Bridge Incident: The Story behind the Story*. Vero Beach, FL: Howard Menger Studio. (p. 4-5).
3. ibid p. 15.
4. https://www.theparacast.com/forum/threads/howard-menger.843/
5. Conversation with researcher Dr. Mario Pazzaglini in the late 1990s.
6. Bishop, Gregory. 2001. "Interview With James Moseley" in *Wake Up Down There: The Excluded Middle Collection*. Kempton. IL: Adventures Unlimited Press. (p. 115).

Allen Michael

MICHAEL, ALLEN (1916–2010)

In 1947—while working as a sign painter in Long Beach, California—Allen Noonan became enveloped in an "ultraviolet light entwined with gold threads" and transported up into a Galactic Mothership operated by an outfit called Extra Territorial Intelligence (ETI). At this time, Noonan was selected to fulfill the role of New World Comforter and human channel for the Everlasting Gospel of the Space Brothers. On direction from on high, he changed his name to Allen Michael, which you must admit is a lot cooler name than Allen Noonan.[1]

In March 1956, Allen attended the Giant Rock Interplanetary Spacecraft Convention and rubbed elbows with the contactees there, including the "3 Georges:" Van Tassel, Hunt Williamson and Adamski. Later that year—on a return visit to Giant Rock—Michael enjoyed his second ET contact experience when a flying saucer appeared with three beings named Favelron, Celeste, and Jameston, who, after introducing themselves, threw Allen kisses before accelerating away in a flash of light.

Afterwards, Michael started a communal experiment called "The One World Family Commune." In 1967, Michael's commune relocated to San Francisco's Haight Ashbury District and opened a vegetarian restaurant called *Here and Now*. In 1970, the group moved across the bay to Berkeley and opened a second restaurant called *One World Family Natural Food Center* and it was there that Michael started once-a-week public channeling sessions with the space brothers. According to legend, on one occasion several members of Michael's commune joined him on a trip to the planet Altamira where they were given the assignment of *Cosmic Masters*. LSD sessions apparently played a large role in these experiences, which explains a lot.

In 1970, the FBI arrested Michael for selling eighth of an ounce of marijuana and he was sentenced to six months in prison. After his release, Michael moved his gang of acid tripping space cadets to a mansion in Stockton, California, where communal tantric sex was added to the curriculum and the group explored the ideal of "Uni-Communism," a concept promoting monogamous love, natural food, and vegetarianism. (In other words, "hippie shit.")

As a further means of promoting the ET message, Michael founded the "Utopian Synthesis Party," which he said was "the party to end all political parties and have a real party!" as part of a presidential campaign he launched for the 1980 election. (Co-author Adam Gorightly actually voted for Michael in the general election that year.)

During the 1990s, Michael hosted a public access TV show called *Galactic Messenger*. His group maintains a website at www.galacticmessenger.com.

1. Allen, Michael. 1977. *UFO-ETI World Master Plan*, Santa Rosa, California: Starmast Publications.

Further listening

Quasar - *One World Family - Extraterrestrial Music From ETI* (1976)

Dick Miller (Joe Fex/APE-X Research)

Miller, Richard "Dick"

In September 1954, Dick Miller joined forces with famed contactee George Hunt Williamson and the duo formed the Telonic Research Center in Prescott, Arizona. The organization was dedicated to ET contact via short wave radio. This partnership ran aground a short time later when the two men had a falling out and Miller moved on to his next space brother adventure.

At the 1955 Giant Rock Interplanetary Spacecraft Convention, Miller said "the Earth is now moving into a huge cloud of deadly cosmic rays but is being screened from the radiation by 3,560,000 spaceships. He added that if the screening fails to prove effective, the Martians are prepared to evacuate the entire Earth to save the people from destruction. Miller said Sol-Tec, the commander of a Martian spaceship, 150 feet in diameter, disclosed the plan when he was picked up by the spaceship near Detroit and made a 12-hour voyage in it..."

During the 1956 Giant Rock Convention, Miller played taped recordings of a Martian named Commander Mon-Ka that were allegedly discovered on previously blank reel-to-reel tapes in his garage. According to Miller, Mon-Ka possessed "wisdom that is light years beyond the most intelligent person on our planet." One of Miller's tapes featured "Mon-Ka's Prediction":

Greetings, people of Earth. I am Mon-Ka. I am what you would call the head of my government. I speak to you this evening from the planet which you call Mars...We, of the Space Confederation... speak now to you, people of Earth. We shall prove our remarks by bringing about an incident which will forever dispel any claims... that would deny our existence. On the evening of November 7, of this your year 1956, at 10:30 P.M. your local time, we request that one of your communications stations remove its carrier signal from the air for two minutes. At that time we will speak from our craft, which will be stationed at an altitude of 10,000 feet over your great city of Los Angeles. This ship

199

will be visible to all of the people, as it will be illuminated by our force fields... People of Earth, it is time you knew the truth...your planet is not ready... May we, your brothers, share the great warmth and friendship of peace, and now, co existence. I, Mon-Ka, have spoken.

In the lead up to Mon-Ka's predicted flying saucer appearance, AFSCA's Gabe Green appeared on Art Linkletter's *House Party* on October 29th speaking in glowing terms about Dick Miller's favorite Martian. When the evening of November 7th rolled around, Los Angeles residents—rife with anticipation—popped some popcorn, pulled out lawn chairs and climbed up on rooftops with binoculars in preparation for the saucer spectacle soon to unfold. Playing along with the gag, L.A. radio stations KATY and KBIA went off the air at the appointed time. Not to be outdone, news reporter Paul Coates of television station KTTV even hired an airplane to go out in search for Mon-Ka's Martian spacecraft.[1]

But alas—like many another saucer prediction—Mon-ka backed out at the last minute and the whole thing turned out to be a bust. UFO researcher Max Miller of Flying Saucers International afterwards noted that Dick Miller's Mon-ka stunt "set saucer research on the West Coast back ten years."

In the aftermath of the Mon-ka debacle, the *Los Angeles Mirror* ran an article accusing Miller of having fabricated a previous short wave radio-flying saucer communication back in 1954 when he was a member of the Detroit Flying Saucer Club. According to UFO researcher and radio personality John Otto:

> I exposed one of [Miller's] attempted hoaxes here when he was a member of the Detroit Flying Saucer Club. Randall Cox, auto dealer and Miller's ex-employer, told me by telephone, "Miller told us he had information that on a certain date we were to contact a saucer in a certain area. When we went out there, he had us remain in the car to listen on the radio. Soon we heard his voice. He said he was speaking from the spaceship. He said he could see us on a kind of advanced-type screen aboard the saucer. Later, when he returned to the car, I was suspicious. I got the radio ham who assisted Miller to break down and tell me the whole story. About half a mile away, in an abandoned truck, we found the radio transmitter he had used to cut in on our car radio with his phony message from the spaceship."[2]

Due to these revelations, Miller made himself scarce for a while only to re-emerge on the saucer lecture circuit a few years later. By this time, Mon-ka had been replaced by an entity named Kla-la from the Aldeberan planetary system.

For those fortunate enough to have attended Gabe Green's 1960 AFSCA convention, Miller was on hand hawking actual Kla-la recordings for the low, low price of $4.95 (Cheap.)

---

1. "The Mon-Ka Business in Los Angeles." *The APRO Bulletin*, Alamogordo, New Mexico, November, 1956.
2. *L.A. Mirror-News*, November 2, 1956.

Helen and Betty Mitchell

MITCHELL, HELEN AND BETTY

In May 1957, Helen and Betty Mitchell of St. Louis, Missouri, were approached at a coffee shop by two men named Elen and Zelas who said they were from Mars. The manly Martian duo further informed the Mitchell sisters that they'd been monitoring them since birth (for a special mission on Earth!).[1]

At first, the Mitchell sisters were a bit suspicious, but when the two purported men from Mars recounted several childhood incidents that had occurred to the Mitchell sisters—that no one could have possibly known about outside of immediate family members—Betty and Helen became suddenly convinced that the mystery men were on the level and most assuredly from Mars!

Shortly after their initial encounter, Helen and Betty returned to the coffee shop to meet again with Elen and Zelas and at that time were given instructions on how to build an advanced communication device that enabled them to remain in constant contact with a Martian mothership piloted by Commander Alna.

In November, Helen was taken aboard said mothership and "told the magnetism of the craft would not affect my watch since it would be balanced by the magnetism of my own body. However, while in the mother craft the magnetism of it caused my watch to stop, and it was de-magnetized in a small machine before I left." It's the little details that matter. After Helen got the whole magnetism thing figured out, the Martians shared with her advanced scientific information and then demonstrated a space-age version of shuffleboard controlled by psychokinetic powers.

In the aftermath of Helen's excellent mothership adventure, the Mitchell sisters maintained communications with their Martian friends, which included information on a wide variety of stuff they were instructed to pass on to the people of Earth. Martians—like their Venusian counterparts—apparently spent a lot of time obsessing over atomic bombs and how the people of Earth might end up doing to our current civilization what the Lemurians did to theirs. (Or to quote George Adamski's friend Orthon: "Boom Boom!")

Beaming with the space brother's message, the Mitchell sisters made the scene at saucer clubs and UFO conventions, where they preached to the contactee choir about atom bombs and Atlantis and the dawning of a new age where mankind needed to get its act together and transcend our war-like ways.

At a meeting of the Kansas City Saucer Club, Helen Mitchell shared her knowledge of interplanetary languages by presenting this example: "Me! Bez de Son. Ras, de ta ol de leon qua sone twila urn bon-ta-bon Zabat dar um ta daga de tra-ce-te de tai o um bont. Zabat rma zabat ott tar ma qua zabat gavon-ta-bon um-quat que. Ban gav ban um ta ban ta zabat, nas qua pa qua zabat ta ol dat urn ta rama. Mel Bez de son."

According to Helen, the above translated to: "Peace be with you. Beloved, in the light of mind evolveness one chooses to serve, and so doing turns the forces of Love in this attraction toward him. When searching is difficult it proves advancement, for adversaries must work strongly to prevent involvement. Let darkness fade to the nothingness that it is, not potential or manifesting as is the light which takes its place. Peace be with you." Unfortunately the translated message seemed almost as incomprehensible as the un-translated version.

In 1965, the Mitchell sisters turned up missing, which suggested to some they'd been taken on an extended trip to Mars.[2]

1. Mitchell, Helen & Betty. 1959. *The Space People We Met: The Story of the Mitchell Sisters*. Clarksburg,WV: Saucerian Books.
2. Beckley, Timothy Green. *On The Trail Of The Flying Saucers*, June 1969 issue.

Buck Nelson (left) with Truman Bethurum at Giant Rock (Joe Fex/APE-X Research)

NELSON, BUCK (1895–1982)

Buck Nelson will forever be known as the guy who sold Venusian dog hair, but is probably best known for the famous photo in which he is holding up a sign for one of his spacecraft conventions with the "S" written backwards. In 1956, Nelson told the world about his ET friends "Bob Solomon,"(a strange name for someone from Venus) an earthling traveling with him called "Little Bucky" and a 385-pound space dog called "Big Bo," who all came by in a souped-up saucer from Venus and landed on his property in the Ozark mountains of Arkansas.

Strangely (or not) Nelson noted that the space brothers he met with also practiced segregation along racial lines, at least on Mars. When visiting Mars, he wrote he was told that "there are other races and colors of people there, but I was taken where the people were most like the ones I was used to."[1] He wrote about his adventures among these cosmic klansmen in his book *My Trip To Mars, The Moon, and Venus*, and his five "contacts" with the space people. Before his trip, Nelson recalled that he "left milk out for my cat, which I call 'Krazy,' and Trixie, my horse, could get feed out on the range. Ted, my dog, went on this trip with me."[2]

The people of Venus had "no roads, [due to their use of hovering vehicles] no police force, no jails, no government buildings, and no wars." The ruler he visited wore overalls just like the denim ones favored by Nelson, but they "didn't have all the buckles and hooks which ours do and they were made of a different material."[3] He also said that the space people had a "book machine" that would read aloud any book placed in it, or play music or show any pictures contained in it.

Nelson favored overalls and a crude crew cut, and basically conformed almost perfectly to the urban-dweller's idea of a hillbilly. He later toured the country selling packets of hair he claimed to have snipped off Big Bo's hide, but looked to many like it may have come from a plastic doll.

Before the fifth and final meeting, his Venusian friends gave him their version of the Ten Commandments, with a couple of extras. A partial list:

(These twelve laws were given to Buck Nelson, at his farm at Mountain View, Missouri, on April 24, 1955, by men from the planet Venus. These laws are followed faithfully and are not just something to mention occasionally.)

Thou shalt not kill...includes accidents and war.

Thou must do as thou wish to be done by.

Your body is God's. Do not misuse it in any way. Do not drink or eat anything that is not food. Use nothing to harm the body, either inside or out. Wear nothing on the body that harms it or is of no use.[4]

His book also included everything else Nelson wanted to say to his eager audience, including an invitation to his farm for yearly saucer meetings, "Bucky's Christmas Message to the World," and the fact that his space friends "shot a ray at me and cured my aching back."[5]

A man named Hank Fulk claimed that Nelson:

...got to meet President Eisenhower on an arranged trip to DC. The President's doctors learned how to do open heart surgery from Buck Nelson. They were able to save Eisenhower's life when he had his first heart attack. This was information given to Buck by the "visitors." Many in Washington DC wanted Buck killed, but the General was a Friend that stood by Old Buck. He was as "HOT" as Area 51.

BO the dog was analyzed, photographed, and x-rayed by students from The University of Missouri, School of Veterinary Medicine in 1953. The Results showed his hair to be unlike standard dog hair, internal organs were also some different. He was said to look much like a giant Sheep Dog.[6]

The trail on Buck Nelson goes cold sometime in the 1970s, but there are rumors that he spent his last years with relatives in California.

1. Nelson, Buck. 1956. *My Trip To Mars, The Moon, and Venus*. Quill Press Company. (p. 8).
2. ibid p. 10.
3. ibid p. 4.

4. ibid p. 5.
5. ibid p. 17.
6. http://gratisenergi.se/hank.htm

Daryle Nieman, "Miss Out of this World" (Joe Fex/APE-X Research)

Nieman, Daryle

The unanimous winner of the "Miss Out Of This World Contest" held at Gabe Green's 1960 AFSCA Convention, Daryle Nieman was described by the *Los Angeles Herald Examiner* as a "beautiful, blonde dancer-model who says she has a way of getting in touch with the real space people via a kind of mental radio."[1] According to Jim Moseley,

> [Nieman] and a group of friends had met a spacewoman named Soloma. Decked out in a white robe, Soloma discoursed at some length about interplanetary life and philosophy and then suddenly disappeared. However, Daryle stayed in "mental contact" with her, had seen saucers on various occasions, and once saw a space animal named Mika, which she described as appearing like a cross between a rabbit and a cat. While Daryle's tale was no more convincing than the others told at Giant Rock (actually, even less so), there was something (!) about Daryle that filled me with the Will to Believe.[2]

1. Crenshaw, James. "Giant Rock Spectacle Perplexes: Was It A Flying Saucer?" *Los Angeles Herald Express*, May 31, 1960.
2. Moseley, James & Karl Pflock. 2002. *Shockingly Close To The Truth: Confessions of a Grave-Robbing Ufologist*. New York: Prometheus Books.

Mel Noel at the 1966 Giant Rock Convention (Joe Fex/APE-X Research)

NOEL, MEL aka Guy Kirkwood (real name Noall Bryce Cornwell)

In 1966, a sharp-dressed, handsome young fellow going by the name of Mel Noel made a splash on the east coast saucer circuit when he checked into a luxury hotel with a pair of stunning ladies on either arm and began wining and dining influential magazine editors and news reporters, recruiting them for a prospective flying saucer flight.

According to the dashing Mr. Noel, the saucer was scheduled to land on the set of the Jackie Gleason television show in Florida, and those interested in taking part would have to apply for a space passport.[1] It was around the time of this supposed flying saucer trip that Noel launched the "Ufology Research Institute" that—according to Don Dornan, an investigative reporter for *Time Magazine*—was a scam to lure investors to pony up for the phony flying saucer trip.

Among other whoppers, Noel claimed the acquaintance of a mysterious "Mr. Genovese" who had been part of a team of scientists that had worked with Guglielmo Marconi developing a "death ray" during World War II. While still in the development stage, Marconi and his group demonstrated this death ray to Benito Mussolini, and of course Mussolini was smitten with it and wanted it for his very own. When the Italian dictator demanded they fork over the ray gun or else, Marconi refused and soon ended up dead. Afterwards, the rest of the scientists fled Italy with their death ray blueprints and resurfaced five years later at a secret UFO base in Argentina where they were supposedly working with some blond ETs who had agreed to provide a flying saucer ride from Los Angeles to Mexico in ten seconds flat.

It didn't take Don Dornan long to figure out that Noel was running a saucer scam, and when he threatened to expose him in a *Time Magazine* article, Noel told investors that Dornan was a dastardly CIA agent who had sabotaged the forthcoming saucer flight, causing its cancellation.[2]

Afterwards, Noel faded from the ufological limelight only to re-emerge in a chapter of Timothy

Good's *Above Top Secret* (1988) where he rolled out many of the same claims that had previously appeared in *The Mel Noel Story: The Inside Story of the U.S. Air Force Secrecy on UFOs* (1967). As the "story" goes, Noel allegedly served in an Air Force unit during the 1950s involved in top secret UFO photo recon flights, all of which Don Dornan had long ago debunked but nonetheless ufology has a short memory about such things, and so Noel again resuscitated the story for a while in the early '90s with an appearance on a Fox Network UFO special. Not long after this appearance, *UFO Magazine* ran an exposé on Noel, after which he made himself suddenly scarce again.

1. Keel, John. 1988. *Disneyland of the Gods.* AMOK Press.
2. "The Mel Noel Story" Don Ecker, *UFO Magazine.* Vol.7, No. 3, 1992.

Ruth Norman with follower Stephen Yancoskie in 1981 (Photo credit: Douglas Curran)

NORMAN, RUTH aka The Archangel Uriel (1900–1993)

In 1954, Ernest (1904–1971) and Ruth Norman founded what was eventually to be known as the Unarius Academy of Science. The organization grew out of the couple's psychic readings in person and by mail as well their small study group, which began to record and catalog the channeled messages that came through the couple.

Ruth (nee Nields) Norman had a troubled childhood and two failed marriages (her second husband died) before she met Ernest, who supported himself during WWII by giving psychic readings to worried wives and girlfriends of servicemen. When they met in 1954, they realized they were soulmates and began to live together, although Ruth's divorce from her third husband was apparently not finalized at the time.

1956 brought the publication of Unarius' first monograph, entitled *The Truth About Mars*, channeled by Ernest and typed up by Ruth. She said she could now transcribe the messages by "typing psychically in her sleep."[1]   Psychic readings were still offered by mail from ads in new age magazines and flyers and in local papers. They continued to move to different addresses in California while gathering more followers and students.

They began to call the Unarian catechism "The Science." This cosmology maintains that all beings in the universe are reincarnations from past lives and the only way to progress spiritually is to recognize this fact and work through past life karma. Students are expected to recognize their past-life trauma and transgressions and re-enact them in what are referred to as "psychodramas." Eventually, Unarius formed an in-house film and video production unit and began to record these events, usually with members in full costume.

When Ernest died in 1971, Ruth became the leader of Unarius and her channeling work went into high gear. With longtime Unarius student Louis Spiegel they produced their first co-channeled book, *The Conclave of Light Beings*. She also began to receive prophecies about a planned mass-landing of flying saucers, which would reveal the space brothers in open contact, as the ships sat one on top of

"It is the dawning of the age of Unarius... age of Unarius..." (Photo credit: Greg Bishop)

the other like a stack of pies to form a new center of learning and a sort of galactic consulate. They would then help mankind to progress to the next spiritual level.

In early 1975, now calling herself "The Archangel Uriel," Norman had a vision that the landing would occur on September 27th, and that she would be whisked away on a universal tour. She prepared her followers for life without their leader and had a brand new spate of formal gowns tailored for her expected duties as Earth's ambassador to the space brothers. Spiegel was tasked with arranging for buses to cart the faithful from the Unarius headquarters in Eastern San Diego to a nearby piece of scrub-covered real estate that Uriel purchased for the expected landing.

When this didn't occur, one of the members told Uriel that her vision was a reliving of a past life as Isis, Queen of Egypt, when she and her husband Osiris (an earlier incarnation of Ernest Norman) were murdered by an angry mob. Most of the followers seemed to accept this explanation. The next year, Uriel and a few well-heeled students placed a bet with a British bookmaker that the spaceships would land within a year. They lost the bet.

In 1977, a new student, Stephen Yancoskie, stopped by the headquarters and joined immediately. The next year, the Unarius newsletter announced that his past life therapy was starting to cure him of his homosexuality. During this time, he was also doing Uriel's hair and makeup, as well as costumes

Greg Bishop with Unarius member Leanne circa 1987 at Unarius headquarters in El Cajon, California.

for the video productions. By 1984, he was ostracized for questioning Uriel's teachings, but accepted back a few years later.

In 1987, I visited the Unarius headquarters to interview the group for my first article on UFOs. They gave me a stack of channeled books and one of their crystal-encrusted flying saucer pins. I was also shown their video production facility, which was surprisingly sophisticated. There was a seemingly great effort put up by all whom I spoke with to be positive and helpful. "Lianne," one of the "nucleus" of followers as they were called, posed with me for a picture. Uriel was in ill health at the time and I was not allowed to speak with her.[2]

After years of health issues and minor injuries, Ruth Norman died on July 12, 1993. In 1997 the Heaven's Gate mass suicides caused the group to have to explain to the press why they were not at all like that bunch, just as the Los Angeles-based Aetherius Society had to do.

Uriel's final prophecy of a mass-UFO landing in 2001 was awaited with anticipation by the Unarius faithful. The events of September 11 convinced many that the Earth was not ready for open contact with the space people.

1. Tummina, Diane G. 2005. *When Prophecy Never Fails*. Oxford University Press. (p. 165).
2. Bishop, Greg. 1990. "The Space Brothers Want You" in *Kooks* (magazine) #6. Allston, MA.

Omnec Onec

ONEC, OMNEC (born ca.1948)

Female UFO contactees are rare. Personalities such as Dana Howard and Mollie Thompson belong to the "classic" era of the space people–the 1950s and '60s. Apart from the notable exception of Pamela Stonebrooke, few women have come forward in the last 20 to 30 years telling tales of outer-space intrigue or spouting new-age homilies.

Omnec Onec has got to be one of the best space sister names in the literature. Onec is not a contactee in the classic sense; she actually claims to be from Venus. Photos of her in her late 30s or early 40s show that she was still attractive in the classical sense. There are reports that she made an appearance at the first International UFO Congress in Laughlin, Nevada, in 1991 clad in silver stiletto heels with "blood red" nail polish.

Onec alleges that she took over the body of a seven year-old girl who died in a bus accident in Chattanooga, Tennessee, in 1955 and was then raised "by the grandmother of the girl whom she had replaced. She grew up in what was to all outward appearances a normal life, never speaking of Venus, and endured the struggles that allowed her to deal with her own karmic past."[1] If she was reincarnated in 1955 at age seven as she claims, that would make her "earth container body" at least 79 years old by now.

Her first book was published in 1991 by well-known UFO personality Wendelle Stevens. The original title was *From Venus I Came* and featured a cover photo of a woman who looked like a fashion model. Surprisingly, on her website, she admits, "Since Omnec says that she physically replaced a girl with the name Sheila Gipson at the age of seven, this is the name that is in her passport."[2]

Her ex-husband believed her story and in 2008 wrote a blog post titled "My Ex-Wife Was Born On Venus":

> We met on Wells Street, Chicago during the hippie era in the middle 60s…She kissed me and the rest, as the cliché goes, is history.

She had a hard time getting taken seriously. Jerry Springer had her on back in the early days of his show, along with our kids and me. The theme was, What was it like to grow up with a mom who said she was from Venus?

They intended to make a mockery of her, with a panel of scientists, etc. But Sheila/Omnec impressed everyone with her dignity and the seriousness and credibility of her presentation.

We split in '76 and soon after she moved to Germany. She was taken more seriously there and spent many years giving talks, seminars and workshops all over Europe. She managed to get featured by all the major media in Europe and basically had a career telling her story and inspiring people with her mind-blowing experience.

Is she authentic? I decided so many years ago, and I got important confirmations from authorities I trusted. Of course this is the sort of thing that you have to decide for yourself.[3]

Omnec has four grown children and currently (2016) three grandchildren, and currently lives in Missouri. She had a stroke in 2009, which has left her partially paralyzed, but she appeared in a video as recently as 2016.

1. http://web.archive.org/web/20110519174153/http://www.galactic-server.net/rune/venuscont3b.html
2. http://omnec-onec.com/
3. http://whatnowgrasshopper.blogspot.com/2008/01/my-ex-wife-was-born-on-venus.html

**Ron Ormond carrying his "Little Green Man" in a cardboard box
(Joe Fex/APE-X Research)**

ORMOND, RON (1910–1981)

During the 1950s and '60s, Ron Ormond directed a slew of exploitation films that are now nearly impossible to find, including such gems as *Mesa of Lost Women* and *The Monster and the Stripper*. Another obscure and impossible to find film Ormond produced was called *Attack of the Flying Saucers*, a UFO documentary featuring contactees Reinhold Schmidt and Daniel Fry.

In the late 1950s, Ormond co-authored a number of psychic phenomena/self help books with a fellow named Ormond McGill (now what's the chance of writing a book with someone whose first name is the same as your last name?) These titles included a book on psychic surgery called *Religious Mysteries of the Orient/Into the Strange Unknown*, in addition to a series of books on hypnosis.

In 1959, Ormond assumed duties as editor-in-chief of Ray Palmer's *Flying Saucers From Other Worlds* magazine and in the August issue penned the curiously titled "I Found A Little Green Man" under the byline of Colonel Ron Ormond (Member United States Air Force Auxiliary.) According to the article, Ormond claimed that a prospector from Arizona had given him a mummified little green skinned man, roughly 15 to 16 inches tall,

Robert Coe Gardner (Joe Fex/APE-X Research)

with an oversized head. The prospector allegedly discovered the creature in a cave nearby his mining claim that had been frequented by flying saucers. A photo from the period features Ormond carrying around a beat-up cardboard box supposedly carrying his little green man, although there's nothing to suggest he ever publically displayed the creature. Ormond claimed that his Little Green Man was similar to a photo that ufologist Robert Coe Gardner was presenting at UFO conferences, alleged to be an ET in the company of German scientists.

A private pilot, Ormond survived a plane crash in 1968 that led to his immediate conversion to Christianity, after which he devoted himself in the following years to producing a number of religious films as a testament to his new-found faith.

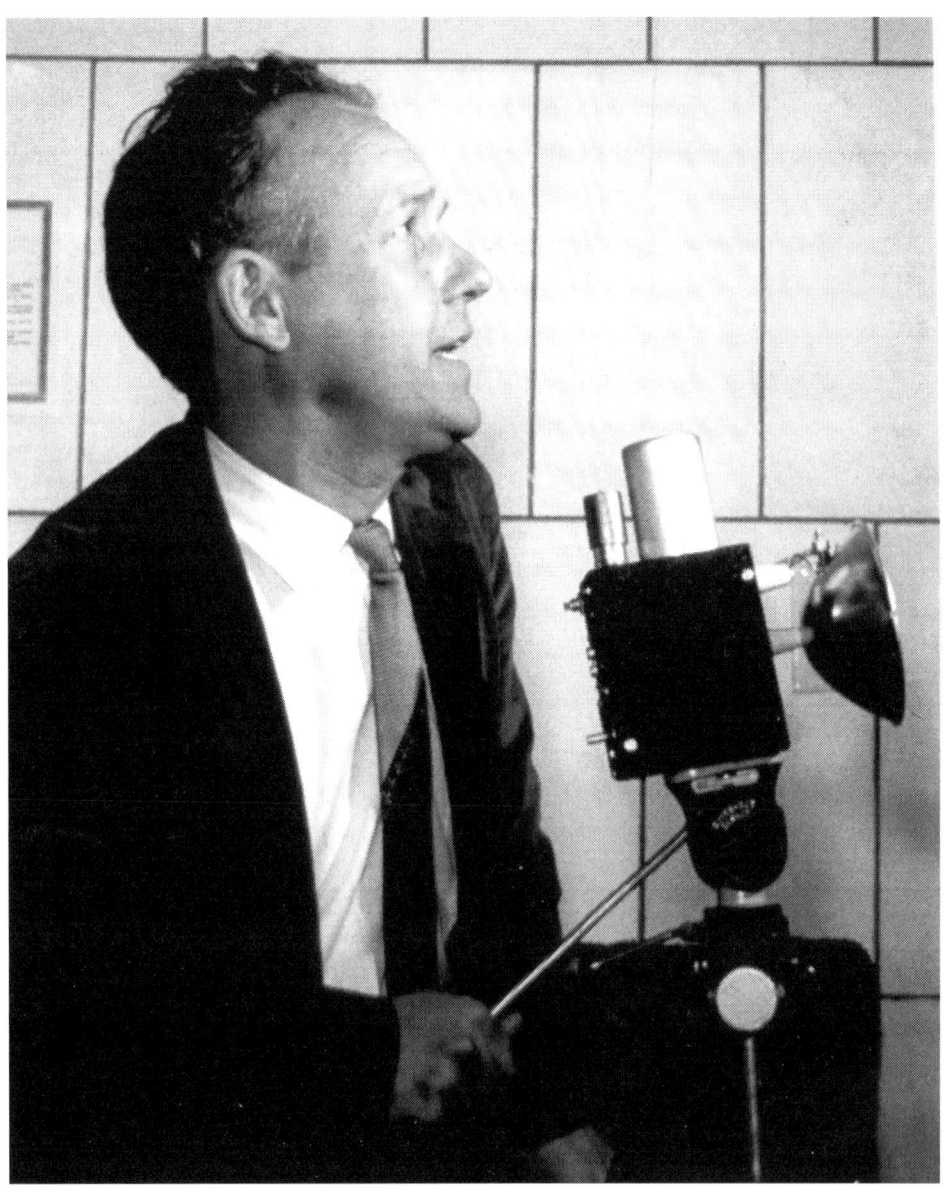

John Otto with his light beam apparatus

OTTO, JOHN

In 1954, John Otto—a member of the Detroit Saucer Club—and fellow club member, Dick Miller (of Mon-ka fame), purportedly made contact with the space brothers using a short wave radio set. During this period, Otto introduced a couple other saucer club members—Charles and Lillian Laughead—to Dorothy Martin (of *When Prophecies Fails* fame), and the rest is apocalyptic contactee history.

Later that year, Otto—in cahoots with radio host Jim Mills of WGN-Chicago—cooked up an ET contact caper, which they rolled out on the evening of November 28th, at 11:15 PM, broadcasting the following stunning announcement across the WGN airwaves:

> This is Jim Mills. I invite you and those in flying discs listening to this program...to standby for a message from the friendly people of Earth! We desire to communicate with you...therefore at exactly 11:25 PM, Chicago Earth Time, we will hold a 15-second period of silence for you to cut in and speak to us through the transmitter.
>
> Give landing instructions if possible...Now, Earth listeners, please, if possible, maintain complete silence at 11:25 and report anything you see or hear to me, Jim Mills, WGN Chicago, by letter or postcard. Thank you.[1]

At the appointed time, Mills announced "Come in, Outer Space" and the microphones in the studio were shut off in anticipation of a cosmic message soon to beam their way. When Mills and Otto went back on air, the switchboard lit up with callers, among them a couple of spinster sisters from Chicago—Marie and Mildred Maier—who claimed they'd tape recorded something that sounded like Santa's sleigh bells. Otto made arrangements to meet with the sisters and made a copy of their tape that he later played on other radio programs, including his own WGN show, *Out of this World*.

The following year, a publication called *Journal of Space Flight* featured a story on the Maier sisters. *Journal of Space Flight*, it so happens, was affiliated with the Chicago Rocket Society, of whom John Otto was a card-carrying member, and it was Otto who was responsible for the article. This, in turn, aroused the interest of the CIA's Office of Scientific Investigation (OSI), who suspected that the sisters may have recorded a clandestine terrestrial transmission of some sort.[2] Afterwards the Maier sisters were visited by a couple of CIA agents (disguised as Air Force officers) who confiscated the tape in the interests of "national security."

In 1957, UFO investigator Leon Davidson wrote to the Air Force Intelligence Branch at Wright-Patterson requesting information on the confiscated tape and was told it had been "forwarded to the proper authorities." When Davidson figured out that it was actually the CIA who investigated the case, he pressed them for their analysis of the recording, and CIA officials responded that the sound on the tape was Morse code from a U.S. radio outpost. Davidson grew convinced that the CIA's response was a cover story designed to conceal UFO activity and when he requested a copy of the tape, was informed it had been destroyed.[3]

These developments led John Otto to conclude that the Maiers' tape recording had been suppressed by the notorious UFO "Silence Group." (Insert creepy organ music here.)

1. Barker, Gray, ed. Spring, 1955. "The Saucerian", Vol. 3, No. 2.
2. Redfern, Nick. 2006. *On the Trail of the Saucer Spies*. Anomalist Books.
3. Gerald K. Haines. 1997. *Studies in Intelligence CIA's Role in the Study of UFOs, 1947-90: A Die-Hard Issue*.

Ted Owens

Best wishes
to Dr. Putoff
and Dr. Targ
from
Owens
†PK 'Man X
1976

OWENS, TED (1920–1987)

Much like Uri Geller and his entities referred to as SPECTRA, Ted Owens said that he was in communication with extraterrestrials. Owens, however claimed that his contacts helped him move objects with his mind, cause lightning strikes, and even aircraft crashes and destructive storms. Much of his story and his wild claims appear to be the ravings of a schizo, but for the fact that some of the more stable people who interacted with Owens essentially confirmed many of his claims and seemed to be perplexed that he could deliver reasonably accurate demonstrations of what he said were his powers, or those of the aliens he said either gave him these abilities or caused the disruptions.

In 1976, graduate psychology student Jeffrey Mishlove received an invitation to visit the offices of Stanford Research Institute (SRI) in Menlo Park, California. Physicists Russell Targ and Hal Puthoff told of their excitement over letters from Owens, who called himself the "PK Man." Owens claimed that he was going to cause thunderstorms and an unprecedented deluge to occur over the drought-stricken state "within the next 90 days." Although intrigued by Owens' pronouncements, the physicists were already up to their necks in controversy and didn't want to invite more by becoming involved with someone whom they correctly assumed had a volatile personality and a penchant for grandiose claims.[1]

However, within less than a month, a "freak snowstorm"[2] descended upon the Bay Area, accompanied by lightning and sleet. Mishlove said that meteorologists were at a loss to explain the unusual weather, which they hadn't predicted. Several weeks of torrential rains followed, which caused flooding, mudslides, and a few fatalities throughout California.

Owens claimed a lifetime of psychic episodes and contact with what he called "Space Intelligences," "Saucer Intelligences," or "SI"s, which was abbreviated to "sis" for the most part. He referred to his main contacts as "Twitter" and "Tweeter" and told Mishlove that they communicated with him by psychic means after abducting him as a child and performing some sort of surgery on his brain to allow them to broadcast their messages, although science fiction and UFO writer (and early ancient astronaut theorist) Otto Binder claimed that Owens' abilities were the result of brain trauma suffered in a series of accidents.[3]

In 1969, Gray Barker, prolific UFO book publisher (and author of the seminal poem "UFO Is a Bucket of Shit") presented Owens' magnum opus *How To Contact Space People*. The cover featured a painting of one of Owens' "SI" contacts, looking a little stocky with slits for eyes and a rather asymmetric face. This was apparently the leader, whom Owens referred to as "Higher Intelligence." In the book, Owens went into great detail about his predictions of wild weather and UFO sightings. He also provided an illustration of Twitter and Tweeter, looking like depictions of "praying mantis"-like beings later made famous in the paintings of contactee David Huggins, among other sources.

Owens not only revealed how to contact space people, he also provided the secret to his weather control powers:

> In my rain-making, and causing lightning to strike, a certain technique is used. I extend my fingers at the skies, and visualize in my mind's eye lightning reaching from my fingers up into the sky. On the sky itself I superimpose, in my mind's eye, the words, "Rain, storm, thunder, lightning." I sense that the lightning from my fingers will cause storm conditions, and crystallize them for the finished product. In my mind's eye I see silent, motionless trees being bent almost double by powerful wind, and I again see, superimposed over the sunny landscape, black sheets of rain beating down.
>
> After doing this for 10 to 20 minutes, I cease. That's it. I know that within hours, or a few days, the storm will come.[4]

...and also revealed his simple method for ET contact:

> It comes to me like a streak of lightning. In an instant, I receive a complete, complicated answer to write to my contacts, composed of perhaps three or four predictions, with details. If you have ever had an idea, or any inspirational thought come to you, that's how it is. One moment you are working at something mundane—the next moment you have received all the Si's information, the message. In the beginning, of course, I had to test it to make sure it was not just imagination. After 180 major predictions had come to pass, concerning earthquakes, hurricanes, etc., —I knew for sure that it was not imagination.[5]

In 1979, Wayne Grover was a reporter at the *National Enquirer* when Owens contacted him:

Over a more than five-year period, Owens phoned me several times a week, usually after midnight and predicted dire events about to happen including earthquakes, hurricanes, tornadoes and violent events worldwide. Within two days or so, I always received the same prediction via letter, often accompanied with some strange drawing of unknown symbols and signed "PK Man." The predictions usually were about five to ten days before actual events took place. When they did, I very often heard them on the news and dozens of times told my wife, "Another coincidence for Owens." When the event took place, he copied the news stories and sent me copies. The pattern was: (1) Predict by phone, (2) Send written backup. (3) Send news clips of the event predicted. As much as I didn't want to believe Owens, the long string of coincidences went on. At one time, I estimated that—with some flexibility on the matter of timing—Owens' predictions were about 80% accurate.[6]

The laundry list of Owens' weather control episodes is long and dramatic, and there is no logical explanation for his hit rate, unless he was one of the greatest weathermen who ever lived (or he duped several investigators.) UFO researcher Dr. James Harder, who once witnessed Owens' apparently accurate prediction of an anomalous aerial object concluded:

I am sure that particular instances of Mr. Owens' demonstrations can be successfully challenged by skeptics, but also believe that the entire story would survive such a challenge. In other words, the work in its entirety constitutes a credible set of extraordinary facts that echo a lesser set that we can find in other humans, but which have seldom made their way into public discourse.[7]

Like many of those who are involved with psychic phenomena, Owens had a volatile personality as well as constant bouts with serious health issues. Ted Owens passed away in December 28, 1987 of sclerosis of the liver, after he moved his family to a secluded house in upstate New York in order to be picked up by his space friends.

1. Mishlove, Jeffrey. 2000. *The PK Man*. Hampton Roads Publishing. (Kindle version.) Chapter 1, paragraph 2.
2. ibid, Chapter 1, paragraph 8.
3. Binder, Otto O. "'Spokesman' For the UFOs." SAGA Magazine (August 1970) n.p.
4. Owens, Ted. 1969. *How To Contact Space Intelligences*. Saucerian Press. (p 56).
5. ibid, p. 56.
6. Grover, Wayne. *My Experiences with the PK Man*. http://www.williamjames.com/grover.htm
7. Harder, James. *The Case of Ted Owens by James Harder*. http://www.williamjames.com/harder.htm

Paulina Peavy (Photo credit: Sam Vandivert)

Peavy, Paulina (1901–1999)

Artists draw inspiration from many sources. Paulina Peavy said that her paintings and other works were delivered through her from an extraterrestrial entity named "Lacamo" which she pronounced "La-I-Come-Oh." Her amazing artwork was sometimes signed by Lacamo, sometimes by Peavy, and at times both. She designed elaborate masks that she wore when she worked, saying that her ET source was better able to work though her when she had them on.

She was born Pauline Ellen White on August 25, 1901, in Colorado City, Colorado (as she claimed) or in Colorado Springs (as her family claimed), to a father who thought that education was wasted on girls and a mother who died of miscarriage before Pauline was 10. In the early 1920s, she was married to Bradley Peavy and living in San Pedro, California, about 20 miles south of downtown Los Angeles. Her second son said that his father was a drunk who beat his wife. She contracted tuberculosis in 1930 and had to enter a sanatorium for a few months to recuperate. After her husband abandoned the family, Peavy, unable to afford for their care, placed her two young sons in the Boys and Girls Aid Society orphanage in Pasadena (which still exists) and moved to Long Beach, CA, in 1932. By 1939, she had rebuilt her life enough to get her children back, although she visited them often while they were separated.[1]

She apparently exhibited her art widely at this time, while working as an art teacher in the Long Beach and Los Angeles school systems to make ends meet. She exhibited at the prestigious Stendahl gallery in L.A., according to an advertisement placed in the *L.A. Times* on February 10, 1933.

Soon after moving to Long Beach, she began attending weekly seances at the home of medium Ida Ewing, where she was instructed to begin writing down her dreams. She said that this practice enabled her to teach herself how to achieve out-of-body experiences at will.[2] Peavy wrote that within two nights, she was able to leave her body and travel beyond her own room "as the soul is electronic; and walls are no barriers to electricity!"[3] The voice of Lacamo coming through Ewing eventually spoke through Peavy and became her lifelong guide. Curiously, she referred to Lacamo not as a space

Illustration of Lacamo from *The Story of My Life with a "UFO"* by Paulina Peavy

being, but as a "UFO."

In 1942, she said it was "her destiny" to move to New York City, where she remained for the rest of her life. It was there, in January of 1958, that Peavy was a guest on the Long John Nebel late night radio show, which also regularly featured many of the personalities described in this book.

The other guest on the show was the "Mystic Barber of Brooklyn," Andy Sinatra, a fellow space brother channeler who was fond of wearing funky metallic headbands that improved his ET communications. Nebel seemed endlessly amused by Sinatra, but apparently took Peavy more seriously.

She wore one of her masks throughout her 20-minute long appearance and channeled Lacamo. Nebel described the mask she wore as "a base color of chartreuse with charcoal gray stripes running through it and...covers at least three-quarters of her face." Peavy began with a very short description of her background and almost immediately began hollering and began to channel her space friends in a measured, robotic-sounding voice. She explained:

> When such powers move in such strange sounds are caused by the powers taking over. We are putting into her being, high voltage. She has had to put up her electrodes to meet our high voltage! This is not the voice of Paulina, for we have not released her entirely. When we come through, we are using her exactly as you use your microphones. You have many ideas regarding us that are your ideas and are not our reality.[4]

After 15 minutes or so, Nebel remarked that Peavy looked drained and suggested they move on. Sinatra piped right up and the show continued. After Sinatra spent considerable time babbling in an incoherent ET language, Long John requested that Paulina return to her trance state and translate the Mystic Barber's manic mumblings:

> We have helped you make your headband. We have given you all the secrets for such a headband we placed upon Paulina twenty years ago—an unseen magnetic headband... We are so happy to find your open-minded attitude toward our contact with you to the state whereby you can broadcast our voice—our voices. Andrew, the bread of life is life!

Some time in her 80s, Peavy wrote an autobiography entitled *The Story of My Life with a "UFO"* and described her concepts of life, her essentially feminist viewpoint, and the nearly 50-year relationship with Lacamo. She predicted that the Earth would soon reject males and women would only produce female children for the next 3000 years. She also mentioned her interest in the 1962 Barney and Betty Hill abduction case and how their reported "treatments of the genitals"[5] was part of the space people's idea that the perfect form of humanity is neither male nor female.

In 1998, Peavy's son Bradley moved her to a nursing home in Bethesda, Maryland, after she broke her hip and slipped into a state of dementia. She died the next year at the age of 98.

> "Early in my painting career I found strange forms developing by my brush. I explained to myself that I had gotten on a beam, that I had tuned in on a power vast and wonderful."[6]

1. http://www.paulina-peavy.com/chronology/
2. Peavy, Paulina. ND (but probably the mid 1980s). *The Story of My Life with a "UFO"*. Self published. (p. 'B').
3. ibid, p. 'B'.
4. Paulina Peavy and Andy Sinatra. [Radio series episode].(1958, January).In *The Party Line*. New York, NY: WOR.
5. Peavy, Paulina. *The Story of My Life with a "UFO"*. Self published. (p. 8).
6. http://www.paulina-peavy.com/

WANTED

William Dudley Pelley

DESCRIPTION

Age, approximately fifty years; height, five feet, seven inches; weight, 130 pounds; has black hair mixed with gray; heavy eyebrows; wears mustache and a vandyke; has dark gray eyes, very penetrating; has straight Roman nose; wears nose glasses; dresses neatly; distinguished looking; good talker; highly educated; interested in physic research.

Capias has been issued by the Judge of the Superior Court of Buncombe County for the arrest of the above-named party for sentence on conviction of felony, making fraudulent representation, and also for violating the terms of a suspended sentence on another charge by failing to remain of good behavior, and by engaging in, among other things, UN-AMERICAN activities.

Arrest and notify

LAURENCE E. BROWN, Sheriff
Asheville, N. C.

PELLEY, WILLIAM DUDLEY (1890–1965)

A newspaper publisher, novelist, and screenwriter, William Dudley Pelley became an Adolf Hitler admirer in the early 1930s and started his own militant fascist organization in the U.S. known as the Silver Legion of America, or The Silver Shirts.

In 1942 (after the attack on Pearl Harbor), Pelley was convicted of sedition and sentenced to federal prison. Following his release in 1950, he founded an organization called "Soulcraft" and published the magazine *Valor* which was a mix of white nationalism, spiritualism, and flying saucer stories.

That same year, Pelley released a collection of automatic writings entitled *Star Guests: Design for Mortality* based on channeled messages he began receiving on May 28th, 1928, after being spiritually transported to Eternity for a total of seven minutes. These channeling sessions revealed that "a vast horde of migrating spirits [from the Sirius star system were part] of a great migration of alien spirits to this planet...who settled down here and began to co-habit with the animal forms it discovered... producing a hybrid race of beings, half-celestial and half-beastial that gave us the unspeakable Sodomic period described in the Bible...Beast forms and celestial forms were fused together in an insufferable bastard creation..."

There was overlap between Pelley's *Soulcraft* organization and Guy Ballard's *I AM*. Like Ballard, Pelley promoted a Theosophical based belief system inhabited by Ascended Masters from a Great White Brotherhood (Aryan bloodline of blonde haired Nordics), which afterwards cropped up in the writings of George Hunt Williamson, John McCoy, and a handful of others who subscribed to the notion that malevolent aliens were working in cahoots with International Bankers to manipulate the global monetary system and poison our precious bodily fluids.

Andrija Puharich and Uri Geller in the early 1970s

PUHARICH, ANDRIJA (1918–1995)

In 1948, Dr. Andrija Puharich launched a privately funded group called the Round Table Foundation in Glen Cove, Maine, which over a ten-year span conducted paranormal research using a stable of psychics, among them Dutch clairvoyant Peter Hurkos.

On December 31, 1952, one of Puharich's psychics, Dr. D.G. Vinod, established contact with a group of Ascended Master types that identified themselves as "The Council of Nine," or simply, "The Nine." As a mirroring of these mystical forces, Puharich organized a group of nine human counterparts he referred to as "sitters" who transcribed and interpreted the Council of Nine's messages.

Concurrent with these "Council of Nine" communiqués, Puharich served as a medical physician with the U.S. Army (from 1952–1954) stationed at both Edgewood Arsenal and Fort Detrick where he was involved with human experimentation projects that overlapped with the CIA's notorious MK-ULTRA program. In this regard, some question how deep a spook Puharich actually was, and if his Round Table Foundation was an intelligence agency front using the cover of paranormal research to mess with people's minds. Puharich was also a master hypnotist, which makes the story even murkier.

In July 1956, Puharich and Peter Hurkos visited the ruins of Acámbaro, Mexico, in an attempt to psychically locate and recover ancient artifacts there. While staying at the Hotel de Paris in Acámbaro, they synchronistically crossed paths with contactees Charles and Lillian Laughead who informed Puharich that they were working with "a young man, a very fine voice channel" named George Hunt Williamson.[1]   A couple weeks later, Puharich received a letter from Laughead that included channeled ET messages from Williamson that identified the exact date of Puharich's first contact with the Nine as well as the second part of a mysterious formula, the first part which had previously been channeled by Dr. Vinod. To Puharich, this correspondence served as confirmation that the Nine were emissaries from outer space and these revelations eventually led to the formation of a group Puharich called "Lab Nine" whose membership included such notables as Arthur Young (designer of the Bell helicopter) and other wealthy socialites, politicians, and industrialists.

In 1971, Puharich hooked up with psychic spoon bender Uri Geller, who had suddenly become a rising star on the celebrity psychic circuit. Curious as to the source of Geller's powers, Puharich placed the young Israeli into a hypnotic trance under which he recalled an encounter from his youth with a "silvery mass of light" that made time stand still. The light identified itself with a name straight out of a James Bond movie: SPECTRA, a "conscious super-computer aboard a spaceship." A recent release of declassified documents reveal that Geller was part of a CIA-funded remote viewing project called Stargate, which only adds credence to claims that he was some kind of a spy using his supposed psychic powers as a cover to travel around the world on covert missions for either Mossad or U.S. Intelligence.

Geller described SPECTRA as his "programmer"—another curious descriptor in light of Puharich's possible MK-ULTRA ties.[2] Puharich came to believe that Geller was "specifically created to serve as an intermediary between a 'divine' intelligence and man" and that SPECTRA was, in essence, an emissary of The Nine. The Nine informed Puharich that his life's mission was to use Geller's 'wild talents' to alert the world about an imminent mass landing of spaceships that would bring representatives of The Nine to Earth, in particular a race of ETs called the Hoovas. In addition to channeling SPECTRA, Puharich and Geller also witnessed a wide range of weird paranormal activity, including messages from SPECTRA that appeared on blank audio tapes, not to mention several UFO sightings and the teleportation of objects.

Geller parted ways with Puharich in 1973, but the good doctor continued on with his psychic explorations, setting up a hippie-like commune in Ossining, New York, called "Lab Nine" where he enlisted a group of children with psychic talents he named the "Space Kids." In the same vein as his work with Uri Geller, Puharich hypnotized the children as a means to enhance their psychic abilities. Puharich's "Lab Nine" operation at Ossining was privately funded by a group of wealthy donors of high social standing, among them the Bronfmans (owners of Seagram liquor) and Italian nobleman Baron DiPauli.[3]

Star Trek creator Gene Roddenberry was part of the Lab Nine circle during the mid '70s, and purportedly authored a screenplay based on the Nine. Some of these concepts wove their way into the *Star Trek* movies, *The Next Generation* and *Deep Space Nine*, which included a character named "Vinod" in one episode.

Another curious character involved in the Lab Nine circle was counterculture figure Ira "The Unicorn" Einhorn, one of the founders of Earth Day. In 1977, the corpse of Einhorn's girlfriend, Holly Maddux, was discovered hacked up and stuffed in a steamer trunk at Einhorn's Philadelphia apartment. Einhorn was subsequently charged with Maddux's murder, but before his trial was scheduled, he skipped the country and was on the lam over the next two decades, a fascinating story chronicled in Stephen Levy's *The Unicorn's Secret* (1988).

In July 2001, Einhorn was extradited from France and convicted for Maddux's murder in October 2002. At his trial, Einhorn claimed he was innocent and that it was all some sort of CIA setup. Maddux's murder occurred during the same period that Lab Nine was dissolved (circa 1978) following an arson fire that destroyed the Ossining property. Afterwards, Puharich fled to Mexico, claiming he was likewise being hounded by mean-spirited CIA spooks.

1. Zirger, Michel and Maurizio Martinelli. 2016. *The Incredible Life of George Hunt Williamson: Mystical Journey: Itinerary of a Privileged UFO Witness*. Publisher: Verdechiaro Edizioni.

2. Puharich, Andrija. 1974. *URI: A Journal of the Mystery of Uri Geller*. New York: Anchor Press.

3. Picknett, Lynn and Prince, Clive, 1999. *The Stargate Conspiracy*. Berkeley Books.

The one and only Sun Ra

RA, SUN (1914–1993)

Sun Ra came into this world with the birth name Herman Poole Blount, and the event that inspired him to change his name (to Ra, the Egyptian god of the sun) occurred in 1937 when a bright light materialized before him:

> My whole body changed into something else. I could see through myself. And I went up... I wasn't in human form... I landed on a planet that I identified as Saturn... they teleported me and I was down on [a] stage with them. They wanted to talk with me. They had one little antenna on each ear. A little antenna over each eye. They talked to me. They told me to stop [attending college] because there was going to be great trouble in schools... the world was going into complete chaos... I would speak [through music], and the world would listen. That's what they told me.[1]

In the early 1950s, Sun Ra formed the Space Trio who sported funky futuristic attire during their live performances: a mix of ancient Egyptian meets science fiction, including elaborate headdresses. By the late 1960s, Sun Ra's band evolved into the Arkestra, an eclectic mix of musicians, dancers, fire-eaters, and trippy stage effects produced by a lighting system called the "Outerspace Visual Communicator."

Always on the cutting edge of musical expression, Sun Ra was among the first to employ the Minimoog. A prototype of the instrument was given to him in 1969 by inventor Robert Moog and incorporated into The Arkestra's "cosmic jazz" repertoire.

In the early 1970s, Sun Ra became an artist-in-residence at U.C. Berkeley, instructing a course called The Black Man In the Cosmos that featured in its studies an eclectic hand-picked reading list including *The Tibetan Book of the Dead*, Madame Blavatsky's *Isis Unveiled*, and that old contactee favorite, *Oahspe*.

During this period, a trippy feature film was produced by San Francisco public TV station KQED based on Sun Ra's life called *Space Is the Place*, which (at the time of publication of this book) is still available for your home viewing enjoyment on YouTube.

1. Szwed, John F. 1997. *Space Is the Place:The Lives and Times of Sun Ra*. New York: Pantheon.

John Reeves leisurely posing with his Venusian flag (Photo credit: Douglas Curran)

REEVES, JOHN (1899–2002)

On March 2, 1965, a 66-year-old retired longshoreman named John Reeves was out snake hunting one afternoon in the scrub flats near his home in Brooksville, Florida, when he came upon a landed saucer that was "bluish green and reddish purple," resting on four legs and roughly 30' in diameter. As Reeves cautiously approached the craft, he encountered what appeared to be the pilot, a "robot-like" creature with a domed space helmet. After they stared down each other for a minute or so, the robo-creature pulled an object (apparently a space camera) from its side, held it up to its dome and clicked, followed by a blinding flash of light. A startled Reeves turned to dash away, and in so doing became tangled up in a bush, stumbled, and fell to the ground, dropping his eye glasses.

The space robot—who it turns out wasn't such a bad guy after all—bent over and retrieved the glasses, handing them to Reeves. The robot then rode an escalator like staircase back up into his ship and:

> A lot of little blades around the rim of the saucer started to move unison like the slats of a venetian blind. They opened and closed, then the rim started going around counterclockwise. It made a whooshing and rumbling sound as it speeded up its spinning. The staircase pulled up inside...Then the four stilts or legs retracted, and the saucer went straight up with that whooshing sound. I watched, and it was out of sight in less than 10 seconds in the cloudless sky.[1]

After the saucer zoomed away, Reeves examined the landing area and discovered a set of the robot's boot prints, in addition to "two sheets of strong but very thin tissue, unlike anything I'd ever touched before. Both were covered with strange writings or marks that looked like Chinese."

The following day, Reeves appeared on St. Petersburg radio station WFFB to share his amazing story. Afterwards, he met with Air Force investigators who accompanied him to the saucer landing site where he directed them to the robot's boot prints. At this time, Reeves turned over the strange papers to the Air Force officers for analysis. Reeves later claimed that when the papers were returned, the Air Force pulled the old switcheroo, substituting fake papers for the real ones. The Project Blue Book Report stated that:

> Two papers that contained unreadable hieroglyphics were reportedly dropped by an occupant of the spacecraft. An analysis was made of these papers by the Institute of Paper Chemistry in Appleton, Wisconsin. This analysis indicated that the paper is composed of fibers which are common worldwide. The fiber composition corresponds to that used in lens and stencil papers. The hieroglyphics on one of the papers was deciphered by simple substitution and was determined to be the work of an amateur. The deciphered hieroglyphics read as follows: "Planet Mars—Are you coming home soon—We miss you very much—Why did you stay away too long?" Since no other implications were apparent, it was not feasible for the Air Force to expend further time and money in deciphering the second sheet. Based on the above, it is the opinion of the Air Force that an attempt was made to perpetrate a hoax.[2]

On August 6, 1968, Reeves came across another landed saucer, but this time instead of a robot creature, he encountered a crew of beautiful space people, tall and thin with porcelain skin who informed him that they came from the planet Moniheya, which we Earthlings know as Venus. The Moniheyans were outfitted in tight-fitting jumpsuits that accentuated their trim, thirty something looking bods. (Reeves later learned that his space friends were actually much older than they looked!) On this same occasion, Reeves was treated to a trip to the dark side of the moon, which transpired over the course of six hours. He described the inside of the spaceship as a glass room full of instruments with three-dimensional TV screens that were used for navigational purposes.

While moon-traipsing, Reeves scooped up a handful of lunar dust and poured it into a medicine bottle to take home with him, as well as a large moon rock that he stuffed into his trousers. However, Reeves never showed any of this moon dust to the authorities back on Earth because he was worried it would be confiscated in the same manner as his alien papers.

On another trip, Reeves visited planet Moniheya which included viewing such natural wonders as two suns, a pink sea (with Loch Ness type monsters in it) and blue rain. Reeves spoke of two amazing modes of public transportation he encountered there, one of which was moving sidewalks, and the other was rockets that cruised around just above the ground, kind of like Volkswagens with wings.

While there, his space friends awarded him the official flag of Moniheya, which like his precious moon dust Reeves decided to keep locked away in a safety deposit box, only showing a few select

Earth friends on rare occasions, although he did make a duplicate of the flag which he hung on a wall in his home for visitors.

Reeves became known as "the Brooksville spaceman." He would often set up a stand at the local shopping mall to show off his display of UFO photographs and news clippings. Reeves gained the reputation as a kind hearted fellow, who for many years ran a trailer park where he would feed people down on their luck or let them slide on rent if times were tight.

As a monument to his outer space friends, Reeves erected a full sized model of the Moniheyan spaceship in his front-yard with a plaque that read: "The spaceship that took John Reeves to planet Moniheya, millions and millions of miles from planet Earth, landed here October 5, 1968." As Douglas Curran wrote in *In Advance of the Landing: Folk Concepts of Outer Space*:

> Harassed by vandals and county tax collectors, Reeves sold his property in 1980 to the state, which razed his house and UFO monument. Letters of protest poured in from throughout Florida objecting to the "desecration of John Reeves' expression of hope." Now eighty-six years old, Reeves lives in a trailer on a side street in Brooksville. His newspaper clippings are kept in an old suitcase that he hauls out for anyone who wants to see. A dog-eared book contains the autographs of people who came to see his UFO monument, among them Jimmy Page of Led Zeppelin, Pat Boone, and Tuesday Weld.[3]

1. Clark, Jerome. 1998. *The UFO Encyclopedia: the phenomenon from the beginning*. 2nd ed. Detroit: Omni Graphics. (p. 162).
2. http://www.bluebookarchive.org/
3. Curran, Douglas. 2001. *In Advance of the Landing: Folk Concepts of Outer Space*. New York: Abbeville Press. (p. 110).

Wilhelm Reich having a bad hair day

Reich, Wilhelm (1897–1957)

While not strictly a contactee in the classic definition of the term, maverick scientist and psychologist Wilhelm Reich belongs in this volume for his belief that he was for a time locked in a desperate battle with space people. The twisting journey from groundbreaking theorist of the human psyche to protector of our planet was a long and not altogether pleasant one.

Reich had begun his career as one of Sigmund Freud's inner circle in Vienna in the 1920s. He soon broke with the famous analyst, believing that inner conflict was not caused by self-repression, but rather the prudish strictures of a Victorian-like society that blocked the free flow of sexual expression.

Penning works like *The Mass Psychology of Fascism* and *The Sexual Revolution* in the early 1930s in Austria and Germany did not endear him to the political ruling party at the time. Freud thought that Reich's ideas on psychoanalysis and the curing of neuroses through allowing patients to experience more fulfilling sex lives were too simplistic, and they soon drifted apart.

Reich was on the run, moving around Europe for much of the 1930s, ahead of governments, groups and individuals who found his ideas distasteful and finally made the decision to immigrate the United States in 1939.

By 1940, he had developed a theory that an energy that permeated the universe called "orgone" was responsible for the physical and mental health of all living things. He was successful enough by 1942 to buy a 280-acre farm in northern Maine near the town of Rangley which he dubbed "Orgonon." He built a cabin, and later a laboratory and observatory, and moved there permanently in 1950, along with his family and a few assistants.

By the mid-1950s Reich had developed his orgone theory to explain its role in not just life, but all natural phenomena, such as the weather. Drought conditions, he proposed, were a simple matter of blocked or unhealthy orgone flow, just as it was in living organisms. To this end, he developed a device he called the "cloudbuster," which consisted of an array of tubes connected to a natural source of water like a lake, stream, or well. Reich claimed that he could redirect the orgone balance of the

Wilhelm Reich and crew with a "space gun" mounted on the bed of a truck

planet and cause or delay rain. He claimed (and was reported in the local papers) to have saved a cranberry harvest with the use of a cloudbuster. He had an agreement with a group of local farmers who would pay him only if they thought he had broken the drought, and they paid up.

Like most people in the United States at the time, Reich became interested in the UFO craze. He soon perceived strange lights and objects gathering in the skies around Orgonon, and pointed the cloudbuster at them. To his surprise, the objects either tried to get out of the way or winked out. Reich eventually convinced himself that he was involved in the vanguard of an interplanetary war against aliens bent on turning the Earth into a desert.

In 1954, Reich led an expedition to the Arizona desert near Tucson with a cloudbuster in tow. He continued his battles with malevolent spacemen and also may have brought rain to the desert after a prolonged drought. Either that, or he happened to arrive right before an unseasonably wet spell. The anomalous rain was remarked upon in the local press. The whole episode was documented in the 1957 book *Contact with Space*. On the introductory page, Reich revealed a very contactee-like attitude towards his interactions with UFOs: "Am I a spaceman? Do I belong to a new race on Earth, bred by men from outer space in embraces with Earth women?"[1]

Meanwhile, the FDA was alerted that Reich and his associates were renting out orgone devices. What they didn't care about was the stipulation that clients would only pay if they believed they experienced positive effects. The issue quickly escalated into a pitched battle led by traditional physicians bent on his destruction. Based on their accusations, agents of the FDA showed up at Orgonon and actually smashed Reich's equipment with hammers and carted off many of his books, which were then burned in an incinerator. One wonders if the object was to save the world from an apparent charlatan, or perhaps something deeper was afoot.

Reich was eventually convicted of transporting fraudulent medical devices across state lines and contempt, and was jailed in 1956. He died of a heart attack in the Lewisburg Federal Penitentiary three

Cloudbuster at Wilhelm Reich museum in Rangeley, Maine (Photo credit: Greg Bishop)

months before his first parole hearing was to take place. He is buried on the grounds of Orgonon, which is still the center of the Wilhelm Reich Foundation.

1. Reich, Wilhelm. 1957. *Contact With Space: Oranur Second Report 1951-56/ OROP Desert Ea 1954-1955.* Core Pilot Press. (p. 1.).

Robert Renaud at the controls of his intergalactic short wave radio

RENAUD, ROBERT (born ca. 1943)

In July 1961, eighteen-year-old ham radio operator and electronics whiz kid Robert Renaud was "browsing around the shortwave bands" when "suddenly from the loudspeaker came a very high pitched beep-beep-beep" followed by a melodic female voice: "I am called Linn-Erri, and my associates and I come from the planet Korendor. We are speaking to you from our spaceship many miles above earth." After introducing Renaud to the rest of her Korendorian crew, Linn-Erri provided detailed instructions on how to modify his shortwave radio equipment to better facilitate space communications.[1]

Later that year, Renaud received instructions on how to adjust his television set to receive visual transmissions from outer space and soon after Linn-Erri materialized on the screen, a beautiful, statuesque blonde possessing the all too earthly dimensions of 37-22-36!

In the early morning hours of December 22, 1962, an average-looking car carrying some average looking fellows (Korendorians in disguise) picked up Renaud and took him for a ride to an isolated area where he was treated to a demonstration of an anti-gravity device that levitated a huge rock one hundred feet into the air and then disintegrated it with a ray gun.

On another occasion, a Korendorian named Algran-Eltar demonstrated a bullet-stopping device by shooting in Renaud's direction and then freezing the bullet in mid-air. These were just a few of the amazing things Renaud witnessed, in addition to the requisite starship trip to Korendor.[2]

After seeing Renaud's story in Gabe Green's *Flying Saucers International*, ufologist Bob Grise (not to be confused with the former Miami Dolphin quarterback) tracked him down at his parents' basement in Massachusetts. Grise—also a ham radio buff—inspected Renaud's short wave set-up and observed modifications to the circuits that "were all appropriate to extend the receiving range." What Grise found even more mind blowing were the dozen or so books Renaud had channeled via "automatic-typing", all of which were single-spaced and roughly 500 pages in length including endless minutiae about Korendorian science and philosophy.

Grise noted that there seemed to be no interest on Renaud's part to market any of this channeled material, and had it not been for Gabe Green discovering and promoting Renaud's work, he probably would have remained in obscurity.

Renaud maintained a large collection of Korendorian tape recordings, including many communications that featured Linn-Erri who spoke with "a kind of hesitancy in speech patterns suggesting a foreign person doing well in English. It had a singsong, melodious quality." Grise seemed convinced there was nothing fraudulent concerning Renaud and that "something quite out of the normal was going on, whatever it was."[3]

1. Keel, John, 1971. *Our Haunted Planet*. Fawcett. (p. 184).
2. Dean, John, 1970. *Flying Saucers Close Up*. Clarksburg, WV: Saucerian Books.
3. Clark, Jerome. 2000. *Extraordinary Encounters: An Encyclopedia of Extraterrestrials and Otherworldly Beings*. ABC-CLIO Publishers. (p 158-159).

Further reading

The TerraKor Files: http://www.berkshire.net/~brenaud/index.htm

Kelvin Rowe at Giant Rock (Joe Fex/APE-X Research)

Rowe, Kelvin (1918–1998)

Kelvin Rowe was buddies with Truman Bethurum (of Aura Rhanes fame) and some suggest he jumped the Aura Rhanes shark (or saucer, as the case may have been) by concocting a yarn quite similar to the one Bethurum spun in *Aboard a Flying Saucer*.

Rowe's story started on March 9, 1954, while driving his pick-up truck through the San Bernardino hills when a voice popped into his head and said "Pluto" three times.[1] A few days later, Rowe paid a call to George Adamski, who confirmed it was indeed space people that were beaming these Plutonian messages his way. Via telepathy, Rowe was introduced to the "Brother of Uranus" who informed him that "I am very pleased to meet you. We hope to contact more people like you on your planet. It will be of great benefit to all." Later that year, Rowe made direct physical contact (or so he said) with his own version of Aura Rhanes in the form of a curvaceous spaceship captain he called the "Lady of Pluto."

Rowe's first trip to the stars took place in March 1956, courtesy of a Plutonian scout ship that transported him to a cigar-shaped mothership hosting several hundred guests from other planets. Rowe claimed to have traveled to outer space on 350 occasions by way of "large space lanes at speeds that defy imagination."

Among other miraculous happenings, the space brothers taught Rowe to walk through a metal wall and come out on the other side, all of which you can read about in *A Call at Dawn: A Message From Our Brothers of the Planets Pluto and Jupiter* (1958).

1. Clark, Jerome, 2000. *Extraordinary Encounters: An Encyclopedia of Extraterrestrials and Otherworldly Beings.* ABC-CLIO Publishers. (p. 150-151).

Reinhold Schmidt at Giant Rock (Joe Fex/APE-X Research)

Schmidt, Reinhold (1897–1974)

On November 5, 1957, Reinhold Schmidt was driving through rural Kearney, Nebraska, when he noticed a cigar-shaped object land in a field. Driving toward the craft, Schmidt's car engine suddenly stalled as two humanoids appeared and led him aboard their ship. The crew inside consisted of four men and two women from Saturn who spoke "high German." After a brief conversation about the U.S. space program, the crew bid Reinhold farewell.

Schmidt reported his encounter to local newspapers and, soon after local, Kearney law officers responded to the scene of the supposed landing where they discovered three sets of footprints and a "mysterious green residue." When the cops learned that Schmidt had previously served time for embezzlement, they grew suspicious of his Saturnian tale. During a follow-up investigation, an empty can of green motor oil was discovered near the "landing site" and some of this same oil was also found in the bed of Schmidt's pickup truck.

The following day, a psychiatrist examined Schmidt and concluded that he'd been suffering from delusions. Afterwards, Schmidt was committed to Hastings State Hospital, and then released a few days later.[1] Schmidt later claimed that his confinement at the facility was an attempt by the Silence Control Group to discredit his Saturnian encounter.

In the years to come, Schmidt enjoyed many more visits from the crew of the Saturnian starship and was treated to several trips into outer space. The Saturnians—it was revealed—enjoyed a damn good cup of Joe, their preferred brand being MJB. To ensure coffee supplies never fell to perilously low levels, the crew kept a Volkswagen Bug stored in the cargo hold of their ship in case they needed to travel incognito to the nearest town to resupply during Earthside visitations.

On May 28, 1961, a cinematic rendition of Schmidt's encounters called *Edge of Tomorrow* premiered at the Wilshire Ebell Theatre in Los Angeles, a film produced by Ron Ormond (of The Little Green Man fame.) The June 1961 edition of *Saucer News* described the film as "hopelessly boring, technically inadequate, poorly photographed hodge podge of inanities."

Around this time, Schmidt partnered with Major Wayne Aho and John Otto, and the three men rolled out a tripleheader UFO show they took on the road. This partnership eventually ground to a halt when Schmidt was convicted of swindling little old ladies (who attended his lectures) out of their life savings.

Schmidt's scam included the fanciful yarn that—during one of his many spaceship flights—he observed an unique form of quartz crystal (while flying over Earth) which could cure cancer, but to be able to extract these miraculous mining deposits he'd need investors, of course, and that's how the little old ladies got roped in. When all was said and done, Schmidt bilked his marks to the tune $30,000. On October 26, 1961, he was sentenced to 10 years in prison.

1. Clark, Jerome. *The UFO Encyclopedia: the phenomenon from the beginning*, 2nd ed. Detroit: Omni Graphics Inc., 1998. (p. 822-23).

Richard Shaver

SHAVER, RICHARD (1907–1975)

There is a short list of those figures who can claim to have changed the course of UFO-related history. Dr. Josef Allen Hynek did, certainly. Marshall Applewhite, definitely. But there are those who lurk just below the surface of mainstream consciousness whose stories broke loudly, captured wide attention for a short time, and then faded quickly. The saga of Richard Sharpe Shaver still captures the attention and imagination of saucer fans today, mainly because of its unabashed outlandishness and Shaver's absolutely sincere belief in the truth of it.

Shaver was a mild-mannered welder on an assembly line during the depression, and lucky to have the work. However, he recalled that sometime in about 1932, he began to hear what he believed were the thoughts of his fellow workers coming through one of the field coils of his arc welding equipment, along with other, more sinister voices that he couldn't identify. They told Shaver that they were called "Deros," which was short for "*De*trimental *Ro*bots" even though they were not robots, but merely slaves to their desire to torture humankind from their lairs deep underground.

Understandably disturbed, he quit his job and became a wandering hobo for a time, and was apparently admitted to a psychiatric institution after 1934. He may have spent time in and out of psych wards and prisons until sometime in the mid-1940s. At least, that is what Shaver's hazy memory recalled when he was asked about the period. He also claimed that one of the beautiful female "Teros" (or I*n*te*grative Ro*bots") had engineered his escape from prison, but was killed by a marauding band of Deros.

In 1943, "S. Shaver" sent one of the strangest manuscripts ever submitted to Ray Palmer, the wonderboy editor of *Amazing Stories* magazine. John Keel once called Palmer "the man who invented flying saucers"[1] since he published stories on "aircraft with round wings" in 1946 and hired Kenneth Arnold to describe his 1947 encounter, as well as to do some research on the Maury Island UFO incident, which became its own sort of adventure.

Another *Amazing Stories* editor, Howard Barne, threw Shaver's manuscript into the wastebasket

**An example of Richard Shaver's channeled rock carvings
(Photo credit: W.G. Bliss)**

after mumbling something about "crackpots," but Palmer, with a soothsayer's guile, fished it out. The letter contained what Shaver insisted was an entire ancient alphabet called "Mantong,"[2] which he said was the original language of Earth. The fact that Shaver believed that his story was not fiction (in spite of the fact that he was sending it to a fantasy fiction magazine) must have intrigued the wily Palmer, and the mental marketing wheels began to turn. He cleaned up the text and published it in the January 1944 issue.

Encouraged by the response, he turned Shaver's next submission into an extended novella and devoted much of the March 1945 issue to the story, which he called "I Remember Lemuria!" According to Palmer, the "Shaver Mystery" increased the readership of *Amazing Stories* by nearly 40%. Certainly, thousands of letters poured in to the office, begging for more details. Palmer was happy to provide them. In subsequent installments, readers learned from Shaver that a race of giants once lived on the Earth, but were driven underground 12,000 years ago by increased radiation from the sun. Some couldn't even withstand it there and escaped on space ships. The ones left behind either migrated back to the surface after evolving to withstand the radiation, or remained underground and morphed into a degenerate race that lived for murder, torture, and weird sex. They also used their machines to cause trouble for us here on the surface, even as trivial as stooping to "trip people walking down the stairs."[3]

Readers seemed to tire of the stories by 1948, and amid protests from the more vocal sci-fi fans, Palmer was fired. He moved to rural Wisconsin and began publishing his own magazines, such as *Mystic* and *Flying Saucers*, and the most famous one of all, *Fate*, which satisfied fans of the fantastical whom Palmer had come to see as his own. Shaver continued to feed him more stories, including one that described three different types of flying saucer pilots: "One kind comes from space to see the sights, or to loot the caverns under our feet, the other kind have lived here in hiding for centuries—

and loot the would-be looters."[4] He described the third group as merely artificial projections caused by the Deros.

Around 1960, Shaver became obsessed with cutting rocks open and looking at the patterns contained within. He somehow became convinced that the Pre-Dero/Tero race of giants used these random rocks as memory storage devices which contained images of their time and world. He called these rock books "Rokfogo" and chronicled his discoveries in the book *The Secret World*, which Palmer published in 1975.

Richard Shaver died on November 5th of the same year and is interred next to his "long suffering wife"[5] Dorothy in the Layton Cemetery near Yellville, Arkansas.

1. Keel, John. "The Man Who Invented Flying Saucers". *Fortean Times*, #41, Winter 1983.

2. Clark, Jerome. 1998. "Shaver Mystery" in *The UFO Encyclopedia: The Phenomenon from the Beginning, Vol. 2, L-Z*. Pmigraphics, Inc. p. 845.

3. J.J. Marino. Richard Shaver & the proto-language of Mantong" https://joelmarino.wordpress.com/2012/02/10/richard-shaver-the-proto-language-of-mantong/

4. Shaver, Richard. "The Flying Saucers", *Mystic* #16. July, 1956. p.56-62 (As cited in Clark, 1998.) p. 847.

5. Clark, Jerome. "Sermons in Stones", Review of *Rokfogo: The Mysterious Pre-Deluge Art of Richard S Shaver, Vol. 1. Fortean Times*, #321, December, 2014. p. 60.

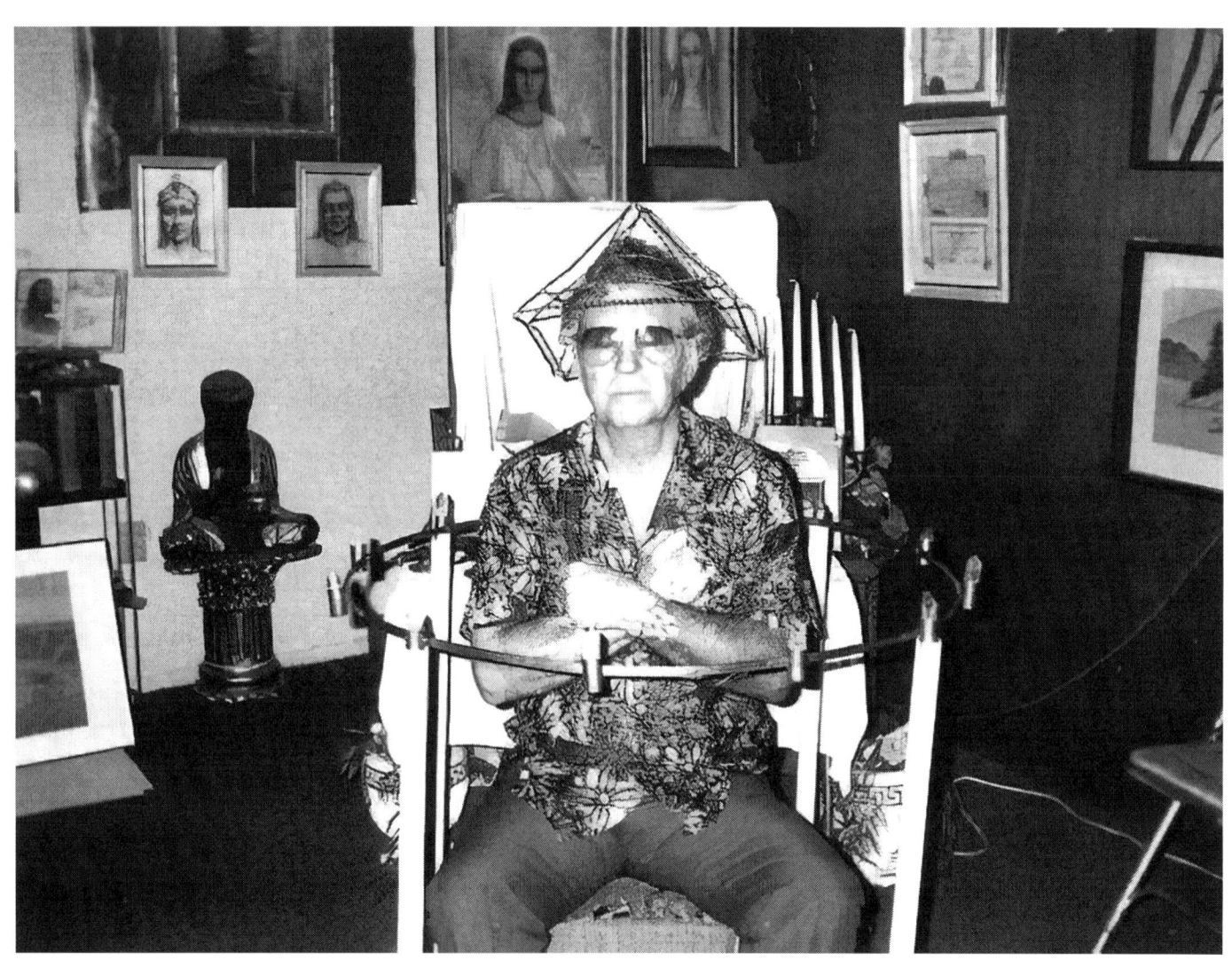

Rev. Robert Short synchronizing his chakras

Short, Rev. Robert "Bob" (1929–)

In 1952, Robert Short—then living in Los Angeles—had a calling to travel out to the desert courtesy of an ET named Jon-Al who directed him to "Go to the Big Rock in the Desert."[1] That big rock, of course, was Giant Rock, and when Short laid eyes on this magnificent 23,000-ton boulder, it was love at first sight. Short became fast friends with George Van Tassel and a frequent attendee of the Giant Rock Interplanetary Spacecraft Conventions.

Short was an associate of George Hunt Williamson with whom he engaged in short wave ET communications in Winslow, Arizona, along with a radio operator named Lyman Streeter. According to Reverend Short:

> Many times during my association with these two men, UFOs hovered over where we were receiving messages. They (*Space Intelligence*) would even answer questions we hadn't asked! We began to contemplate the possibility of bypassing the ham operator altogether and using direct mental telepathy in our communication with the *Space Intelligence*. However, our efforts to explore this possibility were hampered, when in 1952, the government closed our operation. Their explanation given for this action was that we did not have proper legal grounds for "extraterrestrial" or "alien" contacts. Because of this, I eventually left Winslow, disappointed at the mindset of those "authorities" who sought to limit our understanding of the Extraterrestrial Intelligence and their presence on Earth...[2]

Like Van Tassel and a number of other contactees, Short channeled Commander Ashtar and by the mid-1950s (using the non-de-plume of Bill Rose) started an organization called "Ashtar Command" to monetize his otherworldly communications.

At the 1967 Giant Rock Convention, "as Short was being introduced to the assembled audience,

Robert Short's high tech table at the 2004 UFO Congress in Laughlin, Nevada. (Photo: Greg Bishop)

a reddish-orange craft flew overhead and was seen by all for approximately two minutes. Short then channeled a message from Korton, a resident of the planet Jupiter who had flown over Earth in a mother ship—the light the audience had seen was described as a spacecraft from that mother ship..."[3]

Rev. Short and his spunky wife Shirley oversee the Blue Rose Ministry out of their home in Cornville, Arizona, and publish *The Solar Space Newsletter* where "You can learn the mystic connection between the Hopi's, the Pope's and the UFO's!"[4]

For many years, the Shorts were familiar figures on the flying saucer lecture circuit where the good reverend was usually more than happy (for a free will love offering of around $20 or more) to put on a pair of eye shades and perform psychic readings courtesy of Ashtar or Korton or whatever entity was possessing his vocal chords at the time.[4] As co-author Greg Bishop recalled:

At the International UFO Congress in 2004, Bob Short set up a TV tray in the merch room (because he couldn't afford a table) and gave psychic readings. I gave him $20 and he gave me a $20 performance. He went into a trance and began to spout extreme generalities which could apply to almost anyone. I was not very helpful with any feedback to lead him, so he continued in this vein. It was a fun session, mainly because I just wanted to help him out with a few bucks and see how good he might be. I recorded the session, but mistakenly recorded over it with a bootleg recording of a Hasil Adkins concert.

The July 9, 1968 *Long Beach Independent Press-Telegram* featured an article entitled "Outer Space Chef Tosses Bewildering Salad" chronicling a lecture by Rev. Short at the Los Altos Public Library. Staff writer Frank Anderson described Short as a

...outer space chef, [who] cut some green cheese from the moon, mixed it with horse radish and served it up on flying saucers...

274

Billed as a lecturer of unidentified flying objects, Short confined most of his remarks to communiqués from extra-terrestrial sources which have been published in the Solar Space Letter of his Solar Space Foundation at Joshua Tree.

The audience of 30 persons appeared mystified by it all, for the knowledge by Short flew by faster than the cafeteria line at a tape worms' convention.

Short was introduced by Rev. Raymond Broshears, pastor of the sponsoring Church of God of Light. After some Hawaiian music, the lecture began with Short telling his audience how outer space beings tune in on earthlings.

It's done, he said, by means of a resotron, a device that fits on the head like a hair-dryer and immediately translates earthlings thoughts and language into super space intelligence.

Having cleared up this awesome technology, Short read some documents, the substance of which is that the United Nations just isn't interested in UFOs and "please stop writing to this office."

Next came the slides. The first one purported to be outer space lights seen through pink clouds—but if you thought it was a slice of liver left too long in the hot sun, you wouldn't be far off the mark.

This was followed by what appeared to be a human eyeball the day after New Year's—or an under-fried egg.

Short —perspiring freely in his royal blue turtleneck, dark blue blazer and canary yellow slacks—got the next slide in upside down and backwards. But his apology was wasted—the audience didn't know the difference...

Pity the poor Martian trying to decode Monday night's proceedings on his resotron. He'll think he blew a fuse.

1. Farewell, Good Brothers, 1992. Robert Stone Productions.
2. Short, Robert, 2003. *Out Of The Stars: A Message From Extraterrestrial Intelligence.* Infinity Publishing Company.
3. Melton, Gordon J., 2009. *Melton's Encyclopedia Of American Religions.*
4. Stang, Ivan. 1988. *High Weirdness by Mail.* Simon & Schuster. (p. 51).

Joe Simonton showing off one of his otherworldly pancakes

SIMONTON, JOE (1901–1972)

Joe Simonton was a chicken farmer in his sixties who lived in a rural enclave near Eagle River, Wisconsin. While not a contactee in the traditional sense, he did experience (or claimed to experience) a singular meeting with humanoids who parked their silvery craft in his driveway on the gloomy day of April 18 of 1961 and offered him a "communion" of sorts (not to be confused with a later famous book by Whitley Strieber... or maybe it should.)

After first hearing a noise like a jet engine over his house, then something like "knobby tires on wet pavement," Simonton exited his house to see an object that looked like "two washbowls turned face to face" he said.[1] The surface was smooth and shiny and appeared to be some sort of metal. Walking around the object, Simonton noticed an opening through which he could see what appeared to be the interior of the craft.

The scene which greeted him was both strangely familiar and totally insane. Three completely normal-looking (albeit short, at about 5 feet) men stood in the interior, which was jet black "like wrought iron"[2] said Simonton. They were dressed in blue turtleneck knit outfits with small knit caps of the same material. They had no facial hair save for eyebrows and were dark-complexioned.

One appeared to be interested in a set of control or dials, while another appeared to be cooking something on a stove or flat grill. A few small, oblong cookie or pancake-like objects rested on top of the "grill." If this wasn't strange enough, the third being handed an empty container to Simonton and made a drinking motion. Simonton went inside the house and dutifully filled the jug, bringing it back to the craft. The little man took it and gave Simonton four of the baked objects and then saluted as if to say farewell and Simonton returned his salute. The one who was the fry cook hooked himself into the grill with a strap that attached to his uniform, and the craft rose up about 20 feet and sailed off over the trees.

U.S. Air Force investigators later obtained one of the cakes and when tested, they consisted of "hydrogenated fat, starch, buckwheat hulls, soya bean hulls, wheat bran." Air Force scientist Josef

Allen Hynek kept one, and Simonton ate one of the other two, which he said "tasted like cardboard."

As far as we know, and unlike many close encounter witnesses, the incident did not change his life in any lasting sense, but it may have been one of the strangest contact cases on record. Two weeks after the event, he told a reporter that if it happened again, "I don't think I'd tell anyone about it."

Simonton died on August 24, 1972, and is buried in the Eagle River Cemetery.[3]

1. Lorenzen, Coral and Jim. 1967. *Flying Saucer Occupants*. Signet (p. 130).
2. ibid p. 131.
3. https://www.findagrave.com/memorial/21117456/Joseph-Simonton

Andy Sinatra, "The Mystic Barber"

SINATRA, ANDY (1901–1978)

No relation to Frank Sinatra (or at least none that Frank was ever willing to admit!), Andy Sinatra (aka "The Mystic Barber" aka "The Mystical Tonsorial Artist from Brooklyn") claimed that at the tender age of one he underwent a medical procedure that led to his oh so young death. "It was a wonderful experience," Sinatra later reminisced to a captive reporter from the *Fort Scott Tribune*."[1] As they were getting ready to bury me I suddenly came back to life. And from that moment on I knew that I was different!" And oh, how different he was.

Originally from Mars, Sinatra at some point was psychically transported to Earth where he came to inhabit the body of an Italian barber from Brooklyn. However—as Sinatra was quick to point out—his present appearance was quite different from that of the average Martian that stood four feet tall and was covered with white hair and reproductive organs on their heads.

Sinatra—an occasional guest on Long John Nebel's Party Line—claimed he had astrally traveled to the moon, Mars, and the center of the Earth, and was fond for adorning himself with what he called a "psychic machine" consisting of a metal band that wrapped around his head. Not only did Sinatra's headgear function as a telepathic device, it was also a way to prevent malevolent space people from reading his thoughts, sort of an early version of your classic tin foil hat.

Over time, Sinatra's psychic headgear evolved into a grander version of its original primitive design and featured a beanie topped with something resembling a bazooka. This is the version Sinatra wore on February 4, 1962, when—with the assistance of an "invisible army of Martians"—he saved the United Nations from destruction (from evil aliens!) by performing a mystical ritual before a group of curious onlookers who wondered who the hell this guy was with the crazy bazooka beanie.[2]

The Mystic Barber's greatest claim to fame came on September 10, 1962, when he attempted to make contact with flying saucers on a live broadcast of *The Tonight Show* with Johnny Carson. According to Jim Moseley, Sinatra got stiffed for his $100 appearance fee because Sinatra's performance was "incoherent."[3]

1. *Fort Scott Tribune*, Sept 21, 1966.
2. James, Moseley. 1967. *Jim Moseley's Book of Saucer News.* Clarksburg, WV: Saucerian Books. (p. 118).
3. Moseley, James & Pflock, Karl. 2002. *Shockingly Close to the Truth!* New York: Prometheus Books. (p.159-160).

Hélène Smith

Smith, Hélène aka Catherine-Elise Müller (1851–1929)

Although little-known and referenced in contactee literature, Smith/Müller fits comfortably into the mold. In the late 19th century, she claimed spiritual contact with the inhabitants of Mars, and in her trances wrote down what she said was their language. She also drew and painted fanciful depictions of her impressions of Martian flora, fauna, and architecture.

The daughter of a Hungarian merchant, she grew up in Switzerland. Her childhood was filled with fantastical visions that disturbed her so much that she once asked her parents if she was a changeling (a child which has been taken and replaced by a substitute by supernatural beings such as faeries). By age 30, captivated by the worldwide Spiritualist movement, she had moved to Geneva and was channeling the likes of Alessandro Cagliostro and Victor Hugo. She "produced telekinetic phenomena, strange apports, found lost objects, predicted future events, saw spirit visitors, clairaudiently heard their names and received the explanation of visions which unfolded before her eyes by raps."[1] In a strange similarity to the founder of the Unarius society, Ruth Norman, Smith also believed that she was the reincarnation of many historical figures, most notably Marie Antoinette.

Foreshadowing the infiltration of the UFO group around Dorothy Martin in the early 1950s by academics, in 1895, Professor Thomas Flournoy was introduced to the circle of admirers which had formed around Smith, although he did not masquerade as a true believer. For a period of five years, he attended Smith's sessions and spoke with her extensively. He was skeptical of her claims, and gathered as much material on her as possible to make a reasoned verdict. Flournoy and other investigators who were allowed into her circle were occasionally assigned supporting roles as other reincarnated players in her recollections of past lives.

In November of 1894, she had a vision that her spirit was transported to Mars, where she described life on the planet over a series of subsequent sittings. She also began to speak and write in what she said was the Martian language. Flournoy pointed out that the language was very close in sound and structure to French, whereupon Smith developed a new variant she referred to as "Ultra-Martian." He also thought that her drawings of the architecture on the planet were very similar in appearance to pictures and painted depictions of China and the Orient. She also developed another complete and unique language and depiction of life further away on the planet Uranus. Despite the skepticism of the researcher in their midst, Smith and her circle always believed that she was truly in contact with an ET source.

The result of Flournoy's study was revealed in the 1900 book *From India to the Planet Mars*, along with images and languages channeled by Smith. He concluded "I am inclined to believe that Mlle. Smith, in truth possesses real phenomena of clairvoyance, not however, passing beyond the limits of telepathy."[2] In other words, he accepted her feats of knowing earthly things beyond the normal senses, but not the more exciting and fantastic claims of life on other planets. He also lamented the believer's refusal to consider his skeptical stance on things that could not be proven in any objective way. *Plus ça change.*

1. Fodor, Nandor. 1966. *Encyclopedia of Psychic Science*. University Books, Inc. (p. 348).
2. Flournoy, Thomas. 1963. *From India To The Planet Mars: A Study of a Case Of Somnabulism with Glossolalia*. University Books, Inc. (p. 397).

Wilbert B. Smith (Joe Fex/APE-X Research)

SMITH, WILBERT B. (1910–1962)

In 1950, Wilbert Smith—an engineer employed by Canada's Department of Transport (DOT)—established psychic contact with a group of ETs called the "Boys from Topside," certainly one of the more colorful monikers in the annals of saucerdom. That same year, Smith was granted after-hours access to a DOT laboratory which he used as part of a research project dubbed "Project Magnet." The principle idea behind Project Magnet was that UFOs traveled within magnetic fields.[1]

In 1953, Smith released the Project Magnet Report, which concluded that flying saucers were most likely of otherworldly origin. (Surprise!) After that, he somehow convinced the Canadian Government to sign off on a UFO observatory located on Shirley's Bay, near Ottawa. Like his DOT lab, this was an after-hours operation where Smith was assisted by civilian astronomers and government scientists. When news leaked out about the project, it was shortly after shut down on account of what government officials considered "embarrassing publicity" regarding Smith's belief in the "Boys from Topside."

1. Clark, Jerome. 2000. *Extraordinary Encounters: An Encyclopedia of Extraterrestrials and Otherworldly Beings.* Santa Barbara, CA: ABC-CLIO.

Ray Stanford at Giant Rock (Joe Fex/APE-X Research)

STANFORD, RAY (1938–)

To say that Ray Stanford has led an interesting life would be an understatement. Along with his twin brother Rex, the two blazed a trail across the early contactee movement while they were still in their late teens. He was one of the first investigators on the scene after the legendary Socorro UFO CE3K, and he remains the only one of that early group of contactees who later organized a project to record and measure UFO activity. If that wasn't enough, in the last decade or so, now well into his 70s, Stanford has carved a place for himself in the world of paleontology.

In a quest for understanding, Ray Stanford and his brother met with most (if not all) of the friends of the space brothers in the mid-to-late 1950s, most notably spending time with George Hunt Williamson, whom Stanford accused of trying to molest him (see Williamson, George Hunt.) Stanford is also the original source of a marvelous impersonation/recollection of George Adamski on his motivation for entering the Spacebrother Biz, when he recalled this classic line supposedly once uttered to him by the "Professor": "Dat man Roosevelt, he take away da Prohibition, if it wasn't for him, I wouldn't had to get into all of dis saucer crap."[1]

After their episode in the desert with Orthon, Williamson and Adamski had a falling out over whether actual contact was required for true contactee status. Williamson's continued channeling sessions convinced him that the space people could be accessed by certain individuals (such as himself) without the need for rides in saucers. By 1954, emulating Williamson and his cohort John McCoy, Stanford was convinced that he had opened his own channel to voyagers between the stars. Eventually, Stanford apparently had his own falling out with Williamson over book royalties for his titles such as *Look Up* and others, which he said Williamson had lifted information from his own work without credit or permission.

On April 28, 1964, Stanford arrived in Socorro, New Mexico to conduct his own investigation of what was to become one of the most famous UFO landing cases in history. According to his account,

Stanford arrived four days after the incident, which was still fresh in the minds of the witnesses. J. Allen Hynek and the Air Force were already there. Stanford called ahead to secure an interview with the main witness, Lonnie Zamora. Stanford found and interviewed others who saw the same object flying by, as well as a report of a similar one seen over Albuquerque just 25 minutes earlier. He also secured what appeared to be a sample of metal which was left by the UFO's landing gear on one of the rocks at the site. He says that the sample disappeared when he loaned it to NASA scientists for analysis.[2]

Along with his investigative pursuits, Stanford continued to channel wisdom from what he called his "source" in the early 1970s. Based in part on these messages, he founded the Association for the Understanding of Man (AUM) in 1971. One of AUM's projects was an undertaking called "Project Starlight International" (PSI) in which Stanford assembled a team of researchers and instrumentation designed to attract and record evidence of UFO activity. Stanford and his biographer Chris O'Brien say that the results of this study are some of the most well-documented evidence for the physical reality of the UFO phenomenon.

A new chapter and unexpected turn in the saga of Ray Stanford emerged in the early 1990s. In August of 1993, Stanford was exploring a creek bed near his Maryland home with his children, when "we happened upon an isolated iguanodon footprint, which as we soon learned, was of Early Cretaceous age."[3] He continued to log amazing finds in areas that were previously unknown as hotspots for fossil dinosaur tracks, so much so that he attracted the attention of professional paleontologists and the Smithsonian Institution, which currently exhibits some of Stanford's discoveries. In early 2018, his work was featured in an exhibition at Maryland's Goddard Spaceflight Center, which is the location where he made a discovery of dinosaur footprints alongside those of early mammals in "one of the densest concentrations of dinosaurs and mammals ever found."[4] Strangely, the Goddard facility was where, 53 years before, Stanford's Socorro metal sample had mysteriously gone missing.

Perhaps some sort of advanced intuition now guides him to these sites, although O'Brien believes the finds are due to Stanford's "amazing powers of observation."[5] Stanford sent out an email newsletter describing his sense of accomplishment and excitement about this new chapter of his life:

> The Goddard Space Flight Centers' party celebrating my discovery's unveiling and publication of the scientific paper…was surely the "high point" of my entire social life. The place was maximally packed with Goddard people voicing enthusiastic commendations…Hopefully, this discovery…coupled [with] my new species of dinosaur, *Propanoplosaurusmarylandicus*, installed for seven years, now at the Smithsonian's National Museum of Natural History, will enable the realization that I just might be pretty good at noticing things most people easily miss, and also at scientific interpretation

of things noticed.[6]

These new activities have gained him the mainstream acclaim he has not achieved with his earlier research, and could lead to more investigators examining his vast film, video, and data files on UFOs, when he is willing to share them with whom ever he chooses.

1. Ray Stanford.[Podcast episode]. (2009, June 25). *Radio Misterioso,* http://radiomisterioso.com/2009/06/25/ray-stanford-part-2/

2. Stanford, Ray. 1976. *A Socorro "Saucer" in a Pentagon Pantry.* Blueapple Books.

3. (no author). "Interview with Amateur Paleontologist Ray Stanford." Smithsonian National Museum of Natural History. n.d. https://naturalhistory.si.edu/exhibits/backyard-dinosaurs/ray-stanford.cfm Accessed February 1, 2018.

4. Reid, Chip. "Scientist stumbles over dozens of dinosaur tracks in discovery of a lifetime." *CBS Evening News.* January 31, 2018. https://www.cbsnews.com/news/dinosaur-tracks-fossils-discovery-goddard-space-flight-center/ Accessed February 2, 2018.

5. Personal conversation with Christopher O'Brien 1/30/18.

6. Email from Ray Stanford, February 4, 2018.

1960 - LAST PHOTO OF GIRL FROM EARTH

1961 - FIRST PHOTO OF VIVENUS ON EARTH

STARCHILD, VIVENUS

A young woman calling herself Vivenus Starchild came to the attention of saucer enthusiasts in June 1967 after an appearance on Long John Nebel's *Party Line*. During this interview, Miss Starchild informed Long John that the people of Earth have an exact double on Venus, and that our Venusian doubles can only visit Earth if their counterpart here has died, which is exactly what happened on September 24, 1960, when Vivenus was transported to our planet in a Venusian spaceship (known as a "swoop") and dropped off in Central Park. It was there that she came to inhabit the body of her human doppelgänger, a "failed singer of love songs" named "Viv" who had committed suicide. Vivenus took over Viv's body and soon after launched her own short lived music career crooning Venusian love songs.

Although Long John was eternally skeptical about most of the contactees who appeared on his show, he just the same found Vivenus to be a sincere and compelling guest, and had this to say of the Venusian crooner: "Here was this tiny and very well-dressed young woman, telling me a wild tale of coming from Venus in a flying saucer. Yet, after talking with her for fifteen minutes, I was absolutely convinced that this lovely lady blindly believed in what she was saying and in her Venusian origin."

Vivenus tells her story in *Vivenus: Starchild* (2001), a tale that probably had more to do with the planet Venus as a metaphorical/emotional escape hatch than it did with any actual interplanetary travel:

> Twin souls, identical in looks, but not necessarily identical in expression. My twin soul was the voice of the cries I heard. She had agreed to play a role on Earth and hoped that through it, she could make the Earth a better place, a place of love. Perhaps because I knew the Earth language now, I was able to tune in to her and speak to her...
>
> She told me nothing of her role on Earth nor why she wanted out—not then. She could

only speak of her sorrow while she was in her sorrow. I had to tune in to her while she was on the Earth, and "awake" and conscious. She told me that missions must not be called "missions" on Earth, that they must be called "dreams," and dreams—like wishes, may or may not come true.

She told me the Earth laughs at those who dream a dream, admires determination, but ridicules it. She told me too, that feeling souls had difficulty surviving on planet Earth, for the people were embarrassed or frightened by too much feeling. She said her only help in all her years was that she sang. It helped her to express feelings and the people did not silence her when she sang.

She said she had hoped that her mission called dream on Earth would be to be able to sing love to the Earth people and lift them out of their indifference to life and caring. But in her pursuit she felt nothing but pain and hurt. And in her pursuit the rejection was too great to bear...

The obvious metaphor here is that Vivenus killed off her old self to be born anew in Venusian flesh—a symbolic way to leave her old life behind.

After making a splash with Long John Nebel, Vivenus appeared at "The Big Flying Saucer Show" on June 24, 1967, at the Hotel Commodore in New York, said to be the largest UFO conference in U.S. history, with an attendance of 15,000 humans over a three day span. Opening her presentation, Vivenus delivered this stunning pronouncement: "Ladies and gentlemen, indeed, there is a God!" which was met with a standing ovation.

Following her fleeting rise to flying saucer fame, Vivenus set off on a trek across the country to spread the good space brother word. From 1974 to 1981, she walked an amazing 17,756 miles—through 290 cities—to "enlighten this planet with love." The July 13, 1980 edition of the *Oakland Tribune* featured a write-up on Vivenus including a song she composed for a certain write-in candidate:

It's God for President! So go become a resident! Write him in and we can win! And come election day we'll say, "Oh, it's not odd to vote for God."

By the mid-1980s, Vivenus removed herself from the spotlight and last word was that she'd relocated to Ventura, California.

Dr. Frank Stranges at 1966 Giant Rock Convention (Joe Fex/APE-X Research)

Stranges, Dr. Frank (1927–2008)

The Reverend (or Dr., depending on how he wished to present himself) Frank Stranges, author of such contactee classics as *Stranger At The Pentagon* and *Flying Saucerama*, led a multifaceted life as a saucer promoter, contactee, ordained minister, and law enforcement dilettante (although he also served tours on the other side of the law).

Born in New York state in 1927, he founded the National Investigations Committee on Unidentified Flying Objects (NICUFO) at age 40. This was six years after being kicked out of the more well-known and quasi-respectable National Investigations Committee on Aerial Phenomena (NICAP) for promoting his contactee ideas through a supposedly scientific civilian UFO group.

Stranges' most lasting legacy may be his book, *Stranger at the Pentagon*, the story of Venusian Captain "Valiant Thor." According to Stranges, after Val had met with the president and members of the Joint Chiefs, he had a meeting with Stranges at the Pentagon. Val Thor sounded (and looked) like Michael Rennie's portrayal of the ufonaut Klaatu in *The Day the Earth Stood Still*:

> Being a minister of the Gospel of Jesus Christ, as well as a student of the Bible for many years, coupled with my experience as an special investigator, I felt as though my senses were functioning properly and that I knew exactly what I was about to do. I was on my guard for fakes and frauds. In walked a man, about six feet tall, perhaps 185 pounds, brown wavy hair, brown eyes.
>
> His complexion appeared normal and slightly tanned. As I approached him and he looked at me IT WAS AS THOUGH HE LOOKED STRAIGHT THROUGH ME. With a warm smile and extending his hand, he greeted me by name.
>
> His genuineness astonished me, but quickly I understood. As I gripped his hand, I was

Dr. Frank Stranges with Adam Gorightly at the 2007 Retro UFO Convention at The Integratron (Photo credit: Greg Bishop)

somewhat surprised to feel the soft texture of his skin... like that of a baby but with the strength of a man that silently testified to his power and intensity.

Other contactees met their space brothers in deserts, along deserted highways, and in coffee shops. Frank Stranges met Val Thor in the hallowed halls of military power, making him the only contactee to be able to claim the imprimatur of officialdom.

Stranges was also involved with a man by the name of Raymond Broshears, who led a colorful and checkered life as a self-ordained minister, conspiracy theorist, UFO enthusiast, and even a gay rights activist. Sometime in the mid-to late 1960s, Stranges met Broshears and the two began conferring religious degrees on each other. Broshears featured articles and advertisements for UFO lectures and radio appearances by Stranges in his *Light of Understanding* newsletter. Broshears was apparently familiar with some of the characters in New Orleans who were suspects in Jim Garrison's JFK investigation, and was actively questioned during their investigation, which placed Stranges at the periphery of their inquiries.

1966 saw Ken Kesey's first "Acid Test" in San Francisco, John Lennon's "We're bigger than Jesus" comment, the founding of the Church of Satan, and Russia's Venera 3, which became the first manmade object to reach another planet. It also marked the June premiere of Stranges' UFO documentary *Phenomena 7.7* at Los Angeles' Wilshire Ebell Theater. The "7.7" referred to an official figure (perhaps from the U.S. Air Force) of the percentage of unsolved UFO reports. So far, the trail has gone cold on attempts to locate the sole remaining 16mm print. Stranges also released a short 45 RPM record to accompany the film, consisting of a shortened documentary on the reality of the phenomenon. Stranges wisely kept the alien contact material out of his narration, opting to convince skeptical listeners that the UFO subject was real and deserved scientific scrutiny—an issue that is still an object of bickering amongst UFO fans.

Stranges was no stranger to brushes with the law. In 1972, an aircraft with a bent propeller attempted to take off from Thermal, California. Besides the pilot, the only other person on board was Stranges. Police found about 400 pounds of marijuana in the plane. Stranges was convicted of attempting to transport an illegal substance and sentenced to eight months in prison and three years probation.

In 1974, Stranges staged the "8ᵗʰ Annual UFO Space and Science International Convention" in Anaheim, California. He advertised William Shatner, astronaut James Irwin, and U2 pilot Francis Gary Powers as featured speakers. All said they had either refused, cancelled, or never heard of Stranges.

In the last decade of his life, Stranges continued to quietly spread the gospel of the space people and made a few public appearances, perhaps the last of which was the Retro UFO Convention held at George Van Tassel's Integratron in April of 2007.

Chief Frank Buckshot Standing Horse

STANDING HORSE, CHIEF FRANK BUCKSHOT (1891–1977)

On the evening of July 12, 1959, Chief Frank Buckshot Standing Horse of Sulpulpa, Oklahoma was listening to his transistor radio when it suddenly exploded with a shotgun blast sound followed by the electricity going out at his house. When Chief Frank went to check his fuse box he encountered three average-looking gents who informed him that they weren't so average after all, and in fact had traveled all the way from outer space to pick up Chief Frank for a cruise around the cosmos.

After climbing aboard the spaceship, Chief Frank encountered a beautiful woman, which is always a welcome sight regardless of what planet you're visiting. The space gal introduced herself as Captain Mondraoleeka from the planet Oreon. (On the flying saucer lecture circuit, Chief Frank was always quick to point out that the planet "Oreon" was not to be confused with the star system "Orion.") As for Captain Mondraoleeka, Chief Frank described her thus:

> The lady was tall with pitch black hair and big beautiful blue eyes. She had no rings on
> her fingers. She had a well shaped head and well-featured mouth. She was dressed with
> a blue sort of jacket with an insignia on her right shoulder. I noticed a belt that looked
> as if it was jeweled, with a long dress.

Mondraoleeka, it should be noted, was 417 years old, although she didn't look a day over 30. The other ETs that Chief Frank encountered on his trip possessed equally unpronounceable names, and came from a variety of planets that were part of an intergalactic space brother federation like on *Star Trek*.

With his comely space captain at the helm, Chief Frank was flown around the galaxy to check out several planets, including Venus, Orean, and Clarion, the very same planet that Truman Bethurum had waxed so eloquent about. On the way they listened to the music of Connie Francis over KRMG radio station out of Little Rock, Arkansas, the sound of which was crystal clear even though they were an astounding 100,000 miles from Earth!

At one point, Chief Frank was summoned by the call of nature. After relieving himself in a restroom constructed of shimmering green walls, a flush from the space toilet sent out a wispy blue vapor that filled the air with a wondrous aroma. But that wasn't all. The Orean spaceship was apparently a top of the line, full-service facility that provided Chief Frank with a soothing bath, a sumptuous meal, and also the opportunity to catch some quality shut eye in a futuristic revolving bed that made Hugh Hefner's Playboy Mansion set-up look like a cheap army cot.

On subsequent spaceship trips, Chief Frank was treated to a flight to Jupiter on what was called an "Arrow Ship" that was two and a half miles long!

Apparently spaceships weren't the only things that grow large in outer space. On one occasion Chief Frank took the speaker's podium at the Giant Rock Spacecraft Convention to deliver the astounding revelation that "the figs on the Planet Oreon are as big as the watermelons we have on Earth."

Further reading

http://ufologie.patrickgross.org/ce3/1959-07-12-usa-sapulpa.htm

Stuart and Wilkinson's "loathsome, hideous, evil,
disgusting, horrifying" beast (Gene Duplantier)

STUART, JOHN

John Stuart's strange story appeared in *UFO Warning* (1963) published by Gray Barker's (sometimes saucy) Saucerian Press. The back cover blurb for this classic tome states: "FORCED INTO SEX ABOARD A FLYING SAUCER!" In his introduction to *UFO Warning*, Gray Barker mused: "I cannot completely understand this volume, and I don't think that many others can either... In its rawest and most primary sense it will serve as a warning to many UFO students!"

John Stuart's saucer odyssey began in 1950 when he started collecting UFO clippings from around the world and reading any and all books on the subject. One evening in 1952, Stuart received a knock at his door and, lo and behold, when he went to check on it, there was no one there! Stuart suspected that this incident was far more than a mere prank played on him by some mischievous kids and that it was somehow related to his flying saucer investigations. Not long after the mysterious-ringing-of-the-doorbell-affair-with-no-one-there, Stuart was in bed reading late one night when his telephone rang, and on the other end was an anonymous caller (from another planet, presumably) who warned him to "Stop interfering in affairs that don't concern you! You have been warned!"

Apparently this wasn't enough to spook Stuart and in 1953 he joined a UFO research group based out of Hamilton, New Zealand, called the Flying Saucer Investigation Society. After a few months with the group, Stuart had some sort of falling out with fellow members and left to form his own "organization" called Flying Saucer Investigators (FSI). Joining Stuart in this endeavor was a fetching young gal named Doreen Wilkinson (referred to in *UFO Warning* as Barbara Turner.) In fact, the only two members of Stuart's group were he and Wilkinson.

Although Stuart was married at this time, his UFO research activities with Wilkinson formed an intense collaboration, and he seemed to go out of his way in *UFO Warning* to dispel the notion that their relationship had been anything more than platonic. However, things start getting hinky in *UFO Report* when Stuart reveals that—at one point in their relationship—Wilkinson began to make sexual overtures and because of this Stuart suspected she had fallen sudden victim to supernatural possession. This "supernatural possession" occurred around the same time that a "space man" appeared before Stuart and Wilkinson and telepathically instructed the pair to cease and desist with UFO investigations or their lives would be in danger.

During one of their weekly UFO research get togethers, Wilkinson was overcome by a sudden cigarette craving and so they took a pause as she went out to a nearby market to pick up a pack of smokes. Upon Wilkinson's return,

> ...the front door flew open, and a figure rushed into my arms. [Doreen] said in a voice filled with fear: "There's something out there!"

> Quickly reassuring her, I hurried outside, stopping on the top step as a terrible stench struck me. I almost fainted in terror. It was burnt like plastic and sulfur. I stood there for a moment, and then walked down to the front gate, neither hearing or seeing anything. I searched the rear of the grounds, finding nothing, and had just started to return to the door when I heard distinct sounds behind me. I stopped and shone my torch. There was nothing there. I walked on. The sounds followed. I stopped and the sound stopped. I moved. It moved. Again I stopped, was amazed and startled when "it" kept on! The peculiar shuffling, scraping sound went past me, and I felt something solid brush against my shoulder! This was the first indication I had that 'they' were as solid as I!

When the creature at last manifested, it was freaky as all get out:

> The monster's head was large and bulbous. No neck. A huge ungainly body supported on ridiculously short legs. It had webbed feet. The arms were thin and not unlike stalks of bamboo. It had no hands, the long fingers jutting from the arms like stalks. Its eyes were about four inches across, red in color. There was no nose, just two holes, and the mouth was simply a straight slash across its appallingly lecherous face. The whole was lime green in color and it was possible to see red veins running through its ungainly form. The monster was definitely male.

At the sight of this eight foot tall "loathsome, hideous, evil, disgusting, horrifying" beast, Stuart and Wilkinson were suddenly paralyzed as if some psychic force had frozen them in their tracks. The creature moved towards them with its "filthy eyes fixed on [Doreen's] slim body" and started to reach out for her, then suddenly pulled back and disappeared.

Not long after—as Stuart was walking Wilkinson back to her hotel one evening—Doreen spoke "impishly" about the possibility of a space man waiting in her room, and that if he was handsome enough, "I'll take him to bed with me." These words, it appears, proved portentous, as that very night Wilkinson was attacked in her room by an invisible entity that ravaged and raped the poor lass over a two hour period. In December 1954, Stuart and Wilkinson "were forced to close down [FSI] after these very frightening attacks…In that month Barbara fled in terror."

Gray Barker later remembered "reading over the [*UFO Warning* manuscript] with Jim Moseley… and how we broke up at each Frightening Experience, which seemed to end each chapter, and punctuated by the principals in the story lighting another cigarette! It's too bad that at that time I was not fearless enough to print the uncensored original manuscript!"[1]

1. Clark, Jerome,1996. *High Strangeness: UFOs from 1960 through 1970*. Omnigraphics, Inc.

Swan, Frances

Although George Hunt Williamson may have had first dibs on channeling an entity named Affa from Uranus, this very same Affa (or a reasonable facsimile thereof) resurfaced in 1954 in the automatic writings of Mrs. Frances Swan of Eliot, Maine, who—by happenstance—lived just down the road a piece from famous UFO witnesses Betty and Barney Hill.

Affa—orbiting Earth in his spaceship—encouraged Mrs. Swan to contact the United States Navy so that they, too, could receive his telepathic radio transmissions. Mrs. Swan just happened to have a neighbor, retired Admiral Herbert B. Knowles, who was intrigued at the prospect of conversing with ETs and agreed to a Q & A session with Affa at Mrs. Swan's home. Afterwards, Office of Naval Intelligence (ONI) officials visited Mrs. Swan and likewise asked Affa a volley of questions, but that was the last of it until 1959 when an ONI liaison—Navy Commander Julius Larson—happened upon the Swan/Affa file. Larson—who possessed a profound interest in spiritualism—paid Mrs. Swan a visit and tried his own hand at automatic writing and before you knew it the messages from Affa started spilling off the page. Mrs. Swan, however, suspected that whoever Larson was channeling was actually an Affa imposter![1]

During a meeting with intelligence officers in Washington, D.C., Larson delivered a channeling demonstration summoning forth Affa, who instructed the group to look out a window in the office and a flying saucer would soon appear. After staring intently out of a window for several minutes, one of the men actually thought he caught a glimpse of a disc shaped craft partially hidden behind a cloud. Afterwards, Project Blue Book investigators looked into the case, but were unable to uncover any tangible evidence suggesting that Affa was anything more than a shared delusion.

1. Clark, Jerome. 2000. *Extraordinary Encounters: An Encyclopedia of Extraterrestrials and Otherworldly Beings*. Santa Barbara, CA: ABC-CLIO.

Mollie Thompson

THOMPSON, MOLLIE

Most contactees, if they did anything as a result of their experiences (or in the course of making things up) wrote books to tell their stories to the world. Mollie Thompson wrote poetry and then set it to music.

In the early 1950s, Thompson read *The Flying Saucers Have Landed* by George Adamski and Desmond Leslie. She said that "It spoke to me, it tweaked a nerve I couldn't resist."[1] Soon, she was using an Ouija board to contact entities with names such as "Ornoor," "Lon," and "Philemon." This last entity gave her teachings which were eventually published in an early British saucer magazine.

On June 1, 1963, Thompson and a friend heard that George Adamski was staying at Desmond Leslie's home in St. John's Wood, a snooty area of London. They walked right up and knocked on the door, almost demanding to see Adamski. She met the famous man in the kitchen, who told her "The Brothers have work for you."[2]

An anonymous poster at YouTube using the name "I Sleep Now" said of Thompson:

> She was originally the secretary of a saucer club back in 1959. Her contact reportedly occurred on a beach in England in 1964. She says a friend of hers, successful in extrasensory perception, while meditating literally "received," as if she were a radio set, a message from a being who identified himself as the commander of a saucer. The voice in the woman's mind informed her of his desire to contact a group of five "believers."

> Mollie, [British New Age guru Sir] Anthony Brooke, the woman, her skeptical husband, and another friend went to the appointed place at the appointed time. "Ten minutes later," according to Mollie, a "pulsating yellow-white light of great intensity appeared over our heads and simply formed geometric patterns for 20 minutes before streaking away." Almost a year later she claimed to have begun hearing sounds and phrases in

her mind. Weeks later she "began to hear the melody" accompanying them. At the time she claimed that she was "born to help prepare the world for an outer space ruler who is coming in late December of 1967."[3]

In 1965, Thompson recorded some of her compositions, which Brooke was impressed enough with to play for audiences around the world. Based on the reactions, he got Thompson into a recording studio to record an album of her previous compositions, along with a few new ones. She recalls writing three complete songs in an hour and a half, which convinced her that the music and words had come from her space friends.

The lyrics on "Cockeyed Ballad" were indeed inspired, if not by ETs, at least by a talented muse:

There's a cockeyed feeling in the world today
The power of politics is here to stay
For China, Russia, and the USA
Boy don't let them fool you

Take a look at this world of ours
Just one mothball in a sea of stars
Other planets have no color bars
'Cause they've got perspective

Yanks and Russkies put men into space
But it's all a mad politician's race
One-upmanship in this year of grace
It makes you giggle

The population stands and stares
While men in capsules explore upstairs
While we can't even manage our own affairs
Some cheap colonization

Besides they've got people on Venus and Mars
They've got lads and lasses, they've got and Mas and Pas
And they've got better transport than four-wheel cars
Have you ever seen them?

Those flying saucers whisking through our skies
Must make some power to make them rise
The government departments just hide their eyes
And call them meteors

With all the lies that they print and shout
The general public has its work cut out
Figuring what it's all about
But just you keep on trying

I suppose you know why I'm telling you this
So you won't shriek or shake your fist
When you discover Martians do exist
They're real nice fellows

I know 'cause I met one 'bout a week ago
His ship came down for an hour or so
He talked to me but then he had to go
Real interested I was

Got brothers on Venus and Saturn it seems
Fly their ships on magnetic beams
They wear one-piece suits—you can't see any seams
But apart from that—they're just like us

On the liner notes, Thompson said of this song: "I start with a smile on my face, for although living is a serious occupation it also has its funny side. Even so I am not laughing AT 'The Institution,' I am laughing WITH it."[4]

From Worlds Afar was released in 1966 on the Asteroid record label and sold exclusively at UFO conventions and gatherings. At Gabe Green's Amalgamated Flying Saucer Clubs of America annual meeting in Reno that year, Thompson gave 10-minute performances at lunch and in the evenings on July 8th through 10th. A film of this exists and was used in the title sequence to the 2000 television documentary entitled *UFOs: Then and Now*.

She was kept in the US because of a lengthy strike at the airlines and stayed until 1967, basically couch-surfing at the homes of famous ufologists and contactees. When she returned home to the

UK, her interest in the Space Brothers waned, but she did keep the flame alive on a personal level for the next 40 years. Despite the personal nature of the songs and the narratives of meeting aliens, eventually Thompson explained that her lyrics were essentially metaphorical. When one of her songs was posted on a music site she reacted in reply on April 6, 2008:

Mutterings from Mollie.

Yes, I'm still here—alive and—if not kicking, at least the motor is still ticking over.

Somebody said to me the other week,

'So, what are you doing now?'

I had to have a little think about that, but eventually I came up with a reply.

"The secrecy of my work prevents me from knowing what I am doing"

It is over 40 years since I wrote and sang those songs about space people. I didn't know what I was doing then either...but I had great fun doing it.

I'm sure you have guessed by now that I never actually met and spoke with flesh and blood space people in silver suits who had arrived in their vehicles: flying saucers or UFO's.

Vehicle is the key word here; my songs were the vehicle to carry my thoughts and ideas out into the world. But as for who wrote them?? I was NOT telling lies when I said that it was not me...certainly not the "me" that is sitting here writing this.

Every person is far MORE than the sum of their parts, and MORE than they appear to be.
Each individual is more knowing, more understanding, more loving and more loveable, and each of us has the potential to be a truly wonderful human being. That MORE was what created the song words and also what pushed me gently aside and took over the driving of the vehicle—for a while. Then someone was jumping back into the driving seat saying "Step back, let me live this life".

However, the older I get the more I hope to see MORE at the wheel, driving the vehicle.

She is a better driver than I am!

Cheers,
Have a good life,

Mollie Thompson[5]

1. Andy Roberts. "From World's (sic) Afar: The Mollie Thompson Story." Phenomena Magazine - July 2011 - Issue 27.
2. ibid.
3. https://youtu.be/n8yxoXdlQGc
4. Mollie Thompson. *From Words Afar*. Asteroid Records, 1966.
5. http://blog.wfmu.org/freeform/2006/10/mollie_thompson.html

THOMPSON, SAMUEL EATON (1875–1960)

Retired railroad worker Samuel Eaton Thompson claimed that while driving a stretch of rural road on the evening of March 28, 1950, he came across a landed flying saucer in the woods near his home in Centralia, Washington.

As Thompson approached the craft, out stepped a group of attractive Venusians wearing nothing but their birthday suits. These hippie Venusians were also vegetarians, which apparently contributed to their wholesome appearance. Thompson described them as naïve and childlike, and for some reason they had no idea who built the flying saucer they rode in on.[1]

Thompson spent the night with the nude crew, sleeping on a chair in one of the ship's bedrooms. The next morning, he asked if he could run home and grab his camera, then return to take some photos. As Thompson later explained to Kenneth Arnold, it was "just like trying to take a picture of the sun. There was a glow to it. That film was just blank. I wanted to get some of them right onto the ground to take some pictures of them, but they wouldn't come out."[2]

1. "Centralian Tells Strange Tale of Visiting Venus Space Ship in Eastern Lewis County", *Centralia Daily Chronicle*, April 1, 1950.
2. Clark, Jerome, 2000. *Extraordinary Encounters: An Encyclopedia of Extraterrestrials and Otherworldly Beings*. Santa Barbara, CA: ABC-CLIO. (p. 243).

**Hope Troxell at the Cosmic Counsel Center in Los Angeles
(Joe Fex/APE-X Research)**

TROXELL, HOPE (1906–1979)

While hiking in the Los Angeles hills in the mid 1950s, Hope Troxell experienced the following astonishing encounter:

I had just stepped upon the path—when a handsome gentleman entered the path... I shall never forget him. His physique was wedge-shaped, which any athlete would admire. He was clean-shaven and dressed impeccably in that 105-degree heat! His grey flannel slacks were shapely creased, and a spanking white shirt was open at the neck, and rolled up at the cuffs... I noticed also his bright blue eyes and joyous smile. But the eyes really got me! I don't think I've ever seen such China-blue eyes! More than that, he KNEW ALL ABOUT ME, and for the first time in my life, I felt quite spiritually naked! He never took his eyes off me and his smile was steady.

But there was another feature; his walk...My eyes kept being drawn to his feet—for I could not quite tell—but he didn't seem to be touching the ground, yet every time I tried to watch exactly, his eyes called mine back to his face. Yet it was also strange that there was no sound of his footsteps. Was he, or was he not, walking on the path? As he came closer there seemed to be several inches of space between his feet and the ground. I kept wondering if I was just imagining it, or if it were real.

As he passed me on the path, he spoke in the melodious voice, saying like a chord of music: "Hello." A shock went through me—WHERE HAD I HEARD THAT VOICE BEFORE?

Because of these features—his voice, his silent step, the fact that he seemed to KNOW me—though I had never seen him before—a few steps after we passed, I turned to look again—but there WAS NO MAN!

As I thoughtfully drove home, watching the Sierra Madre Range of mountains, suddenly to the right of Mt. Wilson, there appeared low in the cloudless sky, three huge flat, circular disks—WHITE COSMIC CRAFT—which hovered in triangular formation, and then shot silently toward the setting sun![1]

Following her encounter with this mysterious spaceman, Troxell took on the duties of spokesperson for the Pasadena branch of Daniel Fry's *Understanding*. In the March 11th, 1960 *Los Angeles Times*, Troxell said, "The spacemen have told us to go back to the basics of the Bible. Understanding is really a return to God…We are trying to spread the basic beliefs of God, coupled with the science of space. The way we can prepare the people of this earth for the mass landings by the spacemen. If they landed now they would probably be shot."

Troxell authored a number of channeled works including *Wisdom of the Universe* and *Cosmic Attainment*. In the early 1960s, she relocated to June Lake, California, where she got her own metaphysical saucer group going called The School of Thought.

1. Short, Reverend Robert. 1996. *Giant Rock: A Commemorative*. Cornville. Arizona: Blue Rose Ministry. (p. 20).

George and Eva Van Tassel at Giant Rock (Joe Fex/APE-X Research)

Van Tassel, George (1910–1978)

George Van Tassel was a legend among the passel of Southern California contactees of the 1950s, most notably as host of annual "Spacecraft Conventions" from 1953 to 1977. They were the focal point for the burgeoning spiritual UFO movement and attracted thousands of attendees —sort of like a Burning Man for saucer heads.

In the late 1930s, while working at his uncle's garage in Santa Monica, California, Van Tassel met and befriended a German immigrant turned prospector named Frank Critzer. Van Tassel and his uncle took a liking to Critzer and stocked him with food and supplies for a trip into the desert. In return, Critzer promised to cut them in on any riches he found. Critzer staked a claim on a piece of land near a rocky outcropping and built a subterranean home underneath what was then considered to be the largest free-standing granite boulder in the world, known as Giant Rock.

Critzer also built an airstrip and scraped roads through the sagebrush in order to invite more visitors to his remote outpost. In 1942, Critzer was killed in a law enforcement raid on his home under suspicion of working for the Nazis. This last issue was never proven, although he may have helped to hide Japanese Americans in various areas of the desert so that they would not be sent to the internment camps during the war.

A pilot himself since his teens, Van Tassel went to work for Howard Hughes during WWII as an aircraft inspector. In 1947, he moved his wife Eva and two daughters out to Critzer's underground house and renovated the airstrip. He also built a café and pilot's lounge, as well as a sort of dude ranch as a destination for weekend pilots, who were proliferating after WWII.

Early in 1952, Van Tassel said that he began to receive channeled messages from a legion of entities using such monikers as Lutbunn, Molca, Locktopar, and the curiously familiar-sounding "Clatu." He was also the first to mention "Ashtar," who continues to enjoy a wide popularity amongst UFO channeling fans. Soon after, he founded the College Of Universal Wisdom and wrote his first book: *I Rode A Flying Saucer! The Mystery of the Flying Saucers Revealed*, consisting mainly of his

Frank Critzer underneath Giant Rock (Photo credit: Harlow Jones and Morongo Basin Historical Society)

received messages, and no actual rides on flying saucers.

UFO author Gray Barker once recalled a channeling session at Giant Rock. Working himself into a trance, Van Tassel encountered difficulty in transmission: "Confound it! You keep switching around on me! Let's settle on who's going to do the talking tonight!" More rude entreaties finally brought a clear "signal" and he was able to speak in a loud, harsh voice "I AM KNUT. I BRING YOU LOVE." Surviving recordings of Van Tassel's trances bear this out. He seemed to model his sessions on the idea of some kind of "mental radio," since he was familiar with them from his flying days.

Channeling was not enough: his need for popularity and contactee credentials required a physical extraterrestrial contact—or at least a report on one. Sure enough, in August of 1953, he made the acquaintance of a saucer captain known as Solganda and was invited aboard a space ship. He had finally hit the big time.

Thus anointed, Van Tassel began publishing *The Proceedings of the College Of Universal Wisdom*, a semi-regular newsletter sent out to the faithful; in return, they began to send donations for a device that Solganda and his pals instructed him to build on his property in the high desert. Looking more like an insane astronomical observatory than a machine, the Integratron, as it is called, was never completed. It was supposed to enable humans to live well past the expected lifespan, and give us a

Giant Rock in the 1960s (Joe Fex/APE-X Research)

chance to evolve spiritually in this lifetime-without all that pesky reincarnation stuff.

In spite of some differences between his stories about the space brothers and those of his contemporaries, Van Tassel never attempted to contradict his compatriots, and went so far as to feature many of them at his yearly Spacecraft Conventions, which became the largest UFO gatherings of the era. It is said that 11,000 people gathered at Giant Rock for the event in 1959. Tennessee contactee Buck Nelson sold swatches of pink and purple "Venusian Dog Hair," as myriad other hucksters vied for the hard-earned dollars of the saucer nuts with photos, books, strange devices, and homespun wisdom from the space people.

Van (as his friends called him) produced a second volume, *The Council Of Seven Lights*, in 1958. The introduction was succinct: "The information in this book is the result of a developed ability to awaken the nearly dormant consciousness to thoughts existing throughout time. Nothing can be thought of that has not been thought of before... All of the principles of everything that can ever be already exist in the infinity of Universal Mind."

Alternating between scientific-sounding explanations of the history of the Earth and mankind, and spiritual dilemmas and solutions, Van squares this circle to unite science and spirit. The history of our planet, he claimed, is derived from "the twelve densities in the system we occupy... When the

Van Tassel's Integratron, pre public access, mid 1960s (Joe Fex/APE-X Research)

solar system moves from one density to another, it is called a master cycle... The Earth is culminating a minor cycle, a major cycle, and a master cycle all at the same time. This will bring about a rebalancing of the planet on new poles. When this occurs, the great earthquake written of in Revelations will take place." He continues to explain the demise of the dinosaurs and the formation of coal seams based on his catastrophic history-based density theory. The idea that the Earth is completing many cycles at once, and therefore heading for another "density change" in the near future echoes the Hindu Kali Yuga and the prophecies of Nostradamus and Edgar Cayce, among others. Was Van tuning into the Universal message, or was he just paraphrasing reading material through his subconscious, wittingly or otherwise?

Van Tassel died of a sudden heart attack in 1978 while alone in a hotel room in Long Beach, California. His second wife Doris, faced with bankruptcy, sold the property on which the Integratron sits. Following plans to turn it into a disco, Van's followers were aghast and bought the property back. It is now owned by two sisters, Nancy and Joanne Karl, who have faithfully preserved the building and have transformed it into a sort of new age and tourist mecca. Bone white and imposing on the desert floor some 15 miles north of Joshua Tree National Park, it is a fitting memorial to the man and his era. Were it not for this stark and sturdy reminder, the meager literary output and the cherished memories of surviving Giant Rock conventioneers would be all that remained of gentle UFO contactee George Van Tassel.

Paul Villa (Joe Fex/APE-X Research)

VILLA, PAUL (1916–1981)

Paul Villa's interactions with otherworldly entities began in 1953 in Long Beach, California, when he encountered a seven-foot-tall spaceman walking along the beach. Villa's next run-in with the space brothers occurred on June 16th, 1963, when he was telepathically instructed to drive his pick-up truck to the location of a landed saucer. The saucer, in this instance, was a mothership from the Coma Berenices galaxy carrying nine humanoids—a mix of men and women—ranging from seven to nine feet tall. Included in their arsenal were nine remotely-controlled disk

**Paul Villa flying saucer photo, 1966
(Joe Fex/APE-X Research)**

shaped drones (14 inches in diameter) that were used for Earth recon missions, controlled from instrument panels inside the mothership. During this meeting, the UFO occupants "permitted Villa to take photos of their ship which posed and hovered close to the surface."

On April 18, 1965, Villa was telepathically instructed to travel to Bernalillo, New Mexico, and it was there he photographed a spaceship that projected a laser beam, and ignited a small forest fire.

Paul Villa with his scale model saucer (Joe Fex/APE-X Research)

A photo of this arsonist spaceship was among several other Villa saucer photos published in Gabe Green's *UFO International*. Project Blue Book investigators later determined that Villa fabricated these photos using a miniature model of a flying saucer.[1]

1. Randle, Kevin and Estes, Russ, 2000. *The Spaceships of the Visitors: An Illustrated Guide to Alien Spacecraft*. Touchstone Books.

1972 Villa saucer sighting with his pick-up truck in the foreground (Joe Fex/APE-X Research)

Claude Vorilhon aka Raël at his compound in Quebec, 1998 (Photo credit: Douglas Curran)

Vorilhon, Claude aka Raël (1946–)

Claude Vorilhon was born September 30, 1946 in Vichy, Allier France. His life reads like an improbable novel. He reinvented himself three times as a public figure, first as a teenybop singer, then an auto-racer and journalist, and finally as a messenger for an ET race he called the "Elohim."

Vorilhon ran away from home in 1961 at the age of 15 and hitchhiked to Paris, where he hoped to become a vocal star. He was discovered by a radio personality and given a record contract, and a showbiz name: "Claude Celler."[1] From 1966 to '67 he released a string of singles, to minor success. One of the sides was entitled "Madame Pipi," which told the story of a toilet attendant. His teen idol career ended abruptly when his sponsor killed himself in 1970.

Gathering his earnings from his aborted dance with showbiz, Vorilhon founded a magazine based on his lifelong interest in auto racing, which also allowed him to test-drive new cars. Many years after he became an agent of the Elohim, Vorilhon entered at least six official races in the late 1990s and placed well in a few, exhibiting a great deal of competence for someone who had never competed before. He announced his retirement from racing in 2001.

Moved by a strange compulsion, Vorilhon went for a hike in the Pyrenees mountains on December 13, 1973. What he saw on that walk would change his life, and the lives of thousands of his eventual followers. Like Adamski and others, Vorilhon claimed that an alien spacecraft landed before him and space brothers emerged to tell him of their message, which he was chosen to help spread to the people of Earth. Eventually, he said, they also encouraged him to spread their message of sexual liberation for everyone, including liberalized sex education for children, which of course caused Vorilhon more trouble.[2]

His new friends also showed him the unity of all things and the symbol for this unity. Unfortunately for Vorilhon, the symbol faced an incredible uphill battle for acceptance. The logo of a swastika perfectly integrated into a six-pointed Star of David shocked and scandalized almost everyone who beheld it. It was so dazzling (or offensive) that during the 1970s and '80s, the Raelian movement had to order stickers to place over the covers of all the books they still had in stock. The new symbol looked appropriately new-age, but did not have the impact of the original. Eventually, Vorilhon decided that enough time had passed and the scandal had blown over enough to recall its original glory for a new generation.

On a sunny afternoon on June 21, 2012, holidaymakers at beaches along the New York and New Jersey shores were treated to the sight of a small aircraft towing a banner reading

卐 = ☮ + ♥ PROSWASTIKA.ORG

...followed by the Raelian swastika-in-the-star symbol. Thousands were aghast. Vorilhon might as well have marched up the main streets with a few of his followers wearing white hoods. Raelians posted a press release on the proswastika.org site to explain their actions:

> Our objective in this annual "Swastika Rehabilitation Day" is to... rehabilitate the image of this very ancient symbol which has, in recent decades, been equated only with Hitler's horrors, when in fact, the swastika has always meant something very beautiful, peaceful and loving for billions of people all over the world and still is by billions of people.[3]

At the 50th anniversary Roswell festival in 1997, the Raelians rented a booth at the convention center and went for the hard sell with babes in skintight leotards with headset microphones hawking the virtues of sensual meditation and the sex-positive message of Rael.[4]

Not content to conquer just the weird world of UFO fandom, a select few Raelian babes posed in the October, 2004 issue of Playboy, along with text that could almost be termed a recruiting pamphlet with nude women scattered throughout. Rael's "wife and partner for 13 years" quipped, "This is the only religion that teaches that nudity and sexuality are pure and beautiful."[5]

In 1997, the Raelians announced the founding of a biotech company called "Clonaid" to begin research into human cloning, which they said was the first step to immortality. On December 6, 2002, Clonaid director Brigitte Boisselier announced that they had cloned the first human being in their secret lab near Las Vegas. They named the child "Eve," and announced that DNA testing would soon be performed to prove that the girl was an exact genetic copy of her mother. Over the next several months, Boisselier and others from around the world claimed five more successful human clones were born. By March, 2013, they said that the number had risen to thirteen. No evidence was ever provided for any of these claims.

As of 2017, the Raelian movement is still going as strongly as ever, most likely due to its sex-positive message and the fact that female members regularly take part in topless protests against prudish laws that prohibit the baring of female breasts in public.

1. https://en.wikipedia.org/wiki/Raël
2. ibid.
3. http://ja.proswastika.org/about-the-swastika
4. Author's personal recollection.
5. (no author) "The Rael World." *Playboy*, October 2004: p 77-81.

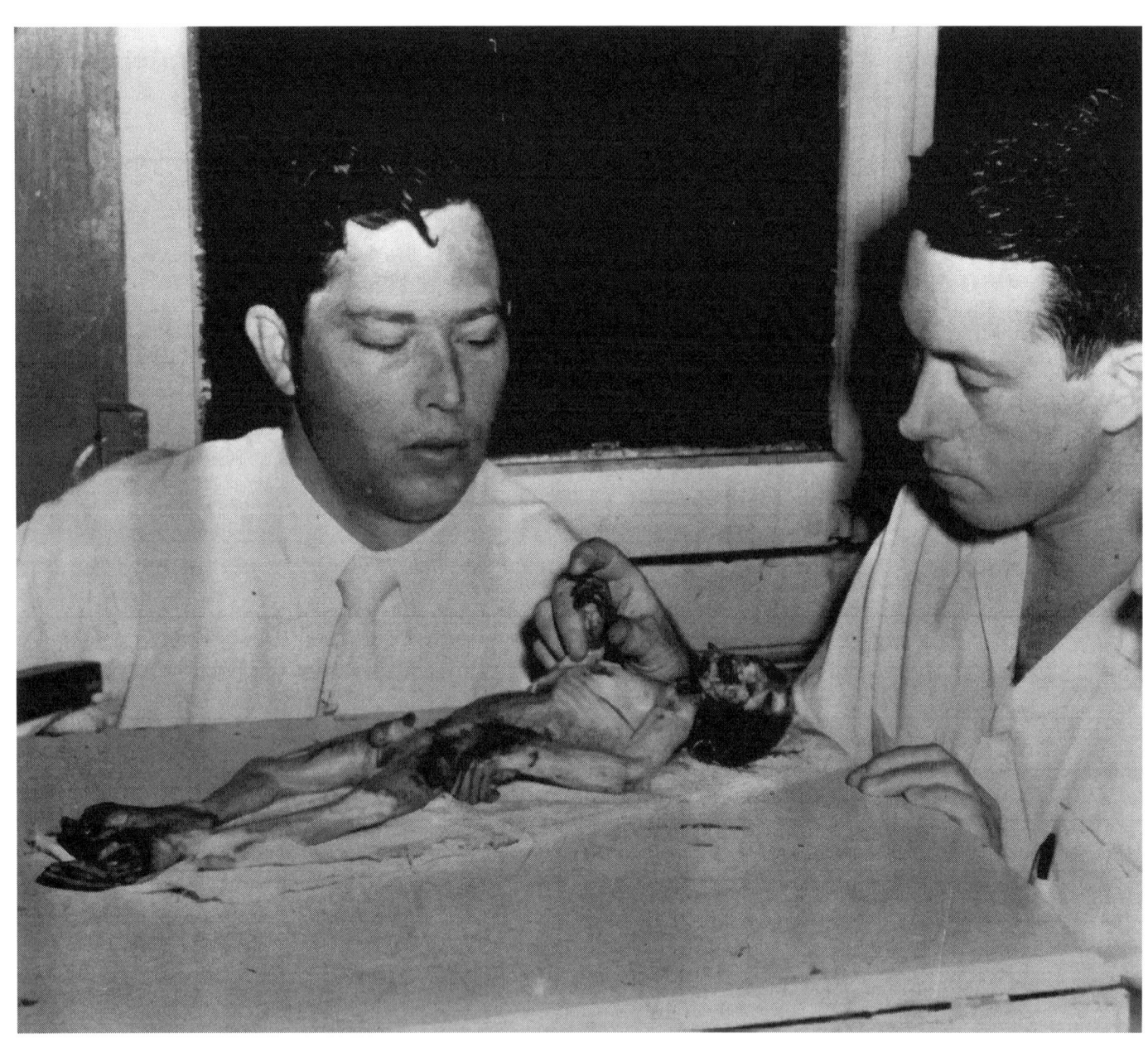

Ed Watters (left) looks on as Dr. Mickle (right) examines the "dead alien"

WATTERS, ED (born ca. 1930)

On July 7, 1953, numerous reports of a multicolored, cone-shaped object were seen in the skies over Marietta, Georgia. The following evening, Deputy Sheriff Sherley Brown was out on patrol when he encountered a stalled truck with its doors flung open and headlights shining on a "hairless, two-foot tall humanoid creature with eerie, round, dark eyes."

The truck's passengers—Ed Watters, Tom Wilson, and Arnold Payne—stood off to the side of the road in apparent shock. When questioned, the young men stated they came over a hill and suddenly found themselves careening towards a landed flying saucer with three small aliens bopping around outside the craft. The driver, Mr. Watters, hit the brakes and attempted to swerve around the object, but unfortunately plowed into one of the little guys.[1]

The two remaining aliens immediately jumped aboard their saucer and high-tailed it, leaving their fallen comrade behind. The next day Watters told the press, "They all jumped for it. Two of them made it. I hit the other one. The red object turned blue and sailed away at a very fast speed."

Deputy Brown didn't quite know what to make of this crazy story, but decided to let the young men go home and take the dead alien with them. Ed Watters put the creature in his refrigerator and the next day called the *Atlanta Constitution* to tell them he had a dead alien on ice.

After giving the creature the once over, the *Atlanta Constitution* reporter brought in a local veterinarian to examine the body who said it looked like "something out of this world." The story soon went old school viral as curious reporters descended upon Atlanta hoping to sneak a peek at the dead little man from outer space.

Suspecting a fraud, Dr. Herman Jones—head of the Georgia forensics crime lab—confiscated the creature and under examination determined it was a shaved monkey.[2] Realizing the jig was up, Watters admitted having bought the monkey at a local pet shop, conked it over the head, then removed its hair and chopped its tail off. He and his buddies then used a blowtorch to burn scorch marks on the highway as evidence of the landed saucer.

The hoaxers were arrested and charged with animal cruelty, but the charge was dropped due to a technicality. Watters ended up being fined $40 for placing the body of an animal in a public thoroughfare. A few months later, Watters left town when he got tired of people calling him the Monkey Man. Afterwards, this caper became known in the annals of U-fool-ology as "The Great Monkey Hoax of 1953."

1. "Flying Saucer 'Monkey Man' Captured," *The Miami News*, July 8th, 1953.
2. Moseley, James. 1954. "Exposing the Saucer Hoaxes," *Nexus Magazine, Book #2, Tome #1.*

John Langdon Watts

WATTS, JOHN LANGDON

During the 1950s, John Langdon Watts was psychically transported to Venus and quickly learned that Venusians lived to be 2500 years old due to their outstanding vegetarian diets. While there, Langdon hooked up with a comely Venusian gal named Mara who was "Commander and Chief of the Federation of the Exploratory Forces of Planets."

After returning to Earth, Watts published a series of pamphlets featuring Venusian beauty treatments (courtesy of Mara) sold through his company, The Dixie Venus Corporation.[1]

1. http://marcianitosverdes.haaan.com/2016/03/john-langdon-watts-el-contactado-que-daba-consejos-de-filosofa-y-de-belleza/

Further reading

Watts, John Langdon, 1973. *Hello, Venus! An ESP Epic*. New York: Vantage Press.

Knud Weiking

Weiking, Knud

In February 1967, two years after George Adamski left this mortal coil, his pal Orthon made a return Earthside, visiting a Danish cab driver named Knud Weiking (which itself sounds like a space brother name.) According to Weiking:

> I returned home from the night's work... I sat down in my living room to have a smoke before going to bed. All of a sudden I heard a male voice saying, "Put out that cigarette, I want to talk to you." I looked around in the room but saw nothing. I'm not easily shocked, so I didn't think any further about it, but calmly kept on smoking. Then the voice repeated its request, and again I took a good puff on the cigarette, like I wanted to show that nobody tells me what to do in my own home.[1]

At some point in this encounter, all the lights went out in the room, and the cigarette-Nazi appeared as a gleam of light, announcing himself as Orthon. Soon after, Orthon began speaking through Weiking, messages that were tape recorded and transcribed for posterity. Weiking described Orthon thusly:

> Orthon is a big handsome man. He is about 188 centimeters tall, brawny but slim. His face is very finely shaped, his hair is golden brown, and his skin is golden. Orthon is always dressed in a tight shiny golden suit, and over this he wears a cape shimmering in purple, black, and scarlet. He is surrounded by a radiant white light.

Weiking's channeled messages from Orthon became associated with a Danish doomsday group known as the Cult of Orthon. On September 28[th,] 1967, Orthon (speaking through Weiking) informed his congregation of doomsday cultists that a global nuclear war would go down on Christmas day.

However, on a more positive note,

> Some are gathered here who absolutely have to survive…We simply transfer the human elementary particles by something we call teleportation up into a spaceship. This means that one second the person stands talking to a friend, and he turns around, and then the friend has disappeared. He has already been taken up into a spaceship while the other must remain when the explosion happens…That is transfer by the power of the mind. This method will be used in places where salvation is a matter of seconds. For instance at the spot where a nuclear bomb is dropped. Immediately afterwards the Earth will be cleansed by being tilted.

In advance of Armageddon, Orthon's cult built a bomb shelter located in a field near Borup in the province of Sealand, consisting of a wooden underground structure covered with 25 tons of lead to survive the forthcoming nuclear blast and fall-out.

Like Dorothy Martin's "Seekers"—and many other doomsday cults that have issued failed predictions—the Cult of Orthon was no exception, as the predicted 1967 nuclear doomsday scenario turned out to be one big, fat dud.

---

1. Wegner, Willy, 1990. *UFO Over Denmark.*

Hal Wilcox at Giant Rock (Joe Fex/APE-X Research)

WILCOX, HAL (born ca. 1932)

As a child, Hal Wilcox had a series of psychic experiences and in his adult years became an ordained Spiritualist minister. In 1951, Wilcox founded the Institute of Parapsychology in Hollywood, CA, which was later renamed the Universe Society Church (UNISOC). Under UNISOC's umbrella, Wilcox brought together several trance channelers, all of whom—along with Wilcox—channeled a group of ascended masters called the Ancient Brotherhood of Fahsz (TABOF).

> Contacts from 1951 to 1961 were maintained by a method the group was taught in order to facilitate regular communications. It consists of a brief ceremony in which a mantrum, "Ino Pazis Gnurum," is chanted, followed by a 30-minute message channeled by one of UNISOC's 12 oracles for directions. The short service, it is believed, activates the pineal gland, connecting it with either the INO, a galactic computer bank, or one of the space brothers within Fahsz's command...

> UNISOC holds weekly classes and has expanded their services to include an interfacing computer network that in 1978 produced a printout of extraterrestrial communications. The associated Galaxy Press has published Wilcox's books, several levels of instructional material, booklets, and a newsletter.[1]

In 1964, a gentleman in a one piece jumpsuit who looked like "like Burt Lancaster in that *Trapeze* movie" showed up on Wilcox's doorstep, put his hands on his hips and announced that he was Zemkla from the planet Selo, a representative of an interplanetary cultural exchange program.

Wilcox, of course, figured this was some sort of gag—I mean who goes around in public in a onesie jump suit?—but just the same he invited Zemkla inside to find out what all the fuss was about. After a half hour of general discussion concerning the Intergalactic Federation of Planets, Zemkla suggested they step outside where he started waving his arms all around. Just at the point that Wilcox was about ready to break out a butterfly net, a full blown Adamski looking bell-shaped craft landed on his front lawn.[2]

In the years to follow, Wilcox enjoyed a series of meetings with Zemkla (dressed more like a regular guy on these occasions, not in the onesie jumpsuit outfit) many of which occurred at coffee shops in the greater Los Angeles area. Over this span of time—and innumerable cups of coffee—Zemkla (and crew members of Zemkla's spaceship) compiled personal information on Wilcox in preparation for a series of forthcoming saucer flights to planet Selo that would commence in 1968.

Zemkla entered Wilcox's personal info into the "universal so-called Ino Computers; incredible data-processing units that are a symbiotic synthesis of mechanisms and creative life or consciousness..." This data was used to produce the perfect female mate for Wilcox, "the most gorgeous thing you could ever imagine, structure-wise. I don't mean just body structure—but mind, body, soul, the whole thing. She was the best person suited for me on the planet [Selo]."

Even though Wilcox was married, he considered it his patriotic duty (as an ambassador of Earth!) to get busy with his alien girlfriend, thus maintaining good relations not only with the women of Selo, but with all ETs throughout the known universe. However—just like Truman Bethurum before him—these extra-curricular activities didn't sit well with Wilcox's then wife and he ended up in the dog house for a while after returning from his jaunt to Selo. Wilcox documented this amazing story in his aptly titled, and impossible to find, *UFO Flight* (1968). The only available copy we've been able to track down on the internet is going for the out-of-this-world price of $5,523.64!

1. Melton, Gordon J., 2009. *Melton's Encyclopedia Of American Religions.*
2. Interview with Hal Wilcox, Winter 1993 issue of "Far-out! The Unexplainable, the Unusual, and the Unreal" magazine.

George Hunt Williamson (left), his charming wife Betty, and a third individual (possibly Lyman Streeter) conducting short wave space brother radio communications in Prescott, Arizona (Fortean Picture Library)

WILLIAMSON, GEORGE HUNT aka Michel d'Obrenovic (1926–1986)

George Hunt Williamson (son of George Williamson and Bernice Hunt) had a mostly self-educated background in anthropology and Western occultism, and in the heady days of the early 1950s, he found his calling as a telepathic contact for the ascended cosmic masters. He claimed out of body and other experiences beginning in his teen years, and borrowed from the supernatural traditions of the Chippewa and Sioux tribes, with whom he said he lived in his early 20s.

He was enrolled at the University of Arizona in 1949 and actually worked an archaeological dig in 1946 in southern Illinois and another in Lincoln County, New Mexico. By 1951, he was expelled from the University and set his sights on other pursuits, although his connection to archeology remained an interest well after his UFO interests ended.

The source of his troubles may have been a rapidly growing interest in the far-right-wing politics of American fascist leader William Dudley Pelley, whom he finally met in 1953. Pelley spent seven years in jail for treason against the United States, and when he was released in 1950, began publishing a radical conservative magazine called *Valor*, which also featured channeled messages from beings who Pelley considered ascended masters. Williamson was the editor for a few months in 1954.

Williamson is perhaps best known for his short association with George Adamski and the latter's famous account of a meeting with an extraterrestrial being in the California desert in 1952. (see Adamski, George) Williamson and his wife Betty, as well as saucer fans Alfred and Betty Bailey took to attending meetings at Adamski's place at Mount Palomar in Southern California. Williamson and Adamski fell out less than month after the desert contact event over the validity of channeled messages. Williamson believed it was a valuable tool to communicate with alien races, while Adamski (strangely enough) thought that it was bunk, or mostly bunk:

"You can never check on the sender of a trance message. Every mock spirit or evil impersonator could come and tell you that his name was Ashtar or Aetherius and that he lived in a space ship. I think that these entities are having a heyday leading astray the gullible mediums and their public... This is not to belittle mediums in any way, but it is to say that most of them have much to learn before they can be sure of just what they are receiving, and from whom and where."[1]

This, despite the fact that Adamski based much of his early philosophy on his idea that "Tibetan lamas" (and "space people" after his UFO gaff took off) were communicating to him telepathically. He perhaps considered his B.S. meter to be more highly developed than others.

Despite their disagreements, Williamson never repudiated his experience with the most famous contactee of the golden era, and in fact continued to claim that it happened exactly as described, except that in his version, Adamski communicated mainly by telepathy rather than sign language.

Williamson and Bailey returned to Prescott, Arizona, and continued their series of ouija-type communications with what they believed were space people. They invented their own circular board and used an overturned shot glass as a planchette. They contacted entities with names worthy of the best science fiction: Ankar 22, Reggah, Nah-9 and Zrs.

As documented in *The Saucers Speak* (1954), the communication soon switched to Morse code by shortwave radio. Lyman Streeter, a ham operator in Prescott, Arizona, was contacted by Bailey in an effort to speed up communication, and speed up they did. On September 28, 1952, the small group received this message: "Be of peace. Happy. Happy. You radioman--are installed in the records. Good. Attention. Surprised my brother?" In a 1954 lecture, Williamson announced that the space people were arriving soon to spread peace and inaugurate a one-world government, and three years later he wrote in *UFOs: Confidential* that the United Nations was a plot to "destroy our sovereignty and void and nullify our Constitution! Don't be fooled by the UN for it is anti-Christ from first to last."[2] Echoes of Pelley still rung in his ears.

In 1953, he began a series of channelings at his home in Whipple, Arizona accompanied by his wife and another minor contactee personality, Charles Laughead, and his wife Lillian. (Laughead has been identified as the mysterious "Dr. Armstrong" in *When Prophecy Fails*, the seminal insider account of a flying saucer group.) After the prophecy failed to materialize in December of 1954, the small group (the Williamsons, Laugheads, and Dorothy Martin/Keech) continued to receive messages which eventually instructed them to go to Peru to look for a place called "the Monastery of the Seven Rays."

They all quit their jobs, sold their belongings and headed to Peru. Arriving in 1956, they actually established a monastic community and lived there until Williamson returned to Arizona upon the death of his wife in August of 1958. Martin stayed on for a while to run the retreat.

In an unpublished interview, UFO researcher Chris O'Brien asked former contactee Ray Stanford about his memories from this period:

I learned that [Williamson] was channeling information and I fell hook, line and sinker for the channeling bit and naively went down to Peru [January 21, 1957] where he was establishing "PriatorioTodos de Los Santos" ("All Saints Priory") of his fictional "Brotherhood of the Seven Rays, Amethystine Order", in Moyabamba, state of San Martin (on the Rio Mayo, head waters of the Amazon), supposedly at the direction of 'channeled' information. When we got down there, it became obvious to us very fast that it was a large farce and there was a lot of hypocrisy involved.[3]

Throughout the 1950s, Williamson kept up a steady stream of book releases as he delved more and more into esotericism and channeled messages. The titles became more metaphysical with each release, beginning with the aforementioned *The Saucers Speak* in 1954, *Other Tongues – Other Flesh* in 1957, and *UFOs Confidential* in 1958, co-authored with his friend John McCoy, as well as *Secret Places of the Lion*. In 1959, he published his final contactee-themed title, *Road in the Sky*. In the course of these books, Williamson was one of the first to propose a theme of what would come to be called the "ancient astronaut theory," which is now the basis of a wildly successful and long-running television program, *Ancient Aliens*, as well as providing the career arc of *Chariots of the Gods* author Erich Von Daniken. He also evinced a running theme of the "international bankers" conspiracy, which, as most conspiracy scholars realize, actually means "International Jewish Banking Conspiracy."

Williamson dropped off the map soon after returning to the U.S. Within two years (1960) he had changed his name to Michel D'Obrevnic, which he claimed was his family's original name, as he believed he was descended from a Yugoslavian royal family. In 1961, he released his final book *Secret of the Andes*, written under the pseudonym of "Brother Philip," which cobbled together his own writing with that of the Laugheads and James Churchward, who wrote extensively on the lost continent of Mu. He embarked on a lecture tour of Japan in 1961, which was apparently successful.[4]

The last 25 years of his life are generally shrouded in mystery, although it is known that he was ordained as a priest in the Orthodox Christian Church and took up residence in Santa Barbara, California before his death in 1986. He was cremated and his ashes are interred in the Arlington National Cemetery under his legally changed name.

In a strange coda to the life of Williamson, Ray Stanford claimed that he had tried to climb into bed with him when Stanford was 17 or 18 years old and staying at the Williamson home sometime in the mid-1950s. Again from O'Brien's interview:

Stanford: I was dubious of him from the start. The very first night [in Prescott]

Williamson invited me to spend the night at his place with him, his wife Betty, and their young son. Betty cooked a nice vegetarian dinner. When it came bedtime, I could have slept on the normal couch but he had her fold it out like a double bed. And instead of going in and sleeping with Betty, he came in and crawled under the covers with me! He snuggled kind of close. I sort of gave him a telepathic "harrrrumph," rolled over and said, "It's been a long trip from Texas. I'm going to sleep. Goodnight." I think I let him know then and there that I wasn't interested in any extracurricular activities.

Chris O'Brien: [Laughter] . . . extraterrestrial or otherwise . . .

Stanford: That was my first encounter with the special proclivities of Ric Williamson. Several years later, I learned a lot more about them from some of the things that John McCoy saw.[5]

1. Zinstaag, Lou, and Good, Timothy. 1983. *George Adamski – the Untold Story*. Ceti Publications,1983. (p. 55, 57).
2. Williamson, George and McCoy, John. 1958. *UFOs Confidential*. Essene Press. (p. 53).
3. O'Brien, Chris, Unpublished transcript of interview with Ray Stanford.
4. Clark, Jerome. 1998 "Willamson, George Hunt," in *The UFO Encylopedia, Vol. 2*, 2nd Edition. Omnigraphics, Inc. (p 1031-35).
5. O'Brien, Chris, Unpublished transcript of interview with Ray Stanford.

Further reading

Zirger, Michel and Martinelli, Maurizio. 2016. *The Incredible Life of George Hunt Williamson*. Verdechiaro Edizioni.

"The spiritual quest of George Hunt Williamson" HakanBlomqvist's blog
http://ufoarchives.blogspot.com/2017/07/the-spiritual-quest-of-george-hunt.html

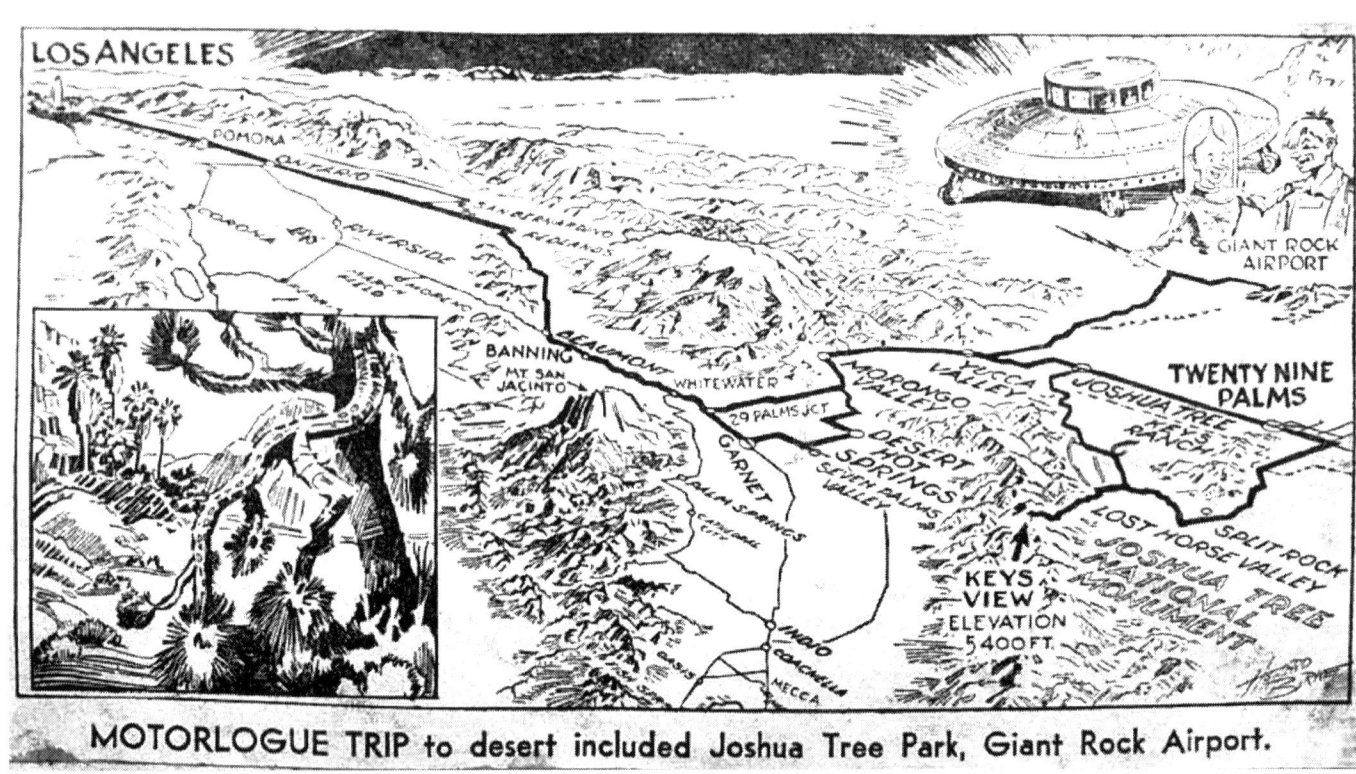

MOTORLOGUE TRIP to desert included Joshua Tree Park, Giant Rock Airport.

The motorlogue section of *The Los Angeles Examiner* ran this April 17, 1955 graphic to promote desert tourism. Cabot Yerxa's Old Indian Pueblo, Joshua Tree Monument and Giant Rock Airport were the featured highlights of this trip.

Interplanetary Spacecraft Visit Desert Hot Springs

by Jane Pojawa

Let's take a flying saucer back in time to 1950. Desert Hot Springs, indeed the whole of California's Mojave desert, was buzzing with a sudden rush of aliens. These fellows—and nearly all of them were male – bore more of a resemblance to Orlando Bloom than to P'lod, the Grey made famous by the *Weekly World News*, and they came with a message of world peace and a warning to humanity to stop its evil ways.

The modern experience of Unidentified Flying Objects (UFO) began on June 24, 1947, when a Central Air Service pilot named Kenneth Arnold spotted nine mysterious, high-speed objects flying along the crest of the Cascade Range near Mount Rainier. He described aircraft that by today's standards look very much like a stealth bomber or flying wing, and he believed that they were experimental aircraft. Soon it was not only aircraft, or lights in the sky that were being documented, it was personal experiences with the inhabitants of the aircraft, generally contacted psychically.

The Desert Sentinel thoroughly documented the invasion. Jean Shannon, the "Feminine Reflections" columnist, spotted the onslaught on July 15, 1949, when she wrote about an article in the obscure new age journal *Fate*, which claimed that a reclusive Native American tribe, the Hav-musuv, developed aircraft and lived in peaceful seclusion in caves in the Panamint mountain range in Death Valley. Accepting the account as factual, UFOs and their peaceful message became a recurring theme in her columns.

On Decemeber 1, 1949 Shannon wrote about George Adamski's lecture to the Fallbrook Rotary Club, "Flying Saucers, Ships from Mars." Significantly for Desert Hot Springs, Cabot and Portia

Yerxa were to become friends of Adamski and another "local boy," George Van Tassel. On January 5, 1950, Portia joined Shannon and Evelyn and Eloise Kane to hear Adamski speak in Banning.

1952 was a big year for alien contact. Adamski made contact first—with Orthon from Venus, who landed near Adamski's home in Desert Center. Van Tassel was not far behind. "His" alien, also from Venus, was named Ashtar. Van Tassel had a better location. He was the lessee of some property around Giant Rock, in Landers. On April 4, 1953, Van Tassel hosted the first Interplanetary Spacecraft Convention.

The Desert Sentinel was right on top of these new developments, declaring "Professor George Adamski, who is a friend of Cabot and Portia Yerxa, claims he has actually taken photos of flying saucers and had an hour's talk with a small man who came and left in an outer spaceship from the sky. This is the first time in the history of the world an occurrence of this kind has been recorded and by a man of recognized scientific standing." Cabot started selling *Flying Saucers Have Landed*, George Adamski's earth-shaking book, at the pueblo. The editors of the *Sentinel* might not have been as impressed with Adamski's "scientific standing" if they knew he had only an eighth grade education.

In September of 1954, the newspaper ran this gossipy tidbit: "Portia and Cabot Yerxa have just returned from a vacation trip of several weeks. The first of August they attended the "Flying Saucer" forum on Mount Palomar and talked with George Adamski, who contacted the flying saucer at Desert Center [and] Truman Bethurum, who is the man who talked with the beautiful woman captain and her crew of 32 men who flew their Flying Saucer here from the planet Clarion. Also, they spent some time with Dan Fry, who it was that boarded a flying saucer and was given a ride of 4,000 miles in 30 minutes, and Desmond Leslie of England, a nephew of Winston Churchill, who told them very astonishing facts concerning Flying Saucers in Europe."

Not quite as riveting as the events on Mt. Palomar, Desert Hot Springs responded with a ufo-themed fundraiser. On Oct. 7, 1954, Cabot introduced Gilbert N. Holloway, whose speech "Flying Saucer Mysteries; Truths and Fallacies Concerning Their Origin and Effect on the World," raised $92 for "new and large highways signs to attract more visitors to our community."

Other Desert Hot Springs residents were literally taken with flying saucers. Mrs. Dana Howard said that she was "whisked away" to Venus, where she married a Venusian named Lelando. Van Tassel's Interplanetary Spacecraft Conventions at Giant Rock were attracting around ten thousand spectators and flying saucers were generally considered good for business. Van Tassel had another project, the Integratron, a hand-made dome-shaped building that when operational was supposed to rejuvenate the human body in a way not unlike recharging a battery. Sadly, it was never operational. Howard and another Desert Hot Springs local, Marie Ropp, started attending Saturday evening "enlightenment meetings" at Giant Rock. By 1959, Desert Hot Springs schools featured "flying saucer cookies" on the lunch menu.

Sightings tapered off, although in 1960 "Report Sight of Saucer in Highlands" grabbed reader's attention on page 10 of *The Desert Sentinel*. "Plainly visible by several citizens in Desert Hot Springs, Genevive Johnston reports she and her companion saw a flying saucer hover over the Highland area emitting high frequency sounds like 'a million tiny bells.' The ship had a warm hair-raising effect on Miss Johnston's companion. And she, according to her testimony, 'had been feeling 'poorly' until the unidentified flying object passed over and 'pow' she took on a 'new look' and was 'fit as a fiddle' in a 'matter of seconds.' The saucer was traveling in a north-easterly direction. 'It left an unexplainable glow,' Miss Johnson reports."

The Interplanetary Spacecraft Conventions continued to draw tens of thousands, even into the early '70s—Cabot attended in 1963. For those who have not visited the Integratron, it is well worth the trip. The new management has spruced the place up, and offer sound baths on the weekends. Address: 2477 Belfield Boulevard, Landers, CA 92285, Phone: 760-364-3126. Giant Rock is accessible about four miles away on an unpaved road.

Now, of course, it would be easy to look at a man from outer space and say "thanks for nothing." In 60 years, alien life forms have not helped cure cancer, stopped the aging process, developed alternative fuel sources, or brought about world peace. But in the 1950s and '60s when humanity hoped for a savior, we looked to the sky.

INTER-GALAXY NEWS

VOLUME 1 ☆ NUMBER 2

PRICE 25c ★ HIGHLAND PARK, CALIFORNIA ★ MAY–JUNE, 1957

Afterword

The Little Green Man That Refused To Die

by Adam Gorightly

Noticeably absent from our Who's Who list are Betty and Barney Hill, Travis Walton, and others of their ilk who fall more appropriately into the abductee bucket.

The common link between contactees and abductees is that their experiences—whether real or imagined—can be categorized as Close Encounters of the Third Kind (CE3s), consisting of direct physical contact with whomever it is that they think they encountered. In some cases, contactees and abductees have attributed these experiences to telepathy, channeling, and astral projection—or a combination of the above.

Not only have contactees claimed CE3s, but many remained in ET communication throughout the course of their colorful lives, maintaining a friendly relationship with the space brothers. Conversely, abductees have been generally viewed as victims: experiencers of physical and mental trauma, including purported sexual encounters frequently bordering on rape.

The abductee experience harkens back to legends of the incubi and succubi: phantasmal figures that appear in the dark of night; psychic vampires who suck us of our souls. In many cases, abductees are drawn ever deeper into this shadow world through the use of hypnotic regression. Generally speaking, these regressions have been conducted by a handful of ufologists that identify themselves as Alien Abduction Regression Therapists (AARTs), a title that presumes the reality of the phenomenon.

Valiant Thor at Howard Menger's UFO Conference in High Bridge, New Jersey, 1959

Although some better known AARTs have PhDs attached to their names, few have actual medical accreditation.

Hypnotherapy, unlike other psycho-therapeutic practices, is unregulated, although some states require certification. With that being said, hypnotherapy has not traditionally been considered a part of mental health education due to the lack of scientific evidence supporting claims of "repressed memories." Most critically, there are ethical concerns that arise from its use (or misuse) and the opportunity for manipulation on the part of the practitioner—whether certified or not.

True believers argue that mainstream medicine and psychiatry are close-minded and that only by thinking out-of-the-box are alien abduction regression therapists able to burrow beneath "screen memories" and arrive at the "truth." It could be argued that such out-of-the-box thinking has become a box in itself: a self-confirming loop creating and reinforcing its own Belief System (BS). None of this, of course, dismisses the possibility of ETs visiting Earth—or of little gray-skinned buggers with fetishes for probes—but just like those who speak directly to God on a continuing basis, the "evidence" is based solely on personal accounts and perceptions.

According to UFO researcher Keith Thompson, the "[Betty and Barney] Hill case stands as a primordial precedent, the mythic First—for future alien abductions." Whatever occurred to Betty and Barney, they seemed genuinely terrified, as evidenced from recordings of their hypnotic regression sessions. The question is how much of what was recalled under regression was external, and how much was an internal projection? Bear in mind, the Hills were an interracial couple at a time when lynch mobs were known to hang black men for sleeping with (or, God forbid, marrying) white women. Hypnotism, in some instances, allows one to tap into a core fear, as evidenced from Barney Hill's regression when he described his first sight of the UFO occupant as a uniformed authoritarian: "He looks like a German Nazi... I got to get my gun!"

Early abduction reports from the 1970s suggested sinister motivations on the part of the ETs, such as Dr. Leo Sprinkle's regressions of Myrna Hansen that included detailed accounts of cattle mutilations and secret underground bases filled with burbling vats of human-alien hybrids. Later accounts (courtesy of Bud Hopkins and Dr. John Mack) presented abduction reports as ultimately positive, indicative of a good cop-bad cop narrative underlying the experience.

Dr. David Jacobs—who could be considered along with Mack and Hopkins, as part of the holy trinity of abduction regression therapists—has in the last decade adopted a distinctly manic tone, subscribing to the belief that evil aliens walk amongst us, their ultimate goal to enslave mankind and create a human-alien hybrid race of rulers, or what Jacobs calls "hu-brids."

None of this, of course, is a new notion: ETs hiding in plain sight, wearing the cloak of human flesh, basically an updated version of the 1960s Quinn Martin production *The Invaders* or films like *Invasion of the Body Snatchers* or *Village of the Damned*.

Mildred Lisette Norman, "The Peace Pilgrim," at Giant Rock (Joe Fex/APE-X Research)

In fact, contactees put forth similar claims, dating back to Dr. Frank Stranges and his bromance with Venusian space pal Val Thor: that human looking aliens were hiding among the population of Earth. The only difference was that Val and his Venusian buddies were busy-body do-gooders here to enlighten mankind and get us off our atom bomb death trip, as opposed to Dr. Jacobs' "hu-brid" boogiemen.

The abductee victimization syndrome stands in stark contrast to the kooky-groovy contactees, who some have called forerunners of the hippies. Supreme Commander James Moseley once mused: "Adamski and the contactees represented an early hippy philosophy of the time—the 1950s version of what came later in the '60s with flower-power protests. A lot of what they were saying merged into the mainstream of liberal thinking at that time. So, in that way, it was a very significant movement."[1]

Bernard Copley at Giant Rock
(Joe Fex/APE-X Research)

On a similar note, contactees could be considered kindred spirits to the Beat Movement. At the same time Orthon was warning Adamski about "Boom-Boom," Beat poets in berets were snapping their fingers in coffee houses, banging bongos, and spouting jazz inspired poetry, railing against atom bombs, the military industrial complex, and "squares" in general. Both groups (contactees and Beats) were looking for an alternative culture light years away from Eisenhower Era consumerism and conformity.

Throughout the '50s, '60s and '70s, George Van Tassel's Giant Rock Interplanetary Spacecraft Conventions served as Woodstock Nation for a Who's Who of contactees who gathered there to swap tales of flying saucers piloted by blonde Venusian bombshells that were "tops in shapeliness and beauty." Like Woodstock, a subtle psychedelic influence gradually seeped into the Giant Rock conventions in later years, due in part to a pioneering acid gobbler named Bernard Copley who frequented the event sharing samples of "cosmic debris." Founder of the Hypnosophic Institute in nearby Joshua Tree, Copley authored *Hallucinogenic Drugs and Their Application to Extra-Sensory Perception* (1962), which chronicled his free-wheeling experiments with acid, mescaline, peyote, and magic mushrooms.

In April 1963, Copley and another psychedelic entrepreneur named Bernard Roseman (together they became known infamously as the "Two Bernards") were the first humans ever arrested for LSD distribution in the United States. Shortly afterward, Copley died while serving his sentence in a Missouri prison.

Evidence of a psychedelic scene flittering on the fringes of the Giant Rock Convention is briefly hinted at in *Gray Barker At Giant Rock* (1976) with a recounting of Barker, Moseley, and Barbara Hudson happening upon a hippie party on the outskirts of the gathering. It should then come as no surprise that the 1960s counterculture was inclined toward a belief in ETs—or at least a fascination with the evolving flying saucer mythos—mainly because it served as a flight of fancy from the norm, symbolizing ascendance to a higher state.

Giant Rock Convention, October, 1961 (Joe Fex/APE-X Research)

Marjorie Cameron-Parsons wasn't the only person named Parsons captivated by the California flying saucer desert scene. Legendary country rock pioneer Gram Parsons likewise possessed a deep fascination for UFOs and spent considerable time tripping on 'shrooms and going out on sky watches in Joshua Tree with his buddy Keith Richards of The Rolling Stones. Parsons entrée into this desert saucer scene was facilitated by film director Tony Foutz, who in 1969 invited Parsons to accompany him to that year's Giant Rock Convention. While attending the event, Parsons visited Van Tassel's room beneath Giant Rock and attempted to play a beat-up old piano there, then abruptly stopped and remarked, "You'd *need* a Martian to tune this."[2]

A similar strain of flying saucer psychedelia blossomed in Glastonbury, England, which became a hot spot for UFO sightings, as more and more hippies made the pilgrimage there to witness strange craft under the divine guidance of LSD. In 1966, author John Michell decided to experience the 'Glastonbury effect' for himself, later chronicled to *The Flying Saucer Vision* (1967) which explored the notion that UFOs and other weird phenomena of the post-war era were portents of a coming radical change in human consciousness.

Pink Floyd picked up on this theme with their album *Saucerful of Secrets*. They were one of many

Major Wayne Aho at the speaker's podium at Giant Rock (Joe Fex/APE-X Research)

bands that incorporated flying saucer imagery into their songs. Music was but one way of spreading the flying saucer meme through the counterculture, as poster artists started using the saucer image as a medium that eventually made its way to LSD blotters, preparing their paisley-garbed passengers for liftoff.

With these influences bubbling to the surface, a new wave of psychedelically inspired contactees emerged in the 1970s. One such was author Robert Anton Wilson who was experimenting with ritual magick and LSD when he received a message from an apparent otherworldly entity on July 23rd, 1973, instructing him that: "Sirius is very important!" Intrigued by this cryptic message, Wilson visited the Berkeley Public Library to conduct more in depth research where he stumbled upon a book passage revealing that July 23rd is the very same day when Sirius rises behind the sun, known as the Dog Days. During this same period, Wilson had been working closely with Mr. LSD himself, Dr. Timothy Leary, on a number of projects related to space exploration and life extension.

Leary—housed in Folsom Prison on trumped-up drug charges during this period—organized a four person telepathy team that came into contact with certain interstellar entities, a story related (in a poetical fashion) in Leary's *Starseed Transmissions* (1973). Synchronistically, these communications

Underground Room at Giant Rock (Joe Fex/APE-X Research)

occurred during the dog days of Sirius in July and August of that year.

At the same time Leary was receiving his Starseed Transmissions, another psychedelic pioneer, Dr. John Lilly, was going through his own series of interstellar communications with a network of ET entities identified as ECCO, an acronym for "Earth Coincidence Control Office." These communications were achieved through the use of the drug Ketamine. But the psychedelic synchronicities don't end there!

While all of the above was going on, science fiction author Philip K. Dick (who had also dipped his toes into those 1960s psychedelic waters) had some sort of "mystical experience" involving beings from the same Sirius star system with which Robert Anton Wilson apparently made contact. This led to Dick's trilogy of books based around the VALIS (Vast Active Living Intelligence System) theme.

Another early '70s psychedelic-flying saucer proponent was Terence McKenna, who suggested (at one time or another) that magic mushrooms were spores sent from outer space to enlighten mankind. During one such psilocybin trip set in the Amazon jungle, Terence and his brother Dennis witnessed an old school Adamski-type flying saucer straight out of some 1950s B movie. Under the influence of *N*-Dimethyltryptamine (DMT), McKenna later witnessed an extra-dimensional world inhabited by "self transforming machine elves." These types of DMT fueled experiences became part of a larger study conducted by Dr. Rick Strassman at the University of New Mexico detailed in *DMT: The Spirit Molecule: A Doctor's Revolutionary Research into the Biology of Near-Death and Mystical Experiences* (2001) and *Inner Paths to Outer Space: Journeys to Alien Worlds through Psychedelics and Other Spiritual Technologies* (2008).

Dr. Strassman theorized that the human pineal gland produces DMT under specific conditions, and it is the pineal gland which mystics have long identified as the seat of the Third Eye. DMT, it so happens, is a chemical compound present in the shamanic drug Ayahausca (or Yage) used for centuries by indigenous peoples. In recent years, westerners like Graham Hancock have made this voyage to the Amazon to drink of the Yage vine, and under its influence Hancock witnessed small, grey skinned entities (not unlike Whitley Strieber's "Greys") who he considers as spirit guides.[3]

One explanation for these ET encounters (experienced under the influence of psychedelics) was explained by Fortean guru John Keel ala his "Superspectrum" theory, "a hypothetical spectrum of energies that are known to exist but that cannot be accurately measured with present-day instruments. It is a shadowy world of energies that produce well-observed effects, particularly on biological organisms (namely people). This superspectrum is the source of all paranormal manifestations from extrasensory perception (ESP) to flying saucers, little green men and tall, hairy monsters. It is hard to pin down scientifically because it is extradimensional, meaning that it exists outside our own space-time continuum yet influences everything within our reality."

In order to observe UFOs—according to Keel's theory—one must enter into a more receptive state of awareness, like a psychic channeler tuning into voices or subtle energies. In addition to hallucinogenic drugs, there are myriad methods that induce altered states, including sensory deprivation, tantric sex, hypnosis, meditation, and chanting. A preponderance of contactees, it so happens, were trance channelers who frequently entered trance states prior to the appearance of their beloved space brothers.

A common description of UFOs is that they often change colors, which suggested to Keel that UFOs are a form of intelligent energy traveling through the visible light spectrum. Keel's Superspectrum Theory posited that UFOs exist at frequencies beyond visible light and can adjust their frequency and descend into the electromagnetic spectrum—just as you turn a radio dial up and down the scale of frequencies. When a UFO frequency nears that of visible light, it will first appear as a purplish blob. As it moves further down the scale, it changes to blue, and then to blue-ish green and so on, finally to white. This is how many UFO sightings unfold. In this regard, Keel suggested that UFOs are energies of a different frequency. Like tuning a radio, you pick up and amplify the signal coming in at a certain point (or frequency) of the electromagnetic spectrum. Your eyes are also receivers tuned to specific wavelengths, as the brain is likewise a receiver.

Greg Bishop with John Keel in NYC circa 2003 (Photo credit: Greg Bishop)

Current day paranormal investigators (or "Ghost Hunters") use infrared detection systems to reveal otherwise "invisible" activity, which is akin to someone using infrared goggles to see what the naked eye cannot. Altered states—such as those induced by mind altering drugs—are a method of seeing into the Superspectrum, which, in essence, is what psychics claim to do. George Van Tassel described the way he communicated with the ETs as being like tuning in a television to decode an electromagnetic signal.

Like John Keel, there have been a handful of ufological free thinkers throughout the years that pushed the boundaries of UFO research beyond simple nut and bolt explanations to examine the effect of human perception on the phenomenon, and the possibility that what UFO experiencers have witnessed (or interacted with) is symbiotic in nature; a force of planetary energy ("non-human intelligence") that often manifests in archetypal forms, or whatever form the current generation considers most appropriate, as suggested by Jacque Vallee in *Passport to Magonia* (1969). Along these same lines, psychologist Carl Jung theorized that humankind's collective unconscious plays

371

a role in UFO manifestations: that the phenomenon is, in essence, an external projection of the subconscious mind at large. A projection of group consciousness.

But as much as UFO research has evolved with occasional deep thinkers like Jung, Vallee, or Keel, the more things tend to stay the same as recurring ufological themes have a habit of recycling time and again only to be forgotten for awhile before resurfacing as the next "big thing." A good example of this recycling is the notion of UFO Disclosure, which has been dusted off repeatedly under different names, but the song remains the same: that the U.S. Government is keeping a lid on the shocking truth about flying saucers from outer space! Adamski and other contactees referred to this shadowy group as "The Silencers" or the "Silence Control Group."

Major Donald Keyhoe was the first semi-serious voice to suggest that the government knew things about UFOs they weren't copping to, and over time this theme expanded into a mythology of Men in Black who were either clandestine agents or ETs in disguise going around hassling UFO witnesses who "knew too much." In response, heroic UFO researchers started petitioning the government to come clean with their dirty UFO laundry and reveal the stunning reality of dead aliens on ice at Hangar 18 (or Hangar 19 or 20, or whatever hangar it actually was) at Wright Patterson Air Base.

More recent incarnations of UFO Disclosure were rolled out in the 1990s by the likes of Dr. Steven Greer and Steven Basset, and are basically new iterations of these same themes, such as the little dead alien legend that dates back as far as the Great Airship Mystery of 1897 and a yarn about a UFO crash in Aurora, Texas. According to the April 19th, 1897 edition of the *Dallas Morning News*, Aurora resident Mr. S.E. Haydon witnessed a cigar shaped craft crash on the property of Judge J.S. Proctor and afterwards its "Martian" pilot was buried in an unmarked grave in the town's cemetery. Conspiracy sleuther Jim Marrs championed the Aurora tale over the years, although by and large most sober-minded researchers consider it just one among many urban legends associated with the airship mystery.

It seems Texas couldn't let the "dead alien" angle go, as a report surfaced in 1913 concerning three brothers out chopping cotton on their farm (in Farmersville, Texas, naturally) when their dog got into a tussle with a strange little man "no more than eighteen inches high and kind of a dark green color." When all was said and done, the creature had been ripped to shreds by the ferocious pooch, leaving only blood and guts.

As for the "crash go the saucers" mythos, it first spun its way into pop culture courtesy of Frank Scully's *Behind the Flying Saucers* (1950), which claimed that a saucer piloted by otherworldly midgets crashed in Aztec, New Mexico, in 1948. Scully's account was later exposed as a hoax based on bogus information passed to him by a couple of hucksters named Silas Newton and Leo Gebauer.

In the aftermath of the phony Aztec story, the flying saucer crash legend took a back seat in ufology until the late 1970s, when researcher Leonard Stringfield helped renew the theme at the

The Roswell UFO Enigma Museum, 1997 (Photo credit: Douglas Curran)

1978 MUFON Symposium. Among the cases Stringfield discussed concerned a crash/retrieval that allegedly occurred in 1948 near the Texas-Mexico border. The source for this story was a retired Air Force colonel who claimed that a dead alien was discovered in the wreckage, as first reported by ufologist Todd Zechel.

UFO researcher Kevin Randle later discovered that Zechel never bothered vetting the "retired" Colonel, who wasn't actually a retired colonel after all but had simply served for a couple years as a Civil Air Patrol squadron leader and hadn't actually seen a crashed saucer—or dead aliens, for that matter. Nonetheless, these spurious stories planted seeds that later sprouted into what is now regarded as the flying saucer crash to end all others.

In 1978—the same year that Stringfield helped revive interest in crashed saucers—up and coming UFO researcher Stanton Friedman came across a purported witness to one such event that occurred near Roswell, New Mexico. The witness—in this case—was retired Air Force Major Jesse Marcel, who

**Jim Moseley in the mid 1990s
(Photo credit: Greg Bishop)**

on the morning of July 9th, 1947, responded to a reported crash of some sort that occurred the previous night on a ranch located 30 miles north of Roswell.

The wreckage—such as it was—appeared to be constructed of aluminum and balsa wood. Aside from these all-too-human characteristics, nothing else resembled anything man-made—at least in Marcel's estimation. Curiously enough, Marcel's account included nothing whatsoever about dead (or live, for that matter) ETs. The dead-alien angle would only later emerge as other claimed Roswell witnesses came forth with accounts that seemed to mimic, in many respects, the spurious Aztec story.

Around the time Stanton Friedman discovered Jesse Marcel, he joined forces with another up and coming ufologist, William Moore, and over the next few years the duo dug deep into the Roswell crash wreckage. These investigations led to the publication of *Incident At Roswell* (1980) authored by Moore and Charles Berlitz, a book that almost single-handedly ushered into popular consciousness a story that, until then, had been not much more than an obscure ufological footnote.

Incident at Roswell was similar, in many respects, to the Aztec story, including hieroglyphic script on the hull of the crashed saucer, and the subsequent transport of dead aliens to a military base. To this end, Roswell seemed a mash-up of previous crashed saucer stories—and, before you knew it, a cottage industry was born. Yearly, thousands make a pilgrimage to Roswell to visit the UFO museum and attend the annual UFO fest. At one time there were plans in the works for an ET-themed amusement park, but after the economy tanked in 2007, funding dried up and the plan fizzled out. At the 50th Anniversary Roswell Festival in 1997, Jim Moseley was asked by a *Washington Post* reporter about the ultimate meaning of the Roswell incident, and Moseley replied, "Only in America can you have the 50th anniversary of nothing."

It seems at least once every decade a new twist on the Roswell crash story takes itself out for another spin. After its introduction into popular culture in 1980, the Roswell crash made its next appearance in 1987 in the form of the infamous MJ-12 briefing papers, a collection of supposedly classified government documents that fortuitously fell into the lap of ufologist William Moore from a supposedly anonymous source who many suspect was sketchy U.S. Air Force Intelligence

Officer Richard Doty. The MJ-12 papers purportedly revealed the existence of "OPERATION MAJESTIC-12... a TOP SECRET Research and Development/ Intelligence operation responsible directly only to the President of the United States..." Majestic-12, as the top secret documents revealed, had been established in the late 1940s to deal with ETs visiting Earth, and among these ETs were some little alien fellows that died (and one who purportedly survived) the Roswell crash. While there are those who still view the MJ-12 papers as authentic, Doty's involvement in the story suggests it was all part of a convoluted hoax. (Read Greg Bishop's *Project Beta: The Story of Paul Bennewitz, National Security, and the Creation of a Modern UFO Myth* for more on this twisted tale.)

The notorious "Silverman" photo

The next big Roswell splash came in 1995 with the equally infamous *Alien Autopsy* film that was eventually found to be a fake. Even today there are those who still believe that the footage was authentic, although the principals involved fessed up that the film was phony.

Photos of little green (or silver) men have long been a fixture in ufology and, like everything else, these oddities get dusted off and trotted out after a period of time has elapsed and run through the grinder again. One such retread that has continued to make the ufological rounds—decade after decade—is a photo that first surfaced in the German newspaper *Neue Illustrierte* on April 1st, 1950, with the title "Der Mars-Mensch" which showed a strange looking three foot tall fellow apparently from another planet—Mars, in this case. The accompanying article claimed that the Martian had been in a saucer crash that occurred in "Death Valley."

A few days later, *Neue Illustrierte* admitted that the Martian story was an April Fool's hoax, but that didn't stop the photo from spreading through the UFO subculture in the years to come, often presented as the real deal. Since then the photo—sometimes referred to as the "Silverman"—has appeared in numerous UFO books, often including the false narrative that the photo depicted an alien who had survived a saucer crash.

Saucer scholar Isaac Koi (www.isaackoi.com) compiled a timeline of the Silverman photo and the publications in which it appeared. The first book to feature this freaky photo was Major Donald Keyhoe's *Flying Saucers from Outer Space* (1953). Keyhoe described it as "two men in trench coats, each holding an arm of a queer, shiny figure about three feet high. Two girls standing nearby seemed to be awestruck by the little man..." Eyewitness G-Man McKennerich, from Phoenix, reports "I was astounded by the importance of this great moment. For the first time I was seeing a being from another world. At the same time I was equally amazed by the desperation of this Aluminum Man. His body was covered with a shiny metal foil. The observatory in Phoenix presumes this is for protection from cosmic rays..."

Conflicting narratives surround the Silverman photo, some of which identified the trench-coated gentlemen as U.S. government agents (G-Men), while other accounts depicted them as German scientists, and that "Silverman" was not necessarily silver-skinned, but outfitted in some sort of aluminum spaceman suit.

In *Space-Craft from Beyond Three Dimensions* (1959), W. Gordon Allen referenced that the creature in the Silverman photo had crawled out of a crashed saucer:

> A "saucer crewman" very much like the moon man (or spirit) described by Swedenborg in his writings about the inhabitants of different planets of the solar system...This photograph is from Germany (note trench coats and North European types), but the "saucer crewman" is from a UFO that crashed near Mexico City; the corpses were sent to Germany for study...

In 1967, a concerned citizen sent a copy of the Silverman photo to FBI headquarters in D.C. inquiring if the trench-coated men were FBI agents, to which J. Edgar Hoover responded: "I can assure you the photograph you mentioned does not represent employees of this Bureau."

Most recently, Harold Povenmire in *UFO's and Alien Abduction Phenomena: A Scientific Analysis* (2016) published a colorized version of the Silverman photo as the real deal, although what "scientific analysis" he conducted is unclear. Thanks to Povenmire, this new iteration of the Silverman photo soon began worming its way through social media, as a new generation of believers clicked and shared to their heart's content.

Another recurring ufological legend is the mummy-alien that—in one form or another—has appeared at such roadside attractions as Ralph Lael's defunct Outer Space Rock Shop Museum. In this regard, Roswell careened headfirst into the mummy-alien mythos in early 2014 when rumors began circulating about the discovery of a 1940s era Kodachrome slide supposedly depicting a dead

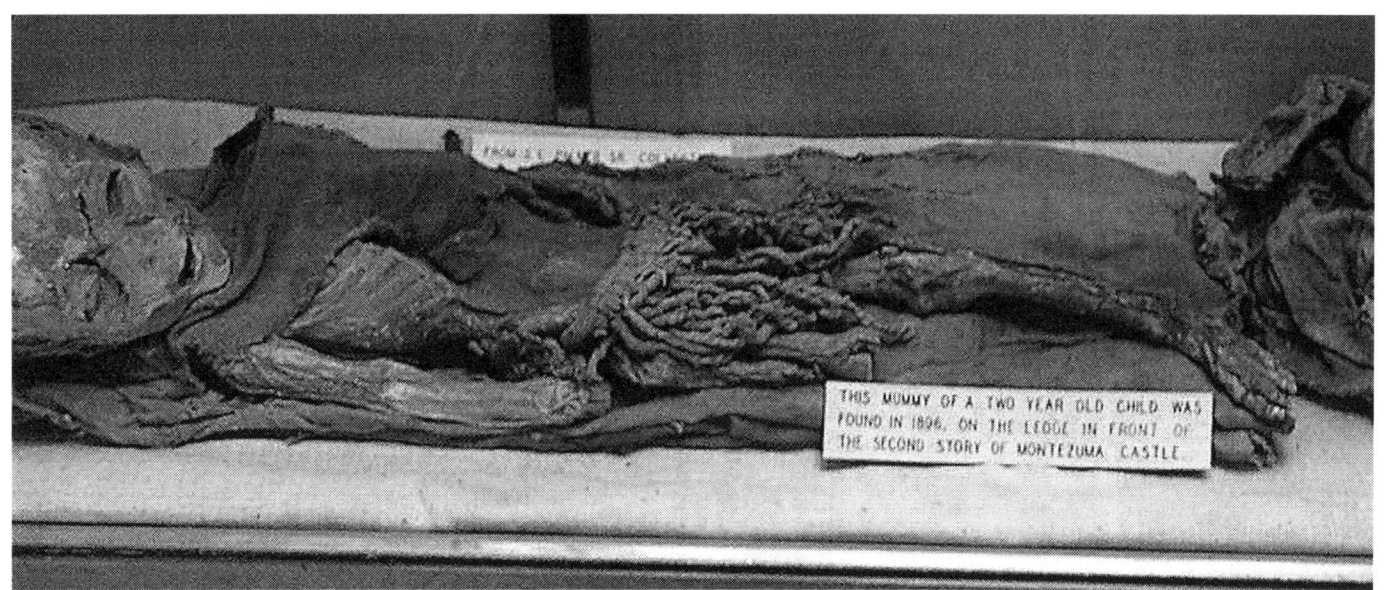

The legendary "Roswell Slide" mummy boy

alien. A low resolution copy of this slide soon made the rounds of ufological social media, leaked by a group of researchers who humbly anointed themselves the "Dream Team" and included in their august ranks Don Schmitt and Tom Carey—authors of *Witness To Roswell* (2009)—and another Roswell crash enthusiast named Anthony Bragalia.

Due to "Dream Team" influence, the slide became associated with the ET that purportedly crashed and burned at Roswell and was dubbed thereafter "The Roswell Slide." The intent of leaking the low-res slide, it appeared, was to generate buzz for a film documentary then in-the-works entitled *Kodachrome* produced by a shadowy character named Adam Dew who had formed a partnership with the aforementioned Dream Team.

A secret Facebook research group—named, appropriately enough, the Roswell Slide Research Group (RSRG)—began analyzing the low-res copy, and part of these efforts included an attempt to decipher a placard that appeared in the slide (placed beside the "alien" body) with blurred writing. These efforts at first proved unsuccessful due to the slide's poor image quality. Meanwhile, pre-promotion hype for *Kodachrome* included an event called *beWITNESS* organized by UFO snake oil salesman Jaime Maussan where (for the first time in human history!) the high res copy of the Roswell Slide would be revealed to a live audience in Mexico City on May 5th, 2015, in addition to a pay per view live stream.

During the course of the event, an RSRG member was able to screen cap the high res Roswell Slide on display and, within the short span of 72 hours, was able to de-blur the placard using open source software which revealed:

MUMMIFIED BODY OF TWO YEAR OLD BOY
At the time of burial the body was clothed in a xxx-xxx cotton shirt. Burial wrappings consisted of these small cotton blankets.
Loaned by the MR. Xxxxxx, San Francisco, California

A short time after the placard de-blur, *Kodachrome* producer Adam Dew fired the first shot across the bow in response to the RSRG, claiming that the placard de-blur itself was actually a fake! In other words, Dew was suggesting that the RSRG had doctored the photo by adding the text about the alien (or whatever it was) being a mummy boy. Around this same time, Dew updated his *Kodachrome* website posting the high-res image of the placard, which of course was still indecipherable. Ironically, this was a stroke of good fortune for the RSRG, as in short order they were able to download and de-blur this high-res version (straight from the horse's mouth) once again demonstrating the same thing they'd accomplished with the leaked image of the slide: that the placard indicated it was a mummy boy.

The RSRG posted a Youtube video demonstrating the step-by-step de-blur process, which in turn led to several UFO researchers doing their own de-blur and achieving the same results. Shortly after, Adam Dew's statement (about the RSRG faking the placard de-blur) was removed from the *Kodachrome* site, which suggests that Dew thought better about issuing such an outrageous (and potentially libelous) claim at the same time that so many others were independently confirming the RSRG de-blur results. Not long after, the *Kodachrome* site was scrubbed and Adam Dew disappeared for good and the "Dream Team" basically threw in the towel, admitting they'd either been mistaken or deceived. However, *beWITNESS* impresario Jaime Maussan decided to stick to his guns and actually went on the offensive, claiming that the mummy in the slide really *was* an alien and that the message on the placard was some type of disinformation campaign perpetrated by the diabolical RSRG. (You can't make this shit up.) Maussan then tweeted: "5 thousand dollars reward to the person who presents a new image of the *beWITNESS* [alien] and 10 thousand dollars" to whoever leads him to the body.

At some point during this fiasco, Nick Redfern blogged that the Roswell Slide may, in fact, have been a mummy on display in years past at the Million Dollar Museum in White City, New Mexico. Redfern posted a late 1980s photo of the Million Dollar Museum creature (in a display case with a ruler measuring its length.) Shortly afterwards, famed mutologist Linda Moulton Howe appeared on Whitley Strieber's *Dreamland* podcast and jumped the shark (or the mummy, as the case may be) by calling the Million Dollar Museum creature "the oddest, strangest, most alien body I personally have seen in my 36 years in trying to get to the bottom of all this" and that she was hot on the trail of tracking it down—presumably in the prospect of pocketing Maussan's $10,000 reward. (The Million

Dollar Museum closed in 2008 and the so-called alien "disappeared" at that time.)

Howe's Million Dollar Museum alien/mummy—as she giddily explained to Whitley Strieber—was different than the Roswell Slide creature, noting that a photo of the Million Dollar Museum "alien" was twelve inches in length, as opposed to the Roswell Slide mummy, which was three and a half feet long. To this, Strieber exclaimed: "This is the most extraordinary interview I've had in the history of *Dreamland*! Between the two of you [Howe and Maussan], you've ended up with two alien bodies! Instead of one fake, we've ended up with two real ones!"

Around this time, I was randomly listening to an ancient episode of Long John Nebel's *Party Line* (circa late 1950s) that featured a panel discussion with Ivan T. Sanderson and Isabel David concerning ETs visiting Earth and supposed evidence of "little green men."

One such claim came courtesy of contactee Howard Menger and a supposed photo he was peddling of a small alien man, a claim that Ivan Sanderson vigorously pooh-poohed, pointing out Menger's penchant for making grandiose claims that he would never back up. Isabel David brought up another purported little man (green or otherwise) that Kenneth Arnold had apparently discovered in a Colorado museum.

"I've seen that creature," Sanderson replied, noting that it had been examined by Ted Kazimiroff, historian of the Bronx Library, who said that this "little man" had been brought to him by "one of these crackpots...it came from Colorado...and it was alleged to have been found in a cave in conjunction with some peculiar bits and pieces of something...It is a well-known abnormality, it's the most peculiar thing, biologically. Apparently human beings and animals can age in the womb before they're ever born. They come out 80 years old...and this was the case of one particular type of deformity, which had a very flattened top of the skull, and that has also gone through a sort of speeded up geriatrics...sometimes you get a tiny old man who is only a year old, you see, and it was probably still born... [Kazimiroff] said these people brought it to him and said, "At last we have a space creature!" and took one look at it and was able to say immediately what it was and he showed it to me at that time...It was sort of mummified." The irony here is that Sanderson was quite possibly referring to the very same creature that would later become associated with the Roswell Slide.

In the aftermath of the Roswell Slide fiasco, researcher Shepherd Johnson identified the slide as a mummy boy that had been on exhibit in years past at a National Park Service museum in Mesa Verde, Colorado, a revelation which, once again, speaks to this theme of recycled UFO myths. Meanwhile, serious UFO research gets shunted aside and drowned out by the hype and wishful thinking that surrounds these apocryphal tales of little green man, and the saucers they spun in on, that continue to go 'round and 'round.

1. Redfern, Nick. 2009. *Contactees: A History of Alien-Human Interaction*. New Page Books.
2. Rubenstein, Raeanne. March 2013. *Space Cowboy*. Mojo Magazine.
3. Hancock, Graham. 2006. *Supernatural: Meetings with the Ancient Teachers of Mankind*. Disinformation Books.

About the Contributors

Red Pill Junkie

Agnostic gnostic, walking conundrum and metaphysical oxymoron (with emphasis on the "moron" part), the mysterious **Red Pill Junkie** leads a double life: By day he serves as Grand Master of the International Sacred Order of Lucha Libre, but at night he pursues his lifelong study of everything considered mysterious and/or "paranormal"—a term he personally detests...

When he's not exploring the web looking for his daily fix of Forteana, he can be found blogging, doodling, fooling around, and offering his services as news administrator and writer at *The Daily Grail*. He also regularly participates in other websites and podcasts like *Mysterious Universe*, *The Grimerica Show*, and *Where Did the Road Go?* He impatiently awaits for the return of the mothership in Mexico City.

absurdbydesign.com

Red Pill Junkie

Greg Bishop

In 1991, **Greg Bishop** cofounded a magazine called *The Excluded Middle*, which was a journal of UFOs, conspiracy research, psychedelia, and new science. *Wake Up Down There!*, a collection of articles from the magazine, was published in 2000 by Adventures Unlimited Press.

Greg's second book was *Project Beta: The Story of Paul Bennewitz, National Security, and the Creation of a Modern UFO Myth*, which documented a government campaign of disinformation perpetrated against an unsuspecting U.S. citizen. *Weird California*, a portrait of strange and eerie history and places in the Golden State, was released in 2006. From December 2007 to November 2011, Greg blogged for the UFO and paranormal site *Ufomystic*. His 2017 book *It Defies Language* was composed for the most part of entries from that blog, along with older material and brand new articles written just for the collection. He contributed an essay entitled "The Co-Creation Hypothesis: Human Perception, the Informational Universe, and The Overhaul of UFO Research" for the anthology *UFOs: Reframing the Debate*, edited by Robbie Graham, also published in 2017.

Greg Bishop

For two years Greg hosted *The Hungry Ghost*, a radio show of interviews and music airing on pirate FM station KBLT in Los Angeles. His current show, *Radio Misterioso*, can be heard live at radiomisterioso.com, and podcasts are available for download. Interviews with fringe-topic researchers and weird music are the usual fare.

He is licensed to fly aerial drones for commercial clients, and is also a certified paraglider and ultralight pilot. He holds a private pilot license.

Adam Gorightly

For well over two decades **Adam Gorightly**'s articles have appeared in nearly every 'zine, underground magazine, counter-cultural publication, and conspiratorial website imaginable. His landmark work, *The Shadow Over Santa Susana: Black Magic, Mind Control and the Manson Family Mythos* (2001, 2009) is considered by some the most comprehensive book on the Tate-LaBianca murders.

In *The Prankster and the Conspiracy: The Story of Kerry Thornley and How He Met Oswald and Inspired the Counterculture* (2003), Gorightly examines the remarkable life of Kerry Thornley—a 1960s Zen radical and founder of the spoof religion Discordianism who was quite realistically being groomed as a Lee Harvey Oswald "patsy-double" before the Kennedy assassination.

Adam Gorightly

Recently, Adam has submerged himself ever deeper into these chaotic Discordian waters with *Historia Discordia: The Origins of the Discordian Society* (2014) and *Caught in the Crossfire: Kerry Thornley, Lee Oswald and the Garrison Investigation* (2014). For more on the origins of Discordianism, navigate to historiadiscordia.com.

Other releases include *Happy Trails to High Weirdness: A Conspiracy Theorist's Tour Guide* (2012), *James Shelby Downard's Mystical War* (2008), and *The Beast of Adam Gorightly: Collected Rantings* (2005). In the latter, he describes the time when Doc Ellis of the Pittsburgh Pirates dropped LSD and pitched a no-hitter and how J.D. Salinger's *Catcher in the Rye* has been used as a control mechanism to trigger mind-numbed Manchurian Candidates.

Adam has been a guest on numerous radio talk shows including *Coast To Coast AM*, *The Richard Syrett Show*, and *Ground Zero with Clyde Lewis*. Television appearances include the History Channel's documentary *The Manson Murders*.

Jane Pojawa

Jane Pojawa's passion is historical research. She has served as secretary/archivist/historian for the Cabot's Pueblo Museum board of directors (2008–2010), the social media and communications director for the Friends of the Michael White Adobe (2009–current), and the media and communications chair for the Morongo Basin Historical Society (2010–2015).

Jane Pojawa

She initiated the nomination process for Cabot's Pueblo Museum to the National Register of Historic Places and served as the editor-in-chief of the Insider magazine in Glendale, California (2008-2016). She writes a blog for her husband, "Raven Jake: Observations of a Western Legend," which is largely related to travel and events in Southern California (http://ravenjake.typepad.com/) and brews award-winning mead.

Pojawa is fascinated by the contactee movement of the 1950s–'60s and has extensively researched Cabot and Portia Yerxa's contributions to this utopian vision of otherworldly visitors.

Pojawa is currently in the Masters of Regenerative Studies program at the John T. Lyle Center for Regenerative Studies at Cal Poly Pomona. Her previous fields of study were journalism and political science. Her thesis work involves interviewing people who are (or were) participants in intentional communities with sustainable values with consideration to theory and practice.

Douglas Curran

Over the span of 35 years, photographer **Douglas Curran** has documented the beliefs and culture of groups ranging from traveling tent preachers in the southern United States to a secret spirit society in Malawi. During a period of 12 years he traveled throughout the United States, often living out a venerable Renault 16, recording those who looked for communion with superior beings arriving from across the cosmos.

In the course of his long quest, Curran recorded—in sympathetic words and perceptive photographs—the ideas and experiences of individuals whose obsession with outer space inspired them to create elaborate homemade spaceships and even more elaborate belief systems. In over 25 years since being first published, his chronicle, *In Advance of the Landing: Folk Concepts of Outer Space* remains as relevant as ever, given the popularity of *The X-Files* and other investigations of alien life.

In his foreword to the book, noted American author Tom Wolfe explains: "Douglas Curran is not only a photographer but also a reporter, and an extremely gifted one. I am tempted to suggest that he also qualifies as an anthropologist, but I think I will leave it at 'reporter.' To be a reporter of Douglas Curran's caliber is a lofty enough achievement. He has discovered an exotic world, and for years he has traveled remote terrains throughout the United States and Canada exploring it. This book is the culmination of a quest that, by terrestrial standards, is as extraordinary as that of the people he brings to life."

Curran presently lives in Victoria, Canada, immersed in the earthbound realities of British Columbia's coastal archipelago.

Acknowledgments

Thanks to the following humans for their assistance in manifesting this reality:

Tim Beckley for his many remembrances of ufological colleagues of yore.

Douglas Curran for his saucerial inspiration, use of photos, and foreword (not forward) to this book.

Joe Fex for his holy work preserving the Dr. Robert C. Beck Memorial Collection.

Space sister Jane Pojawa for her contribution on the 1950s Southern California flying saucer scene.

Red Pill Junkie for his magnificent cover.

Groucho Gandhi for layout and design.

Ed Grant for proofing, copy-editing and overall encouragement.

Barbara Harris and the Morongo Basin Historical Society for documenting and preserving the history of Giant Rock.

David Houchin and the Gray Barker Collection, Clarksburg-Harrison Public Library, for the use of photos and hoaxed documents.

Nick Redfern for photo use and contactee consultation.

And last, but not least, Commander Ashtar, for all that he does.

Index

23248790R00240

Printed in Great Britain
by Amazon